D0073363

CRITICAL INSIGHTS

The Graphic Novel

CRITICAL INSIGHTS

The Graphic Novel

Editor
Gary Hoppenstand
Michigan State University, Lansing Michigan

SALEM PRESS
A Division of EBSCO Information Services, Inc.
Ipswich, Massachusetts

GREY HOUSE PUBLISHING

Library of Congress Cataloging-in-Publication Data

The graphic novel / editor, Gary Hoppenstand, Michigan State University, Lansing Michigan. -- [First edition].

  pages : illustrations ; cm. -- (Critical insights)

  Includes bibliographical references and index.
  ISBN: 978-1-61925-262-2

  1. Graphic novels--History and criticism. I. Hoppenstand, Gary, editor of compilation. II. Series: Critical insights.

PN6710 .G736 2014
741.5/9

First Printing

PRINTED IN THE UNITED STATES OF AMERICA

Contents

About This Volume

Michael Rogers

The graphic novel is arguably the greatest publishing success story in the last twenty-five years. The meteoric rise of the graphic novel serves as a barometer of the sea-change in pop culture as the one-time haven of "geeks" to the mainstream, as personal computers and the Internet became an integral part of daily life for the masses. From the invading army of comics and costume enthusiasts who consume the city of San Diego every summer to attend Comic-Con International to the millions tuning in weekly for TV's incarnation of Robert Kirkman's comics series, *The Walking Dead*, as well as the billions in box-office receipts generated by comics-based movies prove that comics, along with science fiction and fantasy, have gone viral.

During a panel session at the initial New York Comic Con in 2006, one of the speakers queried audience members on how many still were waiting for comics to go mainstream. When numerous hands were raised, the speaker responded that comics, "have been the mainstream for ten years." Much of that widespread acceptance is due to the dramatic rise of graphic novels beginning in the 1980s.

In its original form, the graphic novel was conceived of as exactly what its name implies: a novel-length story told in captioned panels of art. The current incarnation, however, is principally a series of individual issues of comic books, presenting a single storyline, and collected and reproduced as single, oversized paperback volume. Essentially, it is a comic book on steroids. Although the phrase "picture novel" dates back to the 1960s, late comics legend Will Eisner often is credited with coining the term "graphic novel" for his 1978 publication, *A Contract with God and Other Tenement Stories*, a collection of four long stories linked by a common thematic thread. The Brooklyn-born Eisner followed up *Contract* with several more novel-length comic titles depicting the Jewish immigrant experience in New York City.

Though vastly different than Eisner's usual fare, *A Contract with God* garnered immediate attention based on his status as creator of *The Spirit,* a comics series that ran as a sixteen-page supplement in Sunday newspapers from 1940 to 1952. It followed the adventures of a former police officer turned masked crime fighter. Eisner had long contended that the comics medium had far more to offer than just children's fare, and *The Spirit* adventures presented him with the opportunity to write more adult-oriented works. The series was a cocktail made primarily of crime stories as the main ingredient, with dashes of horror and romance for additional flavor. Set against a backdrop of Jewish immigrants living in a Bronx, NY tenement, *A Contract with God* went far beyond *The Spirit* in elevating illustrated stories to the level of literary fiction. Daniel D. Clark's essay in the Critical Readings section quotes Eisner describing the nexus of *A Contract with God*:

> [E]ach story was written without regard to space, and each was allowed to develop its format from itself; that is, to evolve from the narration. The normal frames (or panels) associated with sequential (comic book) art are allowed to take on their own integrity. For example, in many cases an entire page is set out as a panel. The text and the balloons are interlocked with the art. I see all these as threads of a single fabric and exploit them as a language. If I have been successful at this, there will be no interruption in the flow of the narrative because the picture and the text are so totally dependent on each other as to be inseparable for even a moment (Eisner xix).

The four tales are autobiographical: Eisner was born to Jewish immigrants in New York City in 1917 and suffered through the Great Depression. While the stories are dark, Clark, in his essay within this volume, asserts that:

> …Eisner's narratives do not surrender completely to despair. Within the bleakness exists a community that, though enduring poverty, is still capable of acts of humaneness—a bowl of soup offered to the mourning, coins given in exchange for a moment of diversion, a community rushing to protect one of its own. In these small acts, Eisner suggests a better way for a community to live.

While Eisner was at the top of the comics pyramid, racier titles, featuring graphic sex and violence that had long enjoyed classification as "men's" novels, also began appearing in longer comics form, so the concept of graphic novels was expanding in multiple directions. While there, the concepts of the graphic novel reaches back decades (as does the list of those contending for the coveted title of the graphic novel's creator), the medium didn't find a large audience until the 1980s, with the release of Art Spiegelman's *Maus*, which, ultimately, won the Pulitzer Prize—a singular twist of irony, since the story initially was rejected by numerous big-name publishers. Taking a cue from George Orwell's *Animal Farm*, *Maus* casts humans in the roles of animals for a retelling of the Holocaust, in which Jews appear as mice, Nazis as felines, and Americans appear as dogs. Spiegelman based *Maus* on a series of interviews conducted with his Holocaust-survivor father, giving it authenticity. *Maus* differed from traditional comics not only in content, but it also principally was sold through bookstores rather than comics shops, which helped buttress the title as a genuine work of literature rather than simply a "comic book."

As Brian Cogan points out in his own critical reading of *Maus*, which appears in this volume, Spiegelman's use of a subject as sensitive as the Holocaust was not without controversy: "While some critics were appalled by the seeming (to them) trivialization of a one of the most significant and horrific parts of human history," says Cogan, "others praised it as a masterpiece and an example of the potential of the graphic novel. However, the quality and seriousness of the work prevailed over the criticism." Cogan further notes:

> Many agreed that Spiegelman's work was groundbreaking not only in terms of subject matter and style but also because it helped allow a new form of literary autobiography via the medium of the graphic novel. As one critic wrote, Spiegelman's "unique approach to collective autobiography would be the most influential in shaping the reception of the form in the decades to come." *Maus* undoubtedly is one of the most important graphic novels of the twentieth century and a landmark in graphic storytelling.

The awarding of a Pulitzer instantly gave the budding graphic novel format critical legitimacy as a serious art form, and, of course, because publishing is a completely for-profit business, it also generated additional sales, which created a demand for more cerebral illustrated titles to feed the public's growing interest in graphic novels. Therefore, it sent comics publishers scrambling to serve a market that suddenly opened under their feet like a chasm. While legions of comics enthusiasts remained interested in reading longer adventures, featuring their favorite superheroes, the general public hadn't yet embraced their inner geek, making these titles of limited appeal beyond its core audience. Publishers needed stories that featured heroes to please the traditional comics fans, as well as more serious-minded stories to attract readers who believed comics were strictly for adolescents. Ironically, to find success, graphic novels needed to embody the duality of most superhero characters themselves: they had to sport masked champions of justice, who, when off-duty, were just as screwed up as everyone else.

Caped Crazies

By the early 1980s, DC Comics, one of the two leading American comics publishers had yet to release a major graphic novel, although a plethora of popular material was at its disposal. Ultimately, DC collected four releases by writer and artist Frank Miller, featuring an older, retired Batman, who is forced to again don the suit and battle villains Two-Face and the Joker to save a decayed society that may no longer warrant rescuing. Dark is the operative work for Miller's incarnation of Batman, who may be as mentally unstable as the baddies he fights. Jeffrey Johnson, in his essay within this volume, describes this Batman as:

> a Caped Crusader that is no longer a hero in the traditional comic book understanding of the concept. This older, weary, beaten-down Dark Knight is not a rational crime-fighting good guy, but rather an unbalanced individual who has the almost pathological need to impose order in a society that appears to be descending into chaos. It should be noted that the early 1930s Batman was a rough-and-tumble vigilante who battered criminals and seemed to worry little

about following the law. The original Great Depression Batman was a seemingly mentally-stable man, who made the odd choice of dedicating his life to avenging his parents' deaths by dressing in a bat costume to intimidate criminals. This Batman and the numerous versions that followed appear to be obsessive, but rational individuals, driven to fight crime as costumed superheroes, but seem to be lucid and reasonable nonetheless.

Miller's incarnation of Batman proved to be the anti-hero desired by twenty- and thirty-something readers, who were weaned on the nuclear tensions between America and the USSR, the assassinations of the Kennedys and Martin Luther King, the Vietnam War, and the regime-toppling scandal of Watergate. *The Dark Knight Returns* proved a sensation, both selling in great numbers and revitalizing interest in the nearly half-century old Batman franchise while paving the way for a new generation of antiheroes. DC delved further into graphic novels and scored an equally big hit when reproducing the cutting-edge, twelve-issue run of writer Alan Moore and artist Dave Gibbons' *Watchmen* as a single volume. Featuring both costumed heroes and an adult-oriented plot line, *Watchmen* proved the next development in the evolution of graphic storytelling.

For decades, most costumed hero books simply offered stories, in which the golden-hearted good guys triumphed over dastardly villains. Nonetheless, comic book heroes were essentially vigilantes, who take the law into their own hands. *Watchmen* addressed this concept by following a cadre of former masked heroes, who'd hung up their costumes after their actions were outlawed by the U.S. government. Comics readers were raised on costumed crime fighters who are intrinsically good, but *Watchmen* rejected that notion by featuring characters that are deeply disturbed human beings, whose morals are questionable at best: Rorschach, the son of a prostitute, ignores the federal law and continues his crime-fighting work. He is angry, *intensely* violent, and a near psychopath, who embraces the role of judge, jury, and executioner, as he sees fit. And it is hinted that the Comedian, a rapist, may have been the JFK assassin on the grassy knoll.

Like the protagonists of numerous post-modern American novels, the characters populating *Watchmen* weren't super-powered Boy Scouts, standing tall, with legs apart and fists on their hips. These masked avengers were as emotionally, mentally, and spiritually tainted as the criminals they fought, and readers—and critics—ate it up and licked the spoon! Michael G. Robinson's essay, within this volume, delves deeper in Moore's characters:

> In their earliest incarnations in our real history, superheroes enjoyed a certain moral virtue. DC Comics characters, like Superman or the Flash, faced danger with a smile and a blast of brightly colored heroics. Even their grimmest characters, like Batman, had moral certainty. Later, in the 1960s, Marvel Comics complicated the formula a bit, adding tragic figures, like Spider-Man, the Thing, or the Uncanny X-Men. These characters battled through their problems, redeeming their flaws in the defeat of villainy. *Watchmen* essentially argues that in the cold light of reality, all superhero characters are intensely flawed.

Robinson contends that *Watchmen* is not only different because of Alan Moore's intricate characterization and plotting, but a significant portion of the story's sense of foreboding comes from Dave Gibbons' unique visuals. Not only did graphic novels present writers with the opportunity to develop more intricate stories, they also allowed the artist freedom from the traditional format. Robinson, in his essay within this volume, explains that much of the power of *Watchmen* is due to the "extraordinary" artistic style of Dave Gibbons:

> In a structure that was unusual for the time, each page of the series is based on a standard format of nine panels per page. These panels are arranged in three rows and three columns. Many pages use all nine panels of this grid. For dramatic effect, some panels on some pages may become larger, occupying any number of grids. So, for example, the very first appearance in the entire series by Doctor Manhattan takes up six panels, occupying the left and middle columns of the page. The image shows the relative size of the colossal, nude Doctor Manhattan by demonstrating that Rorschach stands only as high as Manhattan's gigantic calf. The effect of using six panels further

highlights Doctor Manhattan's immense debut. In comic book art, a "splash page" is when a single panel or image occupies the entire page. Most comics in the 1980s used splash pages to open stories and add emphasis. *Watchmen* rarely surrenders all nine grid squares to a single image. In fact, the only splash pages in the entire series occur in the first six pages of the final issue. These images linger on the devastation of New York City.

Winners and Sinners

While not a brisk seller, *Watchmen* received critical acclaim and eventually was included on *TIME* magazine's 2005 list of the one hundred greatest novels since 1923. The success of *The Dark Knight Returns* and *Watchmen* altered the concept of what could be achieved in the comics medium and publishers were quick to respond to heightened public demand for additional works by releasing other popular series as single volumes and developing longer original works. Miller and Moore opened the door for other authors to sell longer works to publishers, while they themselves also had additional works to offer. Miller scored another smash success with the equally gritty *Sin City*, and Moore returned with another popular masked vigilante tale, titled *V for Vendetta.*

The explosion of graphic novels also caught the attention of Hollywood, and *Watchmen*, *Sin City*, and *V for Vendetta* all were morphed into live-action feature films. Both *Watchmen* and *Sin City* were noted for their particular style of art, which the film versions managed to mimic remarkably.

Non-comics writers also took notice of the new freedom offered in graphic novels and began producing their own works. British journalist and short story scribe Neil Gaiman became hooked on comics after finding a discarded issue of Alan Moore's *Swamp Thing* comic in a train station. Gaiman credits Moore with opening his eyes to what comics could do as a storytelling medium and began writing his own comics. Gaiman's work caught the attention of DC Comics executives, who offered him the opportunity to revive its *Sandman* property. It was a match made in Heaven, and *Sandman* quickly became a leading multivolume comics and graphic novel series. Like Moore and Miller, Gaiman stepped outside the standard boundaries to reinvent how comics are done. Mary Catherine Harper's essay, within this volume, notes:

> … Gaiman shapes the Sandman character into a complex being, who breaks the "frame" that traditional comics tend to place around superheroes: specifically, the way in which comic books rely on rectangular panels to indicate scenes and the flow of events that make up a plot. When a frame is broken, the panel's image flows past where its frame would go, beyond the "gutter" between frames, and into the space of one or more nearby panels. The form and meaning of the gutter in comics is explained by several literary critics, including Jared Gardner, who discusses the importance of the gutter as a metaphor for "the larger and often less formally explicit gaps that everywhere define how comics tell stories" (xi). The flow of a panel into and beyond a gutter has the effect of stopping the reader, as if it is saying "pay close attention to this out-of-bounds panel." For *Sandman*, the breaking of a frame serves, in part, as a metaphor for Morpheus deviating from the clear set of values and behavioral guidelines of superheroes in other episodic comics.

Best-selling mystery author Max Allan Collins, whose series of novels featuring Chicago PI Nathan Heller had become a favorite among hard-boiled detective fans, was bitten by the graphic novel bug after taking over the famous comic strip *Dick Tracy* from creator Chester Gould. Set during the Great Depression, Collins' volume *The Road to Perdition* was an old-school crime drama featuring protagonist Michael O'Sullivan, a war veteran turned mob enforcer, who seeks revenge against his bosses after they murder his family and leave only his oldest son, Michael Jr., alive. Like Miller's *Sin City*, Collins' *The Road to Perdition* diverts from the standard costumed hero adventures to present a straight mystery story that easily could have been written as a traditional non-illustrated novel. However, as Jared Griffin states, in his essay on Collins within this volume:

> At first glance, *Road to Perdition* does not seem like a typical superhero story, especially in the sense to which Wolk refers. *Road to Perdition* does not have a protagonist who can fly, shoot lasers out of

his eyes, or bear the weight of a supernatural origin story (though his background is foggy, which lends itself to spectacular mythmaking by others). Instead, our "hero," the elder Michael O'Sullivan, is granted the mythos of superhumanness by the narrator (at first), his son, who shares his father's name, and by other characters and true crime writers. While an understated agreement exists between these observers about the elder O'Sullivan's capabilities, superhumanness is still in the eye of the beholder: the younger Michael imagines his father as an incarnation of Tom Mix (a popular paperback cowboy, who influenced John Wayne), with the requisite super-abilities to dodge bullets, speedily react to threats, and sense danger around a corner; Michael's enemies take the myth further and grant him a supernatural moniker—the Archangel of Death. Historians, too, take pleasure in embellishing acts of violence and heroism, a practice that the younger Michael-as-adult is not too fond of, for his view of his father changes from myth to human, from superhero to vulnerable man. Younger Michael even warns his audience in the first frame about this mythmaking through unreliable memory; despite the story being written in black-and-white, there is plenty of gray in this story.

Although Collins had comics experience, he differs from the other authors discussed in this volume because he already was a successful novelist, with numerous titles to his credit before pursuing storytelling through graphic novels—more evidence of the medium's allure and its place as mainstream entertainment. Like *Watchmen* and *Sin City*, *The Road to Perdition* was purchased by Hollywood and became an Oscar–winning 2002 feature film, starring Paul Newman and with Tom Hanks as O'Sullivan.

The essays collected in this volume delve deeply into the background of each title discussed here—and several more—as well as the history and critical development of graphic novels, which have altered the landscape of the comics medium permanently.

CRITICAL
CONTEXTS

The Superhero Narrative and the Graphic Novel

Joseph J. Darowski

For many in contemporary culture, the superhero genre and the comic book industry have become inextricably linked. For example, it seems that, to public perception, a so-called "comic book movie" is synonymous with a superhero movie. It is even possible to overhear people referring to "the comic book genre," although this is a misnomer. As Douglas Wolk explains, "As cartoonists and their longtime admirers are getting a little tired of explaining, comics are not a genre; they're a medium" (11). The medium of comic books, a combination of text and images, which Scott McCloud defined as "juxtaposed pictorial and other images in deliberate sequence, intended to convey information and/or produce an aesthetic response in the viewer" (9), can be used to tell stories in any genre. In fact, the comic book industry has historically found significant success with other genres. There have been periods in the comic book industry when funny animal stories, romantic soap operas, sci-fi adventures, or horror tales outsold the superhero comic books. Also significant is that the superhero genre has been immensely popular in other mediums. The superhero genre has become a staple on film, television, and in video games.

But despite these distinctions, the connection between superheroes and comic books remains strong. It is easy to understand how the genre and mode of storytelling have become identified with one another. It was in comic books that the superhero genre was fully formed and fleshed out in the late 1930s, and the superhero comic books have been the most successful genre for the industry's largest publishers in the last several decades.

The superhero genre and comic books came together when Superman appeared on the cover of 1938's *Action Comics #1*. Larry Tye explains that the "very cover of *Action Comics* No. 1 signaled how groundbreaking—how uplifting—this Superman would be.

There he was, in bold primary colors: blue full-body tights, a yellow chest shield and candy apple cape, booties, and briefs over his tights" (30). Peter Coogan calls Superman the "first character to fully embody the definition of the superhero and to prompt the imitation and repetition necessary for the emergence of a genre" (175). Superman may be the first superhero that codified the elements of the superhero genre into one character and narrative, but Superman didn't just emerge onto the popular culture scene bursting from his creators' imaginations. Jerry Siegel and Joe Shuster, the writer and artist responsible for Superman, were tapping into various narrative traditions that included all of the elements of the superhero genre. Superman comic books put the pre-existing elements together, establishing the generic conventions consumers now identify with the superhero genre.

Pre-History of the Superhero Genre

The superhero genre has two clear antecedents: classic mythology and American adventure stories. Joseph Campbell explained that many myths follow a specific pattern, a pattern Campbell called the Hero's Journey. Many superhero adventures, notably origin stories, which often feature calls to adventure and refusals of the call, follow a similar pattern. Additionally, many ancient myths feature fantastical beings, powers beyond mortal men, secret disguises, and death-defying battles. Clearly, the superhero genre has borrowed from these ancient narratives.

John Shelton Lawrence and Robert Jewett identified an American variation of the Heroes' Journey. In a summary that encompasses the archetypes of the "American Monomyth," Lawrence and Jewett explain the typical plot found in American heroic adventures:

> A community in harmonious paradise is threatened by evil; normal institutions fail to contend with this threat; a self-less superhero emerges to renounce temptations and carry out the redemptive task; aided by fate, his decisive victory restores the community to its paradisiacal condition; the superhero then recedes into obscurity (6).

Significantly, for the early comic book creators who established the genre, there were stories in dime novels, pulp magazines, and radio shows that followed this formula and had elements that would be appropriated into the superhero genre. If we accept that Superman's first appearance in 1938 represents the first full conception of the superhero genre, combining all the elements that would come to be identified as part of the genre, there are still dozens, if not hundreds, of earlier stories featuring do-gooders, mystery men, and adventurers, who come close to fitting into the superhero genre. Coogan identifies four key elements of the superhero genre: Mission, Powers, Identity, and Costume (30–33). All of these are found in Superman's first appearance, but all of these had been seen before.

For example, protagonists with missions to aid the helpless, protect the downtrodden, or provide a service no one else can are found throughout the history of American popular culture (and are certainly not exclusive to American popular culture). Dime novels often featured heroic frontiersmen or cowboys, brave government agents, or detectives who fought to uphold the values of society, even if they themselves did not quite fit in with society's structure. As the dime novels died out, this type of character found a new home in pulp magazines, and subsequently, new versions of this character appeared in newspaper comic strips and early comic books. In non-print media, this character was also popular in feature-length movies, on the radio, and episodic movie serials before naturally transferring into every subsequent form of entertainment media. The character with a noble heroic mission is far from unique to comic book superheroes.

An important distinction for the superhero genre is that the characters often carry out their missions with the aid of superpowers of some sort. These could be powers that are bestowed through science, as with Spider-Man; mystic arts, as with Dr. Strange; technology, as with Iron Man); alien abilities, as with Superman; or a birthright that sets a character apart from normal humans, as with Wonder Woman or the X-Men.

There were several characters that appeared in popular narratives before 1938 and had more-than-human abilities. The comic strip character Hugo Hercules first appeared in 1903 and had super strength. Hugo Danner, the protagonists of Phillip Wylie's 1930 sci-fi novel *Gladiator*, had powers very similar to those possessed by Superman in his earliest stories. The Shadow, a character that began as a narrator of radio dramas in 1930, was eventually spun off into a pulp magazine and had pseudo-psychic powers that aided him in his battles with villains. There were many other examples that predate Superman of comic strip adventurers, pulp heroes, and mystery men with powers beyond those of mortal men.

Another key element of the superhero genre Coogan identified is identity, although this could be tweaked to read dual-identity. There are many stories in popular culture that predate Superman and feature characters with secret identities who act in a manner to dissuade suspicion that they are really a costumed adventurer. Baroness Emmuska Orczy wrote *The Scarlet Pimpernel*, first published in 1905, which features Sir Percy Blakeney pretending to be an upper-class fop, when, in reality, he is a competent and brilliant man who saves French aristocrats from the Reign of Terror. However, the Scarlet Pimpernel doesn't have the identifiable costume of a Superman or Batman.

Costume is the fourth element of the genre that Coogan identified. There were several characters that wore costumes before Superman's first appearance. In 1919, the pulp magazine *All-Story Weekly* published the first of Johnston McCulley's stories that would feature the black-masked Zorro. Don Diego Vega (later his surname would be changed to de la Vega), who, like Blakeney, pretends to be an upper class dandy, wears the costume of Zorro to protect the helpless citizens from corrupt government officials. The Phantom first appeared in newspaper comic strips in 1936, and he wore a mask and brightly colored costume, while operating out of a secret base called Skull Cave.

In retrospect, many of the proto-heroes are clear predecessors to Superman. But for a genre to exist there needs to be clearly established conventions. Superman codified these conventions to the degree that there were, after his first appearance, many imitators and even parodies of the superhero genre. The earlier characters had not put all of the elements together in such a way that a new genre was introduced into the popular culture of America.

The Birth of the Superhero Genre

The superhero genre became one of the most identifiable genres associated with comic books as the industry moved away from simply reprinting newspaper comic strips and began publishing original material. In 1933, a publisher named Maxwell Gaines produced what many consider to be the first American comic book, entitled *Funnies on Parade*. Though there had been previous publications that used images and text to tell a story, *Funnies on Parade* had many of the familiar aspects of the modern American comic book, including its standard magazine size, sequential art, and color printing. However, it lacked original content and was, instead, a reprint of newspaper comic strips. Because of its success, other publishers soon began to reprint newspaper comic strips in comic book format. The first original content in the new comic books came in 1935 with *New Fun: The Big Comics Magazine* (Rhoades 10–12).

In 1938, the Superman comic strip, which had been shopped to newspaper comic strip syndicates, was picked up and the character featured on the cover of National Periodicals' *Action Comics #1*. National Periodicals would later change its name to DC Comics. *Action Comics*, at the time, was planned as an anthology, which contained several different stories and planned to rotate any recurring characters in and out of issues. Superman proved so successful that he was soon the primary feature in the series and was eventually spun off into his own eponymous title. Like most entertainment industries, success bred imitation in the comic books. Soon, other publishers were producing their own costumed, code-named heroes with superpowers. Some, such as a character called Wonder Man, were so derivative of Superman that *National Periodicals* sued (van Lente and Dunlavey 34). This early period has become known as the Golden Age of comic books.

National imitated its own success with Superman by asking Bob Kane to create another superhero to be featured in *Detective Comics*, another anthology title the company published. Bob Kane is legally credited as the creator of Batman, but Bill Finger played a significant role in defining the look and other attributes of the character. With the dual success of Superman and Batman indicating an audience appetite for superhero adventures, the floodgates opened.

Some of the subsequent characters, such as Wonder Woman and Captain America had notably patriotic and propagandistic origin stories. The superhero genre as a whole became associated with the war effort and the concept of American exceptionalism. With the end of World War II, interest in the superhero genre waned, although comic books as a whole continued to sell well. Audience interest and publisher focus simply shifted to other genres. These included the funny animal comics, such as Walt Disney's *Scrooge McDuck*; horror comics, such as EC Comics' *Tales from the Crypt*; crime comics, such as EC Comics' *Crime SuspenStories*; sci-fi comics, such as DC Comics' Adam Strange, who appeared in *Showcase*; and Westerns, such as Atlas Comics' *Two-Gun Kid*. While Superman, Batman, and Wonder Woman comic books continued to be published throughout the 1950s, almost all other superhero comic books disappeared entirely.

The comic book industry came under close scrutiny in the late 1940s and 1950s from public officials. Accusations linking the reading of comic books with juvenile delinquency became prominent enough that the U.S. government held hearings on the matter. Bradford W. Wright argues that "the debate over comic books was really about cultural power in postwar America," and as Cold War fears rose, "influence over young people became hotly contested terrain" (87). Perhaps the loudest voice raising these claims belonged to Dr. Fredric Wertham, a psychologist who first presented his research in a paper called "Horror in the Nursery" and later published a book entitled *Seduction of the Innocent*, which purported to prove that reading comic books was directly associated with criminality, homosexuality, and other perceived social ills of the time (Nyberg 32, 50). The government hearings resulted in thinly veiled threats that, if the publishers did not control the content of its comic books, the government may step in to regulate the industry.

The publishers collectively formed The Comics Code Authority, a self-censoring board that would examine every comic book published and literally bestow a stamp of approval on comics that met their standards. Comics without the Authority's seal of approval would not be sold by most comic book vendors in the United States. The Comics Code Authority produced a strict code that all comic books would have to adhere to in order to be approved, and these guidelines essentially eliminated several of the most popular comic books from distribution. The Comics Code ensured that all comic books published would adhere to a strict moral code and avoid what were perceived as potentially corruptive influences in their narratives (Duncan and Smith 39–40).

The Maturation of the Superhero Genre

In an era when publication guidelines mandated that good always triumph over evil and that strict moral codes be enforced within the narratives, the superhero genre seemed a natural choice to replace the horror and crime comic books that had largely been censored out of existence. DC Comics was still publishing Superman, Batman, and Wonder Woman comic books, but decided to reintroduce a character from the Golden Age, the Flash. They gave the character a new origin, a new secret identity, and a new costume, and launched what many identify as the Silver Age of comic books with 1956's *Showcase #4*. Sales were good enough that DC continued to reintroduce Golden Age characters, and in 1960, the company reintroduced a team comic book, *The Justice League*. This new iteration of the old Justice Society was so successful that other publishing companies took notice.

The publisher of Atlas Comics, which would be renamed Marvel Comics, asked his editor to produce superhero comic books. Stanley Lieber, who published comic books under the pseudonym Stan Lee, would write and collaborate with an extremely talented and prolific artist named Jack Kirby to produce *Fantastic Four #1*. Following the success of this new comic book series, Lee would collaborate with Kirby and other artists to transform Atlas Comics into Marvel Comics, home to one of the two most popular and expansive superhero narrative universes. Among the most popular creations from this period was Lee and Steve Ditko's Spider-Man, an instant and enduring success for Marvel. Some other series introduced concepts that did not succeed at the time, but in time matured into iconic characters. Lee and Kirby's *Incredible Hulk*, for example, was canceled after only six issues, but the character has become a staple of Marvel Comics and has been adapted for film and television. Similarly, the X-Men was canceled after sixty-six issues, but after being re-launched in the 1970s, the series would become one of the most successful franchises in comic book history.

Marvel's Silver Age superhero comic books introduced new elements that were missing from earlier examples of the genre. The characters were more flawed, the stories more complex, and the fans more invested. Whereas impediments had often been external in the Golden Age, such as Superman's weakness to Kryptonite, Marvel's Silver Age heroes were often their own worst enemies because their flaws were internal. Spider-Man's "Kryptonite" is not a glowing rock, rather it is his own guilt, self-doubt, and self-loathing. The Justice League came together to fight as a team, but the Fantastic Four were a bickering family that was thrust into the roles of superheroes. While Bruce Wayne chose to become Batman to fight criminals, Bruce Banner feared becoming the Hulk and facing the U.S. military.

Stan Lee had many roles at Marvel. He was an editor, a creator, a writer, but also an extremely successful salesman. Wright explains that Lee "cultivated an image of Marvel as a maverick within the comic book field, much like the outsider heroes themselves" (217). Lee's role in nurturing the fan culture that has become an important element of the comic book industry should not be underestimated. Lee created a sense of camaraderie between creators and fans through his narration boxes, his editorial boxes, his columns, and in the letter pages. Even when the creators themselves weren't getting along with each other, Lee created the sense that Marvel's fans and creators were part of one big, happy family.

The Deconstruction of the Superhero Genre

In the 1980s another shift occurred for superhero comic books. The Golden Age saw the introduction of iconic, perfect heroes. The Silver Age saw the introduction of flawed, imperfect heroes. In the 1980s dark anti-heroes were introduced or surged in popularity. Another trend was stories that deconstructed the genre. Now that the elements of the genre had been firmly established, and stories had spent decades telling stories while mostly adhering to those conventions, writers began to deconstruct the genre. Stories such as *Watchmen* and *The Dark Knight Returns* were firmly entrenched within the superhero genre, but extrapolated inherent flaws and limitations within the genre while telling their stories.

Watchmen, written by Alan Moore and drawn by Dave Gibbons, carried the end result of superheroes enforcing their values on society to its terrifying conclusion. *The Dark Knight Returns*, written and drawn by Frank Miller, explored the end of the career of a superhero after a society has become dependent on protectors with superpowers. While these are excellent stories with complex themes, one thing that has been frequently noted is that they represent comic books that are distinctly not for children. As Wolk says, "The initial praise outside the comics world for *The Dark Knight Returns* and *Watchmen* didn't mention that they were well-wrought as much as they were 'grown up" (102). The target comic book audience was no longer implicitly children. Comic books could be published carrying the warning on the cover that the content was intended for "mature readers."

Simultaneous with these darker stories from DC Comics, Marvel was enjoying success with darker anti-heroes, including Wolverine and the Punisher. Wolverine had been created in the mid-1970s, but experienced a surge in popularity in the 1980s. He headlined his own series and guest-starred in numerous mini-series, one-shots, and other characters' series. Whereas Spider-Man webbed villains to incapacitate them, Wolverine had sets of retractable claws that emerged from the backs of his hands. This undeniably more violent method of dealing with enemies was a marked departure from the early Silver Age of comics, where violence was often implied and rarely gratuitous. The Punisher was even more violent, as he chose to kill rather than wound or incapacitate most of his enemies.

Other stories from this period, such as DC Comics' *Crisis on Infinite Earths* are indicative of a new style of superhero comic books coming from mainstream publishers. These stories represent a loss of the assumed innocence that seemed to permeate Silver Age superhero comic books. In keeping with the age names from earlier eras, some have proposed that comics after the mid-1980s be called the Iron Age. Although this name has not been used as widely as Golden Age and Silver Age, most agree there was a change in superhero comic books in this era.

Considering the Superhero Genre

The superhero has several clear generic elements already discussed, including the protagonist's mission, identity, and powers. But there are many other elements of the genre worthy of consideration and in-depth analysis, including the concept of continuity and some of the problematic race and gender issues that are embedded within the tradition of superhero comic books.

The narrative universes of the most popular mainstream superhero stories, notably DC Comics and Marvel Comics, include a complex continuity. This continuity is the consistent ongoing storyline of the entire line of superhero comic books published by the companies. This means that the stories found in an X-Men comic book are supposedly happening in the same world and may have an impact in the narratives found in other Marvel comic book titles. Ostensibly, this continuity encompasses the entirety of the published history of Marvel and DC Comics. DC Comics has rebooted their entire continuity more than once, notably with a storyline called *Crisis on Infinite Earths* in the 1980s, and recently following a story called *Flashpoint*, DC launched what was termed the "New 52," a new continuity that restarted their superhero universe. However, both of these reboots came out of stories that began in the previous continuity and ended with the new continuity. Thus, there remains some connective narrative tissue between the pre- and post-crisis DC Universe and the pre- and post-New 52 DC Universe.

This continuity is simultaneously a positive and a negative for both creators and consumers. On the one hand, it invites consumers to read all the comic books published by the company, potentially creating a rewarding depth to the reading experience and adding to the sales for the company. However, with several decades of continuity built up, there are undoubtedly errors and contradictions, which plague stories. Also, the faithfulness a publisher has felt to continuity has varied over the years. For example, in the 1980s, when Chris Claremont wrote a mini-series detailing Wolverine's adventures in Japan, he wrote Wolverine out of the X-Men comic books so that he wouldn't seem to be appearing in two places at once. But in the 2000s, with Wolverine having become one of the most popular characters in the industry, Wolverine appeared in multiple team books as well as several individual titles and mini-series that were all ostensibly occurring at the same time. With a tight continuity, it would be impossible to explain his appearances in so many comic books within the same month, but with Marvel's looser continuity in the 2000s, readers were expected to simply go along with it.

Another aspect of superhero storytelling is the repetition. Superhero comic books belong to two narrative traditions. As Umberto Eco argued, superheroes exist as an unchanging archetype that means the characters "must necessarily become immobilized in an emblematic and fixed nature which renders him easily recognizable" (149). Simultaneously, comic books are telling a grand continuing narrative requiring that characters "be subjected to a development which is typical [...] of novelistic characters" (149). As a result of serving the two narrative masters of unchanging archetype and novelistic advancement, the illusion of change must be provided with very little change actually occurring. Thus, Superman can be killed for a storyline, but he will eventually return and resume his role as Clark Kent, reporter for the *Daily Planet*, love interest to Lois Lane, and protector of humanity. Even seemingly long-term changes may eventually be undone to return the character to an earlier state. Peter Parker was married to Mary Jane Watson for twenty years when, due to an editorial mandate, the marriage was undone to return Peter Parker to a more iconic single status.

Nat Gertler identified four of the most commonly repeated storylines in superhero comic books. These include 1) stories of a hero striving to stop badness—a villain has a plot to take over the world and a hero stops him, 2) stories exploring why heroes strive to stop badness—more introspection from the heroes as they stop the villains, 3) stories of the results or repercussions of heroes stopping badness—deconstructions of the traditional superhero story, and 4) the never-ending cycle of villains attacking the heroes—harming the hero has become the villain's focus rather than robbing a bank or world domination (Duncan and Smith 228–9). Versions of these stories can be found repeated across the decades of DC and Marvel's publications, often repeated in the same title in consecutive stories.

Unfortunately, another aspect that is repeated often is a stereotypic identity of the heroic protagonist. With the genre having been codified in the late 1930s, the standard look and appearance of superheroes was established in a time where many of the protagonists in popular culture fit a particular type. While there were some early female superheroes, most prominently Wonder Woman, the vast majority of superheroes in the earliest superhero comic books were male. The first superhero appeared in 1938, but the first black superhero to appear in mainstream superhero comic books was Marvel's Black Panther in the 1960s. And while romance was a key part of early DC and Marvel superhero comic books, it was exclusively heterosexual romance. The first homosexual character in mainstream comic books was Northstar, a character created in 1979, but not officially outed until 1992. The portrayal of female characters, minority characters, and homosexual characters has improved through time in terms of representation and non-stereotypical characterizations, but the default superhero remains a white, heterosexual male.

Because of the preponderance of heterosexual male protagonists in superhero comic books, female characters have all too often been relegated to supporting cast roles, often as love interests. Even when a female is a member of a team, she has often been cast into a more subservient or domesticated role than her male counterparts. For example, Wonder Woman was the secretary of the original Justice Society of America and Marvel Girl was shown acting as a cook and nurse for the male members of the X-Men in the 1960s.

Minority characters that appeared in the earlier eras of comic books were much more likely to be villains than heroes. Even in X-Men comic books of the 1960s, a series which has a reputation for a progressive thematic core, the only prominent minority characters were a group of villains, while the team itself was entirely white until the mid-1970s.

There are certainly positive aspects of the superhero genre. It can be both inspirational and aspirational. It can demonstrate moral codes that benefit society. It can entertain and provide escape. But to ignore some of the problematic aspects of the genre would prevent necessary correctives from taking place. The superhero genre has lasted for 75 years. It doesn't seem to be going away in the foreseeable future, but it will inevitably change and alter, along with the society that consumes these stories. Hopefully, the positive aspects of the genre will be maximized and the problematic history of stereotyped minorities and objectified females will be minimized.

Works Cited

Campbell, Joseph. *The Hero with a Thousand Faces*. NY: Princeton UP, 1949.

Coogan, Peter. *Superhero: The Secret Origin of a Genre*. Austin, TX: Monkey Brain Books, 2006.

Duncan, Randy and Matthew J. Smith. *The Power of Comics: History, Form, & Culture*. NY: Continuum, 2009.

Eco, Umberto. "The Myth of Superman." *Arguing Comics: Literary Masters on a Popular Medium*. Eds. Jeet Heer and Kent Worcester. Jackson, U of Mississippi P, 2004.

Lawrence, John Shelton and Robert Jewett. *The Myth of the American Superhero*. Grand Rapids, MI: William B. Eardmans Publishing Company, 2002.

McCloud, Scott. *Understanding Comics: The Invisible Art*. Northampton, MA: Kitchen Sink Press, 1993.

Nyberg, Amy Kiste. *Seal of Approval: The History of the Comics Code*. Jackson, MS: U of Mississippi P, 1998.

Rhoades, Shirrel. *A Complete History of American Comic Books*. NY: Peter Lang
  Publishing, 2008.

Tye, Larry. *Superman: The High-Flying History of America's Most Enduring Hero*. NY: Random House, 2012.

Van Lente, Fred and Ryan Dunlavey. *The Comic Book History of Comics*. San
  Diego, CA: IDW, 2012.

Wolk, Douglas. *Reading Comics: How Graphic Novels Work and What They Mean*. Cambridge, MA: Da Capo Press, 2007.

Wright, Bradford W. *Comic Book Nation: The Transformation of Youth Culture in*
  America. Baltimore, Johns Hopkins UP, 2001.

The Horror Narrative and the Graphic Novel

Lance Eaton

The early twenty-first century has given rise to hordes of horror graphic novels and appears to be one of the most successful periods for the resurgence of genre-storytelling within the history of comics. These narratives have served as inspiration for a great deal of storytelling in other media, including television (*The Walking Dead*), film (*30 Days of Night*; *From Hell*, *Blade*), novels (the *Cal McDonald* series, the *Walking Dead's Governor* Series), and video games (*Hellboy: The Science of Evil*, *The Darkness*). Comics and graphic novels have also served as the home for further exploration into the worlds produced by horror creators in other media, such as the ongoing *Buffy the Vampire Slayer* comic book series by Joss Whedon, another series on the *28 Days Later* film series, and a series of mini-series based upon the video game, *Silent Hill*. This essay acts as a guide to the elements of horror comics and their origins within the larger comic book history. In order to the present the state of horror graphic novels, it also identifies the key contributions by individuals, organizations, and the culture at large.

As a genre within comic books, horror relies on several features, in order to instill tension within the reader. Visuals are a major feature of comic book horror narratives. However, visuals can work in many different ways. The two significant ways of playing with visuals in comic books is either by providing as graphic an illustration as possible, thereby emphasizing gore and disgust. However, comic books also play with visuals by denying the reader the ability to see what is horrific. Readers are left to wonder why a protagonist's face is stricken with fear, or what the monster looks like that is casting such a strange shadow. An extension of this approach is the creator's use of closure around the horror. The creator must choose what moments to encapsulate in panels and which moments of the story to envision for the reader. Creators regularly balance how much is shown with how much they want their readers to imagine. A blending of both strategies has become an increasingly popular style that is best represented by Ben Templesmiths' artwork. His artistic style presents characters and environments that have both clear physical attributes, such as vampire's sharp and gnarly teeth, and abstract characteristics, such as that same vampire having no other distinguishing facial features. When violent, brutal, and horrific moments occur, they are a mixture of both specific detail and a lack of clarity that produces its own sense of unease within the reader.

Horror in graphic novels cannot be accurately understood without taking a look at the history of horror comic books and their impact on comic storytelling throughout the twentieth century. It is only in this context that one can appreciate the popularity and significance of horror graphic novels over the last twenty years.

Though comic strips were popular by the end of the 1800s and comic books became popular in the late 1930s, comic books that focused solely on horror would not emerge until the late 1940s. However, the roots of horror comics can be traced back to Gothic novels and the works of horror writers, such as Edgar Allan Poe, Robert Louis Stevenson, and Bram Stoker. These writers fueled the imagination of pulp fiction writers in the 1920s and 1930s, such a H.P. Lovecraft, Robert E. Howard, and Clark Ashton Smith. Horror comics were also influenced by horror films from as early as Thomas Edison's *Frankenstein* of 1910 up through Universal Studios' horror films of the 1930s and 1940s, as well as the horror radio series of the 1930s and 1940s, such as *Inner Sanctum Mysteries*, *Lights Out*, and *The Weird Circle*. These creators laid much of the foundation for horror comic books and still remain inspirational to contemporary horror comic book writers.

Action, adventure, mystery, and comedy were the popular genres for comic strips throughout the early 1900s, and these, too, became popular comic book genres in the 1930s. Then, the publication of *Actions Comics #1* in 1938, featuring Superman, led to the dominance of the superhero genre within comic book publishing. Over the first few years, superhero comic books did branch out and include its share of horror-inspired villains. Superman faced such mad scientists and geniuses as Professor Zee (*Superman #8*, January–February 1941) and Lex Luthor (*Action Comics #23*, April 1940). Yet, it was Batman, whose identity was subsumed by horror and whose costume struck fear in villains, where many horror-inspired characters appeared. Batman fought such characters as Doctor Death (*Detective Comics #29*, July 1939), the vampiric Mad Monk (*Detective Comics #31*, September 1939), and Two-Face (*Detective Comics #66*, August 1942). The latter villain's first appearance directly drew upon Stevenson's *The Strange Case of Dr. Jekyll and Mr. Hyde*, with the opening page of the issue showing Two-Face reading "Dr. Jekyll and Mr. Hyde" and being described as "a twentieth-century Jekyll-Hide."

The first genuine horror stories published in comic books came in the 1940s, mainly as adaptations of written works. Some adaptations, such as Mary Shelley's *Frankenstein* (*Prize Comics #7*, December 1940) and Washington Irving's "A Legend of Sleepy Hollow" (*Classic Comics #12*, June 1943) were published as short comics within a larger anthology, but *Classic Comics #13* in August, 1943 published what is considered the first horror comic book, *The Strange Case of Dr. Jekyll and Mr. Hyde*. The *Classic Comics* series produced comic book adaptations of classic literary works and followed with another adaptation of *Frankenstein* two years later in *Classic Comics #26*.

The end of World War II marked a growing change in comic book themes. An entire generation of readers had grown up with superheroes and light-hearted fare, but the brutalities of war meant that the more gentle comic books of the late 1930s and 1940s would not engage an audience, which had witnessed the devastation wrought by the true horrors of war. Though still dominant in many ways, the superhero genre soon found itself competing with the emerging crime genre. Starting as early as 1942 with the series *Crime Does Not Pay*, an anthology of crime stories inspired by true events, the genre gained momentum as soldiers, who read comics abroad, returned home looking for stories with a bit more edge. More crime comic books followed suit and these grittier tales opened up the door to more horror-themed stories.

Although *Eerie Comics #1* came out in 1947 with clear horror tropes throughout the issue, it failed to produce a second issue for another four years. In 1948, the ongoing *Adventures into the Unknown* produced a regular assortment of horror stories, and between 1948 and 1949, other publishers began experimenting with horror by changing an anthology comic book's focus to horror, or by regularly including horror stories among the other features within the anthology.

As publishers and consumers continued to widen their taste in genres to include the aforementioned crime and even romance comic books, EC Comics quickly rose as the major publisher of horror comic books. Originally known as "Educational Comics" under the original owner, Max Gaines, it was converted to "Entertaining Comics" by his son, Bill Gaines, when he inherited the business. As a less successful publisher, EC Comics followed the changing trends within comic books until 1950, when it moved ahead with launching several horror anthology comic books and subsequently became the most familiar name in horror comic books for the 1950s.

The popular series by EC Comics included *Tales from the Crypt*, *The Vault of Horror*, and *The Haunt of Fear*, each featuring a host akin to the radio horror shows of the time. The host served to introduce each story or transition to other stories within the collection. Using a fictional host to bridge an individual comic book's stories, as well as connect each issue in a series, created a consistency and continuity that was lacking in other anthology comics of the time. Readers knew, with each issue, they would encounter the Crypt Keeper, the Vault Keeper, or the Old Witch, the respective hosts of *Tales from the Crypt*, *The Vault of Horror* and *The Haunt of Fear*. They often used puns and gross commentary or goofy outfits and expressions as they introduced the stories. These characters regularly brought a humorous touch to the otherwise graphic and grim stories.

Another significant attribute of the EC Comics horror line was the use of morbid justice. Predominantly, the stories were not horrific in content just for the sake of gratuitousness. Rather, the violence and gore embedded in each story served the purpose of delivering justice to a person or people who had committed some type of crime. Harm done to the innocent never went unpunished, and often, the perpetrators received punishments that were in sharp contrast to the horrible things they had done.

EC Comics' overwhelming success instigated other publishers to follow suit with their own horror comic series, and the genre quickly took up a significant market share of comic books sold monthly. As publishers competed for readers, they regularly tried to outperform one another. The rivalry resulted in more graphic stories with each passing month. As stories became increasingly gruesome, so too did comic book covers, which by 1954 were catching the attention of many parents.

The moment of crisis for the horror genre in comic books came in 1954. In the years prior to 1954, various cultural critics had spoken out against comic books and made various arguments about the content and quality of such popular entertainment in the hands of young children. The most vocal of these critics was the psychiatrist Dr. Frederic Wertham, who, since the late 1940s, had been publishing academic and popular articles on the subject of comic books as a threat to youth. But in 1953 and 1954, Wertham made a strong case, strategically placed to be heard by parents. Though his book, *Seduction of the Innocent: The Influence of Comic Books on Today's Youth*, was published in 1954, and prior to publication, Wertham had articles and excerpts published in *Ladies' Home Journal* in 1953 and *Reader's Digest* in 1954. These publications' major audience was women, particularly middle-class mothers, who helped to initiate campaigns large and small to remove and destroy horror comic books.

The overall message of Wertham's book was that his professional experience with studying juvenile delinquents had revealed to him that they all had obsessive fixations with comic books and that comic books were, in part, contributing to a dramatic increase in such delinquency. With each chapter, the book addressed a different genre, identifying the key elements that contributed to the corruption of youth. The success of Wertham and his book resulted in hearings by the Senate Subcommittee on Juvenile Delinquency on the subject of horror and crime comics. Led by Senator Estes Kefauver, these hearings took place in April and June of 1954 in New York, and featured Wertham as an expert witness. Publishers, including Bill Gaines, were called to give testimony. Gaines' argument of artistic expression and First Amendment rights were not persuasive enough for the subcommittee and the public to believe horror comic books were acceptable to a young audience.

Rallying to prevent government interference, the Comics Magazine Association of America produced the Comics Code Authority, an internal censorship board to address the issues raised by Wertham and others. The Comics Code Authority would provide a seal of approval to comic books only if they met the standards put forth by the newly established code. The code used language and restrictions derived from the Motion Picture Production Code of the 1930s, but took more draconian measures, particularly around the genre of horror and crime. Under General Standards Part B, the words "horror" and "terror" were not to be included in comic book titles. The same section also stated that "Scenes dealing with, or instruments associated with walking dead, torture, vampires and vampirism, ghouls, cannibalism and werewolfism [were] prohibited."

The impact on horror comic books came fast and put many publishers out of business in the following years. EC Comics attempted to continue to publish comic books without and then with the Comic Code Authority's seal, but regularly faced challenges in getting their comic books onto newsstands. EC Comics continued to exist in part due to their other popular publication, *MAD Magazine*.

The restrictions implemented by the Comics Code Authority limited the complexity of stories that could be told within comic books as a whole, but severely limited the nature and dynamics of horror stories. Throughout much of the 1950s and early 1960s publishers only flirted with horror themes within their comic books. Some companies did venture into horror by adapting classic written works or adaptations of films and television series, such as Gilbert

Company's *Classics Illustrated* series or Dell Comics' *Twilight Zone* series.

Starting in the 1960s, publishers looked to circumvent the Comics Code Authority by publishing horror comics as black-and-white, magazine-size publications instead of the traditional color-based comic books. These magazines could bypass the Comics Code Authority and end up on shelves at newspaper stands. Warren Publications was one of the most successful in this venture with *Creepy* debuting in 1964 and *Eerie* in 1966. The larger publishers, DC Comics and Marvel Comics, also pursued this tactic in the ensuing years.

By the early 1970s, it became clear to the Comics Code Authority that the culture was changing and that its restrictions needed loosening. In 1968, the Motion Picture of America Association stopped enforcing its censorship code and moved to a movie rating system that still stands today, providing a specific rating to indicate the levels of appropriate and inappropriate content. The change brought a new level of storytelling within horror films and generated a lot of new interest in horror storytelling. Comic book publishers also looked to profit from the renewed interest. Though the Comics Code Authority did not change to a rating system like films, it did allow for more horror content to be present within comic books so long as it fell into traditional themes of classic horror fiction.

The 1970s marked the return of horror within comic books in a variety of ways. Marvel Comics slowly began publishing horror comics as magazines under its Curtis Circulation Company brand, which included *Dracula Lives!* of 1973, *Monsters Unleashed* of 1973, and *Vampire Tales* of 1973. Marvel Comics also pushed forward several comic book series based on famous horror characters, including *The Tomb of Dracula* of 1972, *Werewolf by Night* of 1972, and *The Monster of Frankenstein* 1973. Publishers returned to publishing horror stories as part of their anthology series or even returned to horror anthology comic books to include series from DC Comics such as *Ghosts* of 1971, *Secrets of Sinister House* of 1972, and *Secrets of Haunted House* of 1975. In addition to horror stories, these two major publishers also began incorporating horror more directly into their fictional universes with horror-inspired protagonists, such as DC Comics' *Swamp Thing*, which debuted 1971, and Marvel Comics' *Ghost Rider*, which debuted 1972.

The rise of underground comics in the 1960s and 1970s also gave rise to new publishers in the late 1970s through the early 1990s, some of which operated without the code and were free to explore many different themes and genres, including horror. Arrow Comics, Caliber Comics, Dark Horse Comics, and Eclipse Comics were among the dozens of publishers that appeared during these decades and featured various single and ongoing horror narratives. Dark Horse Comics established itself early as a publisher of intellectual properties from film and television and generated comic adaptations and follow-up stories to such film series as *Aliens* and *Evil Dead*. Image Comics quickly became a significant publisher after its premiere in 1992 and produced several series, such as *Spawn*, *Darkchylde*, and *Trencher*. These contained relevant horror tropes, including demons, zombies, and various hellish or nightmarish characters.

By the 1990s, horror comic books and even graphic novels could be found at local comic book stores. Although horror as a genre within comic books was nowhere near as popular as it was in the 1950s, they were slowly gaining wider appeal. The growth was precipitated not only by the rise of independent comic publishers reaching into realms that the mainstream publishers would not, but also because horror was growing increasingly popular in other realms of entertainment. Throughout the 1980s and 1990s, horror films continued to make big returns at movie theaters and established long-lasting film franchises that crossed over into comics, including the *Friday the 13th*, *Nightmare on Elm Street*, *Halloween*, and *Chucky*. Horror fiction writers continued to publish works that regularly made best-sellers lists, including the works of Clive Barker, Ramsey Campbell, Stephen King, Dean Koontz, and Peter Straub. Horror as a genre also became popular with young adults as writers, such as R. L. Stine and Christopher Pike, published numerous individual and serial horror tales.

Another clear sign that the horror genre was ready to return in full to comic books was the HBO television series, *Tales of the Crypt*. Running from 1989 to 1996, this series adapted many of the famous stories from the EC Comics horror series. The inspiration for the show came from the various reprints and republications of the EC Comics series released in the 1970s and 1980s.

The 1990s also featured numerous teams and characters intrigued by the occult and supernatural. Various supernatural characters in Marvel Comics, such as Ghost Rider, Morbius, Dr. Strange, and others teamed up for several crossover series and were referred to as the Midnight Sons. Dark Horse Comics had one of the most interesting runs with its *Hellboy* series in the 1990s, which walked the line between superhero and supernatural. The title character is part of the Bureau for Paranormal Research and Defense (B.P.R.D.), which investigates the supernatural in order to protect the world. Many adventures have Hellboy and other assorted B.P.R.D. members facing off against possessions, Lovecraftian demons, horrific beings from other dimensions, and other such threats. The popularity of the series led to a spin-off series for B.P.R.D. and several other characters on the team, as well as two feature films, two animated films, several novels, and a handful of video games.

The twenty-first century also began with the launch of IDW Publishing in 2000, a comic book publisher whose primary focus was on horror comic books. They eventually branched out to do licensed properties, though many of those were focused on horror such as adaptations of George Romero's *Dawn of the Dead* and *Land of the Dead* and various stories following the adventures of Angel and Spike, from Joss Whedon's *Buffy the Vampire Slayer* and *Angel* television series. The first mini-series of *30 Days of Night* by Steve Niles and Ben Templesmith was published by IDW Publishing in 2002, and it was followed with further mini-series and single-issue releases further exploring the world Niles and Templesmith created until 2009. The series starts with vampires laying siege to a city in Alaska, as it experiences perpetual night. Niles and Templesmith teamed up again in 2003 for *Criminal Macabre*, a noir-horror series following a character, Cal McDonald, which Niles had been created nearly a decade earlier.

The major horror series to emerge in the last fifteen years is Robert Kirkman's *The Walking Dead* in 2003. Premiering just a year after the first *Resident Evil* film of 2002 and *28 Days Later* also of 2002, it stood as one of the earlier representations of the zombie craze that dominated popular culture in the 2000s. The series follows a police officer who awakes from a coma to discover that zombies have overturned society. He sets out to find his family and discover if there is any place left to call home. Published by Image Comics as a monthly black-and-white comic, the series became quite popular and the graphic novel publications were picked up by many bookstores and libraries. The popularity of the series and of zombies in general led Marvel Comics to hire Kirkman to write a mini-series called *Marvel Zombies*, wherein many of the Marvel superheroes and villains become zombies. The success of *Marvel Zombies* led to ten additional mini-series and numerous tie-ins from other ongoing Marvel comic book series. DC Comics also played with the undead in its crossover event, *Blackest Night*. The event consisted of the genesis of a power akin to Green Lantern's, but which revived dead superheroes to help eliminate all life in the universe.

Marvel Comics' Max imprint debuted in 2001, with numerous horror series both new and old. Max included new runs of *Werewolf by Night* and *Zombie*, as well as other series focused on new adaptations of written works by Edgar Allan Poe and H.P. Lovecraft.

Other horror series also garnered acclaim and success during the 2000s and 2010s. Tim Seeley's *Hack/Slash* series of 2004 follows an odd pairing of a young, but tough, woman and a muscular, gas-mask-wearing man, who together hunt down slashers or other evildoers. By the end of the 2000s, even mainstream horror fiction writers were getting involved with horror comic books and graphic novels. In 2008, IDW Publishing began selling Joe Hill's *Locke and Key*, an ongoing series that fixated on the strange occurrences and haunted experiences of the Locke family, when they move into the town of Lovecraft. Marvel Comics began publishing various new works within the *Dark Tower* series by Stephen King as well as additional pieces to his book *The Stand*, while Del Rey Books published several manga volumes featuring Dean Koontz's serial character, Odd Thomas.

The works of H.P. Lovecraft witnessed a renaissance in the 2000s as artists and writers time and again returned to his work with dozens of renderings published, as well as works inspired by his writing, like the aforementioned *Locke and Key* series. Renowned comic book writer Alan Moore wrote several mini-series and graphic novels that were derived from Lovecraft's work, including *The Courtyard* of 2003, *Yuggoth Cultures and Other Growths* also of 2003, and *Neonomicon* of 2010. Some were clear adaptations of his work, such as Eureka Productions' publication of *Graphic Classics: H. P. Lovecraft, 2nd edition* of 2007 or Sterling Publisher's rendering of *At the Mountains of Madness* of 2010. Yet some comic creators took a more intriguing approach by casting H.P. Lovecraft as a fictional character himself, as seen in Vertigo Comics' *Lovecraft* of 2004, Image Comics' *The Strange Adventures of H.P. Lovecraft* of 2010, and Arcana Studio's *Poe and Phillips* of 2011. The last title tells a tale, in which Lovecraft and Edgar Allan Poe explore the supernatural.

Besides traditional literature providing inspiration for horror narratives, the rise of manga (Japanese comic books) also produced a large assortment of horror narratives that were quickly consumed by comic book readers. Just as Japanese horror films provided new approaches to horror, so did the new horror manga, including such works as Kodansha Comics' *Parasyte* series, Viz Media's translation of the *Death Note* series by Tsuguri Ohba and Takeshi Obata, and the *Uzumaki* series by Junji Ito, also by Viz Media. Stylistically, the drawing was not as explicit as American horror graphic novels, but many of the Japanese series often continued for more than one thousand pages, which provided much longer and engaging experiences.

The first two decades of the twenty-first century have demonstrated that horror remains a significant genre within the realm of comic books and graphic novels. As individual comic books, many horror series cannot compete with the sale numbers of mainstream superhero comics. However, the rise of the graphic novel and its marketing to bookstores and libraries has created a strong secondary market for readers who engaged with these editions of various comic series. Horror-themed graphic novels continued to be bestsellers among graphic novels monthly sales.

The 2000s–2010s proves a fascinating time for the horror narrative in comic books and graphic novels, as the traces of several different lineages are made clear. The generations of horror fiction writers from the nineteenth and early twentieth century were clearly influential on the earlier horror comic writers of the 1940s and 1950s, but they still remain a powerful influence on modern horror comic writers. The creators of horror comic books served as key influencers on horror fiction writers and film-makers of the mid- and late twentieth century, including such authors as Stephen King, R. L. Stine, George Romero, and John Carpenter. Those classic horror comic books are still popular today, as they have been republished repeatedly for decades. Those writers and filmmakers served as influences for the comic book writers growing up and starting their careers since the 1980s, and indeed, some of them, like King, have crossed over to also write for comics in the early twenty-first century. This horror legacy, coupled with a mixture of new and refined talents, means that horror comics will continue to hold a prominent place among comics and graphic novels for decades to come.

The Crime Narrative and the Graphic Novel

Rich Shivener

Some serious sleuthing by inquisitive graphic novels readers should reveal that the Golden Age of crime narratives has been in a revival period in the United States for more than a decade, recouping from years of mainstream censorship and scarcity, thanks, in large part, to the Comics Code Authority, formed in 1954 (Nyberg 166). Representing this revival are several relatively recent graphic novels, like *Sin City*, *Road to Perdition*, *100 Bullets*, and *Fatale*, titles celebrated by the industry and the community, which includes scholars, creators, and fans. This essay, which takes a wide view of the crime narrative genre as it relates to graphic novels, focuses on the aforementioned graphic novels and others considered successful, examining the circumstances that surrounded their publications as well as the comics series that inspired them.

Put differently, if a reader takes a magnifying glass and dusts for fingerprints on the celebrated crime graphic novels of recent decades, he or she can undoubtedly see trace evidence of crime stories, not to mention comics, that ran between the 1930s and early 1950s, considered the Golden Age of comic books. And when all the information is put together, one thorough case file emerges, showing a rise, fall, and reemergence of a genre that is far from lighthearted.

American Crimes

In the 1930s, well before the dawn of today's legendary superheroes—including a certain man of steel, not to mention one of the world's greatest detectives—crime narratives had a grip on newspapers, periodicals, books, radio, and film in America (Goulart 233). Embedded in the public conscious were the effects of Prohibition and the true-life sagas it created: from the rise and eventual fall of such gangsters as Al Capone and Charles Luciano, among others. The public's interest in following organized crime and its influence gave rise to various fictional crime narratives across media, as noted by Gerard Jones in the book *Men of Tomorrow*, an important case analysis that itself unpacks the dominance of crime stories—whether it was the pulp magazine *Black Mask*, the film *Little Caesar*, or Dick Tracy, among others (96). While Jones' treatise primarily centers on Superman taking flight in the American comic book industry and beyond, it recognizes the public's demand for crime. The angrier and meaner the crime stories became, it seemed, the better they sold.

Building on what the public wanted during the Prohibition era, as Jones also notes, Chester Gould's comic strip Dick Tracy series, which debuted in 1931, is an early indication of how the comics creators handled crime narratives. For instance, in the first published storyline of Dick Tracy, instead of Superman heroics or payroll robberies and holdups, the level of violence is evident in the following details: a sharp pen is used as a weapon, if a knife is not handy; stones are thrown into car and train windows; young children are beaten or threatened, following the simple formula of older child against younger child instead of Superman against man (215).

Following "What Parents Don't Know about Comic Books," Frederic Wertham's accusations would come to a head in his 1954 book, *Seduction of the Innocent*, a thorough investigation of the effects that crime comics, superheroes, and even Batman's "gay" leanings had on children. What's more, in 1954, Wertham would be an outspoken participant in the Senate Subcommittee on Juvenile Delinquency hearings on American comic books. One could quote from his entire speech, but this excerpt offers an overview of his content: "If it were my task to teach children delinquency, to tell them how to hurt people, how to break into stores, how to cheat, how to forge, how to do any known crime, if it were my task to teach that, I would have to enlist the crime comic book industry" (304).

Countering Wertham's condemnation of crime comics was William Gaines, then publisher of EC Comics, whose *Crime SuspenStories*, *Vault of Horror*, and *Journey into Mystery*, were on the line. Gaines was indeed on the defense, as senators peppered him with questions and comments. At one point, Gaines noted how crime comics fit into the context of crime narratives across media:

Let us look at today's edition of the *Herald Tribune*. On the front page a criminal describes how another criminal told him about a murder he had done. In the same paper the story of a man whose ex-wife beat him on the head with a claw hammer and slashed him with a butcher knife …. Once you start to censor you must censor everything. You must censor comic books, radio, television, and newspapers. Then you must censor what people may say. Then you will have turned this country into Spain or Russia (Gaines).

Try as they might to outmatch the rhetoric of Wertham and the suspicions of the Senate Subcommittee on Juvenile Delinquency, comics publishers and their crime series were doomed, locked into their own sort of slammer, with little chance of bail. Many have viewed Gaines testimony as "disastrous" for the industry (MacDonald).

Collectively, and perhaps begrudgingly, the industry adopted the Comics Code Authority, formed by the Comics Magazine Association of America. Despite being inspired by the Senate, it was not governed by law or commanded by federal authorities. It was, at its core, a regulator that was tasked with ensuring that comics adhered to the Comics Magazine Association of America's Comics Code of 1954. In fact, the very word "crime" was the highlight of the 1954 Code. The "General Standards Part A" notes that "scenes of excessive violence shall prohibited," including "unnecessary knife and gun play," and that "Restraint in the use of the word 'crime' in titles or sub-titles should be exercised" (Nyberg 167).

But all was not lost for crime comics, not even provocative content.

Breaking the Code

Similar to the way federal authorities handled alcohol in the years of Prohibition, the Comic Book Code Authority's heavy hands largely forced comics publishers to move edgier content through circumvention and exception. Warren Publishing, owned by James Warren, is one highlight of a publisher by-passing the code, albeit completely legally. In 1964, the publisher launched the series *Creepy*, filled with stories that took cues from the aesthetics and plots of Golden Age horror, crime, and science-fiction comics (i.e., EC and Gleason). *Creepy* and its 1966 counterpart, *Eerie*, put well-known artists, like Jack Davis and Frank Franzetta, back in the limelight a decade after EC's fall to the Code. Warren Publishing had the freedom to produce *Creepy* because it was designed and labeled as a magazine released on newsstands rather than to the comic book market, as Warren once explained in an interview via TwoMorrows Publishing. "The comic book world in America had not seen material like this since the days of EC Comics. Had I published *Creepy* as a regular comic book, the Code would never have allowed this material" (Cooke).

Warren's circumvention continued for a number of years, and the Code had little power against him. Years later, its *Creepy* collections were reprinted via Dark Horse. Aside from *Creepy*, which is not entirely grounded in the context of crime comics (though Wertham might beg to differ), there are other notable instances of "Code-cracking," especially among comic book publishers. EC's *Crime SuspenStories* were collected and reprinted through the independent publisher Ballantine Books in 1964, several years before the publisher was sold to Random House. An important challenge to the Code came less than a decade later, in 1971. In perhaps a superheroic move, Stan Lee, then editor of Marvel Comics, wrote a three-part story on drug abuse for *The Amazing Spider-Man*, issues 96-98, which was proposed by the United States Department of Health, Education, and Welfare. Lee knowingly released the story in the face of opposition (i.e. the Code) after he got approval from Marvel publisher Martin Goodman. Revisions to the association's code came that same year. In regards to crime, it now noted that "Criminals shall not be presented in glamorous circumstances, unless an unhappy end results from their ill-gotten gains, and creates no desire for emulation" (Nyberg 171).

By the 1980s, the Code was beginning to wane. One popular citation to mark such a return of more adult-oriented crime comics is Terry Beatty and Max Allan Collins' series *Ms. Tree*, first published by Eclipse Magazine, which, like Warren Publishing, didn't face the restrictions of the Code. The series centers on a woman who turns to private-eye work to avenge the death of her husband. At the time, Collins was still writing Dick Tracy comic strips and had numerous crime novels to his credit. Ms. Tree, he later explained, "was created in part to do the topics that were too hot for 'Tracy'—abortion clinic bombings, gay bashing, date rape, etc." (Singh).

Edgier content, not unlike crime, was also making its way to mainstream comic books. In 1986, the comics industry saw another response to the censorship on stories regulated by the Authority, this time in the form of DC Comics' mini-series *The Dark Knight Returns*, created by writer/illustrator Frank Miller, with art by Klaus Janson. When in conversation about working with the Batman mythos, the creator has posited that superheroes, in recent decades, had lost much of their power, noting that:

> ... I set out to remark upon them. And seeing how all these heroes had been castrated since the 1950s, and just how pointless they seemed to be... In this perfect world of comic books, which was what it was back then, why would people dress up in tights to fight crime?" (Robinson)

With such ideas in mind, Miller offered an edgier Batman story, depicted as an aging Batman fighting in a world gripped by the Reagan administration. One year later, he was the mind behind *Batman: Year One*, focusing on the Dark Knight's origins.

But Miller's treatise was just the beginning of landmark stories of the decade. In terms of other edgy works that responded to the comics industry's shifting away from the Code's decades-old standards, the DC Comics series *Watchmen*, written by Alan Moore and illustrated by Dave Gibbons, is another popular example. Also released in 1986, it is often compared in tandem with Miller's work, owing to its depictions of masked superheroes facing the threats of politics, anarchy, and nuclear power (Conan). Two years later, building on *Watchmen*'s successes, Moore and collaborators were responsible for *Batman: The Killing Joke*, another gritty depiction of the Dark Knight and his villains, this one including an infamous scene in which Batgirl is shot by the Joker. Moore's reflections around the time of the book's release illustrated how DC Comics felt about censorship: "DC encouraged me in giving them something that was more adult which seems to be a pretty straightforward transaction. And as such, because those are the sort of stories that I enjoy doing. I was still quite able to carry on working at DC" (Groth).

Indeed, as the decade was rounding out, mainstream comics were seeing a revival of the adult-oriented content that thrived decades prior. The Code was updated again in 1989, giving some leeway to crime stories. As it noted:

> While crimes and criminals may be portrayed for dramatic purposes, crimes will never be presented in such a way as to inspire readers with a desire to imitate them nor will criminals be portrayed in such a manner as to inspire readers to emulate them. Stories will not present unique imitable techniques or methods of committing crimes (Nyberg 177).

The Dawn of the Modern Crime Graphic Novel

Publications in the 1990s would make good cases for keeping such a revival going. Building on his mature content and that of the likes of Moore and Collins, Miller would signal a strong return to noir books in 1991, the year Dark Horse began publishing his *Sin City* series, the first stories of which appeared in the company's anthology *Dark Horse Presents*. Overall, *Sin City* depicts a bitter and provocative world of crime, riddled with dames and bullets, and *That Yellow Bastard,* the sixth and final work in the series, never shies away from explicit illustrations of each (Miller, et. al). In several ways, it was a challenge to the comics industry's ideals of censorship, something it self-bestowed in response to the 1954 Senate hearings. What's more, even though Dark Horse released it, Miller owned the rights to *Sin City*, and he refused to include a rating/seal of approval on it. His condemnations of censorship are ripe throughout the letter columns that bookend *Sin City* stories, important artifacts of modern crime narratives. In letters that followed the first issue of *The Big Fat Kill*, which ran in November 1994, Miller reiterated that authorities—at the time, such figures as Janet Reno and Senator Paul Simon—were not coming after comics, as they were with Beavis and Butthead. He also reiterated the comics industry's penchant for self-censoring, and he took another stab at advisories and ratings:

We have dedicated talent. We have dedicated fans. We've even got a few dedicated publishers. We have never censored by anybody but ourselves. Any freedoms we surrender are inexcusable. Candy-ass apologies like cover advisories or rating systems are equivalent to giving the farm away to an enemy who hasn't even asked for it (Miller 27).

The editorializing of Miller and his mostly supportive fans continued throughout the *Sin City* series, outweighing letters regarding the work itself. In the years since its original publication, *Sin City* has been reprinted as a collection by Dark Horse, and, in 2005, it saw a film adaptation, directed by Robert Rodriguez and Frank Miller. Paying close attention to Miller's layouts and writing, Rodriguez envisioned the latter this way: "Let's take cinema and turn it into a living graphic novel" (Smith).

In terms of crime comics that debuted in the 90s, *Sin City* wasn't the only series paying homage to the past and addressing the future of crime comics. In 1998, Image Comics debuted Brian Michael Bendis and Marc Andreyko's limited series *Torso*, set in 1930s Cleveland, where a now-infamous murderer had a penchant for decapitation. Bendis was influenced by newspapers and media from the Depression era. "The fact that there was a drawing of a bogeyman on the front page of a major metropolitan newspaper, telling you that the Torso murderer might come and get you, was absolutely fascinating to me" (Mulholland Books). Years after its release, *Torso* is still under consideration for a film adaptation (Comic Book Resources).

DC Comics' criminal investigations had better luck on the film side. The year 1998 saw the release of the graphic novel *Road to Perdition*, a fictional account of gangsters, namely John Looney and Al Capone, in the Great Depression. Max Allan Collins wrote the story, which was illustrated by Richard Pier Rayner. As Collins explained to Comic Book Resources, "What made it an 'irresistible creative opportunity' was my need for work: I'd just been fired from the 'Tracy' strip and wanted to do something else in comics...preferably something adult, without the restraints of the 'Tracy' strip" (Singh). *Road to Perdition* was released through

DC's Paradox Press, and the film adaptation was distributed in 2002 through DreamWorks Pictures.

DC had more than one imprint that was reviving crime comics. In 1999, its Vertigo imprint debuted the series *100 Bullets*, created by writer Brian Azzarello and Eduardo Risso. Rooted in mystery and noir themes, the series' plot centers on a certain weapon, which allows those to exact revenge, for better or worse, without criminal consequences. Azzarello, in an extensive interview with *The Comics Journal*, noted that his work was influenced by Golden Age comics, namely EC, and that Miller's work "legitimized" crime comics (93). The interview is a rather noteworthy artifact of creators discussing the state of crime comics at the time. Not only did Azzarello and his colleagues discuss *100 Bullets* and works that preceded it; Azzarello also questioned the very definition of a crime comic. "Pretty much every comic is a crime comic, you know? Just because he wears a cape and has an 'S' on his chest doesn't mean he's not a cop, you know? And the Joker's a criminal" (96).

However the creators handled crime, their aforementioned works have been celebrated by adaptations and/or with awards, like those presented at Comic-Con International: San Diego. By the beginning of the twenty-first century, the future of crime comics looked far from grim.

New Crime Scenes

The advent of crime comics and graphic novels in the twenty-first century is indeed signified by 2009, a year that one might venture to call the year of crime comics. In February 2009, Marvel released *X-Men Noir*, part of a Marvel Universe-spanning alternative storyline in which characters, such as Wolverine, Spider-Man, and Daredevil are styled in the pulp aesthetics of the 1930s. In an interview with Comic Book Resources, writer Fred Van Lente and artist Dennis Calero cited Raymond Chandler; the film *Chinatown*; and Marvel's direct predecessor, Timely Comics, as influences.

In April 2009, Vertigo's *100 Bullets* completed its one hundredth and final issue. As that was finishing up, Vertigo was also planning its sub-imprint, Vertigo Crime, set to release a series of original graphic novels. In August 2009, its launch titles included *Filthy Rich*, created by Azzarello and artist Victor Santos, and *Dark Entities*, written by Ian Rankin and Werther Dell'Edera. As Vertigo Crime's launch loomed, its writers and editors noted its allusions to crime stories of yesterday and today (Lorah). Vertigo Crime lasted a mere two years (MacDonald), and perhaps fittingly, it concluded with the *Road to Perdition* sequel, *Return to Perdition*, also written by Max Allan Collins (Dueben).

Following the events of 2009, crime comics and graphic novels still have a notable presence, thanks primarily to writer Ed Brubaker and artist Sean Phillips. The team's neo-pulp series *Incognito*, launched through Marvel's adult-oriented Icon imprint in December 2008, has been collected in two volumes, and Marvel has released four volumes of the team's *Criminal* series, which started in 2006. Their collaborations haven't stopped. In June 2012, Image Comics released the first volume of the team's horror-noir series *Fatale*. In one publication or another, Brubaker has reflected on blending horror and noir.

> My general rule to myself is if I have to choose which way to go on a scene, noir or horror, I'll lean more on the noir, because to me the horror elements work best the less they're shown, anyway. But I really feel those two genres blend incredibly well -- I mean look at a film like "Angel Heart," which is sort of like "Chinatown" with a horror twist (Dietsch).

However they move forward with *Fatale* and their *Criminal* series, the approaches of Brubaker and Phillips—plus those of others not mentioned here—will be remembered as crime narratives continue on in the twenty-first century. The case file on the genre is far from closed.

Works Cited

"2010-Present." Comic-Con International: San Diego. Comic-Con International: San Diego, n.d. Web. 01 Nov. 2013. <http://www. comic-con.org/awards/eisner-award-recipients-2010-present>.

"Bendis & Andreyko's 'Torso' To Be Adapted by Sundance Favorite Lowery." *Comic Book Resources*. Comic Book Resources, 17 Apr. 2013. Web. 25 Oct. 2013.

Comics Alliance Staff. "Stan Lee on the Spider-Man Drug Story Too Hot for the Comics Code Authority [Video]." *Comics Alliance*. Screencrush Network, 26 July 2010. Web. 04 Nov. 2013. <http://comicsalliance.com/stan-lee-amazing-spider-man-drugs-comics-code-authority/>.

Cooke, Jon. "James Warren Interview–Comic Book Artist #4–TwoMorrows Publishing." *James Warren Interview –Comic Book Artist #4–TwoMorrows Publishing*. TwoMorrows, n.d. Web. 01 Oct. 2013. <http://twomorrows.com/comicbookartist/articles/04warren.html>.

Conan, Neil. "Batman' Author Frank Miller." *Talk of the Nation*. National Public Radio. NPR, Washington, D.C., 15 June 2005. Web. Transcript. <http://www.npr.org/templates/story/story.php?storyId=4704766>. Dietsch, TJ. "Ed Brubaker Gets Modern With 'Fatale'" *Comic Book Resources*. Comic Book Resources, 22 Apr. 2013. Web. 01 Nov. 2013. <http://www.comicbookresources.com/?page=article>.

Dueben, Alex. "Collins Returns to 'Perdition'" *Comic Book Resources*. Comic Book Resources, 4 Jan. 2012. Web. 1 Nov. 2013. <http://www.comicbookresources.com/?page=article>.

Gaines, William."Testimony of William Gaines." *The Comic Books*. James Coville, n.d. Web. 1 Oct. 2013. <http://www.thecomicbooks.com/gaines.html>.

Gaines, William M., Albert B. Feldstein, Jonathan T. Craig, Marie Severin, Wallace Wood, Graham Ingels, Harvey Kurtzman, Jack Kamen, Jack Davis, and George Roussos. *Crime SuspenStories*. Timonium, MD: Gemstone, 2007.

Gleason, Lev. "Crime Does Not Pay." *Crime Does Not Pay* 1:22 (July 1942). *Digital Comics Museum*. Web. 1 Oct. 2013. 14. <http://digitalcomicmuseum.com/index.php?dlid=5867>.

Goulart, Ron. *Ron Goulart's Great History of Comic Books: The Definitive Illustrated History from the 1890s to the 1980s*. Chicago: Contemporary, 1986.

Gould, Chester, Max Allan Collins, and Jeffrey Kersten. *Chester Gould's Dick Tracy*. Vol. 1. San Diego: IDW Pub., 2009.

Groth, Gary. "The Alan Moore Interview." 1987. *The Comics Journal*. Fantastagraphics, 13 June 2012. Web. 04 Nov. 2013. <http://www.tcj. com/the-alan-moore-interview-118/>.

Jones, Gerard. *Men of Tomorrow: Geeks, Gangsters, and the Birth of the Comic Book*. New York: Basic, 2004.

Lorah, Michael. "NYCC '09: The Vertigo Crime Panel." *Newsarama*. Newsrama, 8 Feb. 2009. Web. 04 Nov. 2013. <http://www.newsarama. com/2171-nycc-09-the-vertigo-crime-panel.html>.

MacDonald, Heidi. "Many New Vertigo Trades Announced, including an INVISIBLES Omnibus." *The Beat*. The Beat, 22 Nov. 2011. Web. 1 Oct. 2013. <http://comicsbeat.com/many-new-vertigo-trades-announced-including-an-invisible-omnibus/>.

MacDonald, Heidi. "MUST LISTEN: Audio of the 1954 Senate Comic Book Hearings." *The Beat*. The Beat, 31 Aug. 2012. Web. 01 Oct. 2013. <http://comicsbeat.com/must-listen-audio-of-the-1954-senate-comic-book-hearings/>.

Nyberg, Amy. *Seal of Approval: The History of the Comics Code*. Jackson, MS: U of Mississippi P, 1998.

"Random House – About Us." Random House, n.d. Web. 01 Nov. 2013. <http://www.randomhouse.com/about/history.html>.

Richards, Dave. "Fear And Hatred: Van Lente & Calero on 'X Men Noir'". *Comic Book Resources*. n.d. Web. 04 Nov. 2013.<http://www. comicbookresources.com/?page=article&id=17970>.

Robinson, Tasha. "Interview: Frank Miller." *The A.V. Club*. Onion Media Network, 5 Dec. 2001. Web. 01 Oct. 2013. <http://www.avclub.com/ articles/frank-miller,13748/>.

"TORSO Revisited." *Mulholland Books*. Mulholland Books, n.d. Web. 1 Nov. 2013. <http://www.mulhollandbooks.com/2012/03/19/1959/>.

Singh, Arune. "Just the Facts Ma'am: Max Collins Talks 'Road to Perdition'" *Comic Book Resources*. Comic Book Resources, 16 June 2002. Web. 01 Oct. 2013. <http://www.comicbookresources.com/?page=article>.

Smith, Kevin. "'Sin City': Guiding a Comic to the Silver Screen." *Morning Edition*. National Public Radio. NPR, Washington, D.C., 1 Apr. 2005. Web. 1 Oct. 2013. <http://www.npr.org/templates/story/story. php?storyId=4569989>.

Wertham, Fredric. "Do The Crime Comic Books Promote Juvenile Delinquency? PRO." *Congressional Digest* 33.12 (1954): 302.

Wertham, Fredric. *Seduction of the Innocent.* New York: Rinehart, 1954.

Wertham, Fredric. "What Parents Don't Know About Comic Books." *Ladies' Home Journal* Nov. 1953, n. d. Web. 1 Oct. 2013. <http://www.seductionoftheinnocent.org/LadiesHomeJournalNovember1953cover. htm>.

The Reality/Fantasy Narrative and the Graphic Novel

Rikk Mulligan

Reality is an event, occurrence, state, or thing that exists or has existed; fantasy is the imagining of things removed from reality—the impossible or improbable. Graphic novels or comic books are a medium or mode of visual storytelling; some make a point of depicting reality with as much fidelity as possible, but far more blend reality and fantasy in creating their narratives. Comics that depict history, biography, and autobiography tend to adhere more closely to reality using literary or Platonic mimesis as "artistic representation—be it visual or verbal—of agents and events in the world" (Nightingale 38). Stories of myth, legend, folklore, alien worlds, far-flung futures, and the vast majority of comic books that focus on the adventures of costumed superheroes could be considered narratives of fantasy, yet these stories employ formulaic elements, settings, and conventions to construct internally consistent pseudo-realities. In *Adventure, Mystery, and Romance*, John G. Cawelti explains that such formulas began in the 19th-century dime novel, but began to stabilize in the pulp magazines and paperback fiction (literature), radio shows, film, and television during the first half of the 20th century. In 1938, comic strips provided the form, but pulps, radio dramas, and film provided the initial formulas—plots, character archetypes, and settings—of the comic book. However, as historian William W. Savage, Jr. observed, comic books transcended the limits of form imposed on radio and film because their writers and artists could produce anything they could conceive (7). This freedom allowed comic book creators to recombine the older archetypes of other genres, like the western gunslinger, urban detective, inventor-adventurer, and radio mystery men in any setting, but the result required these new formulas be reestablished by creating consistent narrative reality as continuity. Because formulas and archetype are mixed and melded, the function of the fantastic in comic books and graphic novels defines or delimits reality through the hero's ability or freedom to act, and the continuity of the story or story arc in a series.

According to Bradford W. Wright's cultural history, *Comic Book Nation*, the first titles reprinted popular comic strips, including *Popeye*, *Flash Gordon*, *Li'l Abner*, and *Tarzan*, among others, from a range of genres, but in 1938, *Detective Comics* published what would become the new crime-fighting formula that would eventually overwhelm the rest (3–5). Over the past seventy-five years, the crime-fighter became the superhero, and these narratives have come to vastly outnumber all other genres combined, including westerns, war, mystery and detective, horror and suspense, and humor. Still, most superhero narratives draw and combine their formulas primarily from the genres of fantasy and science fiction, and as these genres have continued to evolve during the late 20th century and into the 21st century, the relationship between reality and fantasy has become more sophisticated and, at times, conflicted.

Graphic novels are closely related to literature in their use of metaphor, myth, and symbol. Cawelti's analysis of formulaic stories tends toward the myth and symbol approach, but he explores these in terms of the creation of a "slightly removed, imaginary world," the use of suspense, or the reader's need to identify with the protagonist (17). When comic books appeared in 1938, the settings tended to be big cities, but they were fictionalized, in order to attract the most readers and to create the suspension of disbelief that, perhaps, a man could fly in the right place. Richard Reynolds argues "the New York (or Gotham City, or Metropolis) that dominates the superhero story . . . is a city that signifies all cities, and, more specifically, all modern cities, since the city itself is one of the signs of modernity" (19). In this urban setting, as Wright points out, several heroes including Superman, Batman, and Green Lantern fought corporate greed and corruption, a particularly real issue given the context of the Great Depression (22–26, 45). While Captain America (*Captain America Comics #1*, March 1941) became a super-soldier and fought fifth columnists before America entered World War II, he, Wonder Woman (*All Star Comics #8*, December 1941), and later the

Sub-Mariner (*Marvel Comics #1*, October 1939) fought Axis on a number of fronts (Wright 40–47).

Cawelti's discussion of formulaic suspense tends to privilege the mystery, but much of his discussion can be reframed in the context of other formulas. In the superhero narrative, suspense is created in a number of ways, including: resolving a crime, discovering the villain, protecting the innocent, the possible defeat of the hero, or the defeat of the villain. Readers of formulaic stories must identify with a character who is "typically better or more fortunate" than they are (18); this superiority can be ranked in terms of literary critic Northrop Frye's concept of the hero's power of action, "which may be greater than ours, less, or roughly the same" (33).

All superhero comics contain a fantastic conceit: not that the protagonist has skills, abilities, or powers greater than other humans, but that those abilities are "real" and comply with the laws of physics (and often metaphysics) in these narrative worlds. Even non-superhero genres tend to feature protagonists who have special abilities or are improbably competent. Frye defines the power of action as the protagonist's ability to do or failure to do something; in the context of graphic novels, the power to act comes from knowledge, skill, training, or powers (biological, technological, or supernatural), as well the ability to overcome the resistance of not only the villain, but also the mundane or normal world created by the authorities and the personal relationships or responsibilities of the hero.

Frye's categories result from his analysis of literature as whole, beginning with myth, moving into the romance as legend and folklore, then the "high mimetic" modes of epic and tragedy or "low mimetic" mode of "most comedy and realistic fiction" from the eighteenth century onward (33–34). In Frye's terms, if the hero's ability to act is superior in *kind* to both men and environment, the hero is divine (god or demigod) and the story mythic; if superior in *degree* to other men and his environment, the hero remains human, but is marvelous; if superior to other men, but not his natural environment, the hero is a leader; and if superior to neither men nor environment, then the hero normal—one of us (33-34).

Frye only engages "literature" in his taxonomy, not works of formula or genre, but what is interesting is that he suggests that the older romances "lean heavily on miraculous violations of natural law for their interest as stories," and sees this mode in "drama, particularly tragedy, and national epic" (34). The hero of non-superhero adventure, war, and detective narratives often rises to specific challenges to temporarily become superior to other men, marking him as a hero, but not to his environment; those who stretch the bounds of the improbable, as Marv does in Frank Miller's *Sin City Volume 1: The Hard Goodbye*, stray into the realm of the marvelous hero—the category of most superheroes. But in 1938, the United States and the world were in the midst of the Great Depression, with the possibility of another world war looming larger every day, which might suggest that the costumed superhero manifested as a modern national epic based on the rising power of technology or to help create a modern mythology drawn from science fiction.

The Golden Age of comic books (1939–1951) used cutting-edge, real-world technology as well as the inventions of science fiction and science fantasy to empower their protagonists, with abilities ranging from the mythic and marvelous, to those "merely" at the heroic pinnacle of human achievement. The first and often most popular superhero, DC Comics' Superman (*Action Comics #1*, April 1938), is the orphan of an ancient and incredibly advanced alien civilization, who, when he comes of age on Earth, develops nearly god-like abilities, including strength, speed, and near-invulnerability. By contrast, the Batman (*Detective Comics #27*, May 1939) is a normal man, who has trained his mind and body to their greatest potential, to use fighting skills, deductive reasoning, and a vast array of advanced tools and weapons provided by his personal wealth to fight super villains and mundane thugs and crooks. The equally human and highly skilled Green Arrow (*More Fun Comics #73*, November 1941) has near-heroic abilities with the longbow, and has equipped his quiver with a range of trick and special purpose arrows, supplied by his own vast fortune.

Against the backdrop of the Great Depression, access to millions is itself a marvelous quality. Timely Comics, the precursor to Marvel Comics, introduced three characters whose origins are arguably scientific: Captain America, the Human Torch (*Marvel Comics #1*, October 1939) and Namor the Sub-Mariner. A scientist using "vita-rays" and a super-soldier serum transforms skinny, 4-F Steve Rogers into Captain America, whose strength and fighting skills rise just above the pinnacle of human ability. A human inventor created an android with a human form and emotions in The Human Torch, who also has the marvelous capabilities of flight and the ability to project and control flame. Namor the Sub-Mariner, is a hybrid of man and merman and has near-mythic levels of strength and invulnerability, as well as the ability to fly and survive in the oceans depths. However, where the creators of Superman attempted to justify his strength with a scientific fig leaf by appealing to the "proportionate" strength of ants and grasshoppers, Timely Comics unapologetically exploited the science fantasy of the pulps for its super-soldier, android, and mutant.

Magic, sorcery, and gods of the Greek and Roman pantheons also provide the origins and powers of other Golden Age heroes, but most rank amongst the marvelous, and only rarely stray into the mythic. The original Green Lantern, Alan Scott, gained his powers from a sentient magic lantern forged from a burning green meteor that landed in China; his ring granted him vast powers, but also an inexplicable vulnerability to wooden objects, a frequent environmental element (*All-American Comics #16*, July 1940). Doctor Fate (*More Fun Comics #55*, May 1940) fights crime and supernatural foes using a magic helmet, amulet, and cloak given to him by a revived Egyptian wizard, and the original Hawkman (*Flash Comics #1*, January 1940), Carter Hall, is an archeologist who discovers not only that he is the reincarnation of Prince Khufu, an ancient Egyptian, but also the antigravity "ninth metal" that allows him to fly, although how resisting gravity also provides propulsion remains a mystery. The origins of Hawkman and Doctor Fate draw on the exotic Orient, specifically ancient Egypt, perhaps in response to the success of Universal Studios' film *The Mummy* (1932) and its earlier reincarnation plot.

The Green Lantern, however, might suggest its contemporary Sax Rohmer *Fu Manchu* novels, their 1920s and 1930s film versions, or the 1940 Republic Picture's serial. Although Wonder Woman's powers are of the mythic kind, her origin borrows from the pulps to make her a warrior princess of a tribe of Amazons hidden on the island of Themyscira in the Mediterranean. She is an exceptional athlete, and is as strong as her contemporary Superman, but here her golden Lasso of Truth and indestructible bracelets (or bracers) are magic objects linked to the goddess Aphrodite. Fawcett Comics created Captain Marvel (*Whiz Comics #2*, February 1940) to compete with Superman. An ancient wizard named Shazam grants the boy Billy Batson the powers of five Classical (Greek and Roman) heroes, demigods, and gods when he becomes Captain Marvel: the strength of Hercules; the stamina of Atlas; the power of Zeus; the courage of Achilles; and the speed of Mercury, as well as the wisdom of Solomon. Many of the villains these particular heroes face have corresponding levels of power and ability, also conferred through magic and sorcery, or different divine entities, as in the case of many of Wonder Woman's foes and Captain Marvel's opposite number, Black Adam (*Marvel Family Comics #1*, December 1945). By the end of the Golden Age of comics, advanced science, magic, and pagan divinity had been established as part of the continuity and reality of these narratives.

Although most of the superhero titles other than those involving Batman, Superman, and Wonder Woman were cancelled by the early 1950s as publishers shifted their focus to other genres including science fiction, Westerns, humor, and romance, the superhero narrative had created a modern mythology that would continue to mature as literary science fiction and fantasy evolved. Beginning in 1956, under the direction of Julius Schwartz, himself tightly linked to science fiction writers and publishing, the origins of many DC heroes, beginning with the Flash, had their genesis-stories and powers rebooted or re-explained almost entirely in terms of science fiction rather than magic; this launched the Silver Age of comics books that lasted until 1970. Superman and Batman remained unchanged, but Wonder Woman was an exception. She became more tightly tied to

Hellenic culture and Greek deities, as her new origin-story included the details that she had been formed from clay and breathed into life by the gods Aphrodite, Athena, Hercules, and Hermes, who then bestowed gifts on her (Wonder Woman [vol. 1] #*105*, 1959).

The rest became tightly bound to narratives of science fiction: Hawkman was recreated as a police officer from the planet Thanagar whose powers derived from alien technology; Green Lantern became a former test pilot recruited by the Green Lantern Corps, an intergalactic police force whose power rings have a vulnerability to the color yellow; but the Flash received his powers from being splashed by lightning-activated chemicals in a police laboratory... perhaps some of the new origins did not stray as far from magical-science fantasy as they could have. The Golden Age Justice Society was rebooted as the Justice League. However, within a few years, the Flash of the Silver Age Justice League met up with the Golden Age Justice Society thanks to the Flash vibrating between their two worlds—Earth One and Earth Two—in a process that is today explained in terms of quantum tunneling (Kakalios 250), although other writers have found all Flash's powers impossible according to logic and science (Gresh and Weinberg 117–128).

The success of the Justice League has been widely credited as the impetus for Stan Lee and Jack Kirby to create the Fantastic Four, which ushered Marvel Comics into the Silver Age (*Fantastic Four #1*, November 1961). Marvel Comics used science (or science fiction), specifically radiation, to create its heroes: the members of the Fantastic Four were irradiated by cosmic rays during a space launch, to develop marvelous, if not mythic, powers loosely derived from the four elements. Meanwhile, gamma radiation from a military bomb test turned Bruce Banner into a modern day Jekyll and Hyde, with mythic levels of strength and near-invulnerability as the Incredible Hulk (*Incredible Hulk #1*, May 1962). An irradiated spider created Spiderman (*Amazing Fantasy #15*, August 1962), and radiation was behind the mutations that created the teenage team, the X-Men, whose marvelous powers include telepathy, telekinesis, cryokinesis, winged flight, and eye blasts (*The X-Men #1*, September 1963).

Tony Stark is a millionaire industrialist, scientist, and engineer forced to create a suit of powered armor to keep him alive, and to free him from Vietnamese guerillas (*Tales of Suspense #39*, March 1963). However, when Lee and Kirby needed another hero stronger than the Hulk, they turned to another source of divine power: the Norse myths. Thor was introduced in *Journey into Mystery #83* (August 1962). In a mix of science fiction and fantasy, a handicapped doctor, Donald Blake, is trapped by alien invaders, and when he tries to free himself, the stick he uses transforms into the hammer Mjolnir, and he becomes Thor, who chases the aliens back into space. Thor became a founding member of *The Avengers* (*#1*, September 1963), but another demigod, Hercules also joined the Marvel "pantheon" (*Thor #126*, March 1966).

Marvel's fantastic and supernatural characters were not limited to pagan pantheons. Perhaps as a reflection of the counter-culture or the British New Wave of science fiction that "began to peel open the ideological myth of supreme scientific competence" (Broderick 52), some of Marvel's new heroes turned inward. Many New Wave authors began to explore psychological and metaphysical realities, as Michael Moorcock uses his eternal champion and the multiple-dimensions of his multiverse—one that preceded the multiple realities of both DC and Marvel Comics. Doctor Strange (*Strange Tales #110*, July 1963) drew inspiration from Eastern mysticism and expanded into a number of abstract pocket realities and realms, including Limbo, which reflected the psychedelic and surrealist turn of pop art (and drug culture) in the late 1960s. Although Strange used mystic scrolls, tomes, and artifacts, including his Cloak of Levitation, Eye of Agamotto, and Orb of Agamotto to combat villains and supernatural forces, his stories stretched beyond the science and magic dichotomy to incorporate anthropomorphic manifestations of Nightmare and Eternity—one of the cosmic entities—in this case, the personification of the universe depicted as a humanoid outline filled by a sea of stars.

More than any other Marvel character, including Doctor Strange, Adam Warlock, under the control of Jim Starlin in the early 1970s, appears in adventures that engage cosmic concepts, metaphysical constructs, and the nature of reality through comic book narratives. Warlock began as a failed messiah figure, but when Jim Starlin took over the character, he became a paranoid schizophrenic before being forced to travel into the future to harvest his own soul and prevent his insane future-alter ego, the Magus, from traveling into the past to create the genocidal Universal Church of Truth (explained in detail in Karen Berger's interview with Jim Starlin). Before his second death, Warlock came into conflict with the Mad Titan, Thanos, whose foremost desire was to win the love of the personification of Death; to that end, he reached and attained near omnipotence several times, only to be defeated by the efforts of Warlock, various Marvel heroes, and his own subconscious (*Infinity Gauntlet #5*, November 1991). By the end of Starlin's stories in the mid-1970s, Warlock had been killed by Thanos after frustrating his plan to annihilate the universe. Thereafter, Warlock was pulled from the afterlife within his soul gem by the cosmic anthropomorphizations of Chaos and Order to kill Thanos, and he thereby saves Earth's solar system from being destroyed (*Warlock #9-16* [1975–1976], reprinted as *Warlock, Special Edition, #1-3*, 1982; *Avengers Annual #7*, November 1977; *Marvel Two-in-One Annual #2*, December 1977). Starlin had created cosmic plots around near-infinite, reality-bending power with the cosmic cube in the first Thanos plot lines and then with the infinity gems that were almost used to end the universe. With the death of Thanos and final sacrifice of the cosmic messiah, the story of Adam Warlock was complete.

But rarely does Marvel Comics or superhero narratives in general keep a good man or woman down. In the 1990s, Starlin was asked to resurrect Warlock in the *Infinity Gauntlet* limited series; Thanos had already been restored in other comics. In this story arc, Thanos acquires all the infinity gems, forges his gauntlet, and then defeats the collected champions of Lord Chaos and Master Order before engaging the pantheon of cosmic entities themselves. Thanos handicaps himself to savor the challenge, but his remaining powers dwarf that of many of Marvel's greatest heroes, including the mythic power of Thor, the Silver Surfer and his Power Cosmic, Dr. Strange,

Doctor Doom, the (intelligent) Hulk, and an assembly of some of the most powerful members of the Avengers.

After Thanos defeats Earth's heroes, he takes, swiftly defeats, and imprisons Marvel's cosmic entities—Lord Chaos, Master Order, Chronos, Eon, Mistress Love, Sire Hate, Galactus, the Stranger, and the Celestials—on his path to briefly becoming omnipotent by defeating Eternity. This miniseries was followed by the limited series, *Warlock and the Infinity Watch*, and another, *The Infinity War*; again, various cosmically-potent and anthropomorphized concepts appear, but as with the original *Infinity Gauntlet*, the sheer scope of concept and power seems beyond the ability of writer and artist to communicate using images other than those of extraordinary power and destruction.

Concepts such as order, chaos, the cosmic balance, time, love, and hate are existential and dwarf even the most divine or mythic protagonist's power of action unless they, like Thanos, have become imbued with a number of existential or omni-powerful abilities. In attempting to engage sublime metaphysical concepts, the superhero narrative exposed the limits of its ability to represent reality by continuing to descend into cycles of combat and conflict—cosmic tragedy.

DC Comic's *Vertigo* comics were suggested for adult readers and began appearing shortly before Marvel's cosmic tragedy, but they also picked up the threads of tragedy and dipped them in existential horror in two of their ten titles: *Hellblazer* and *Sandman*. The former featured John Constantine as a horror hero; an occult investigator, who eventually uses his knowledge of magic and lore to challenge the Lords of Hell. Constantine is able to play the Lords of Hell against each other, have them lose, and then regain his soul. In the process, he loses loved ones and is hideously wounded, both physically and psychically. *Hellblazer* renewed the existence of devils, demons, and Hell in the reality of the DC universe continuity, even if it was through a tenuous overlap with the character of Batman in the pages of *Swamp Thing* and later in the early issues of *Sandman*.

Neil Gaiman's *Sandman*, however, rarely dipped into the mainstream DC superhero continuity, although the story begins by jumping between horror-tainted superhero continuity, the Realm of Dreams, and Hell in its first eight issues, collected as the graphic novel *Preludes and Nocturnes*. Over the course of its seventy-five issues, Gaiman, as the sole writer, shifts the narrative from horror to dark fantasy, but it always focuses on its tragic hero, Dream of the Endless. Before Dream is killed by the Greek Furies at the end of his portion of the story arc in issue #69, Gaiman has introduced the rest of the Endless as anthropomorphized existential concepts, including Desire, Despair, Destiny, Delirium, Destruction, and most importantly, Death. Beyond these manifestations, the stories also include a variety of settings—Asgard, Faerie, Hell, and points in the distant past; a number of gods—Odin, Loki, Thor, and Bast; and devils—most significantly Lucifer—but also unnumbered legions that accompany him on his visit to Hell to recover his helm (#4). Dream not only inhabits the realm of the Dreaming, but he is the collective manifestation of sentient intelligence to dream; yet for all this, Dream remains vulnerable to the manipulations of others (most notably Loki), which results in his death and the ascendancy of a new Dream. Unlike the belligerent, impotent omnipotence of Marvel's existential personifications, Sandman presents its anthropomorphizations in human terms that reveal not only their power, but how we as humans apprehend and make sense of the space between the panels of our life—the moments and details we apprehend—to continually reshape our reality.

In *Reinventing Comics*, Scott McCloud says that comic books came of age in 1978 with the publication of Will Eisner's *A Contract with God* (1978, 2006), a series of short stories that he called a graphic novel to set it apart from comics and in the hopes that it might be taken more seriously as literature (28–30). Although Eisner enjoyed some modest success, graphic novels did not begin to hit their stride and be noticed by a wider, less fan-based audience until the release of Art Spiegelman's Pulitzer Prize-winning *Maus* in 1986. Initially, the term graphic novel also indicated a self-inclusive story or set of closely-related stories, such as Eisner's collection or the first Marvel Comics graphic novel, Jim Starlin's *The Death of Captain Marvel* of 1982, but in contemporary usage, it has come to refer to a collected series of issues that follow a specific story arc, including some within this collection: Robert Kirkman's *The Walking Dead: Volume 1 Days Gone Bye #1-6* and Neil Gaiman's *The Sandman: Preludes and Nocturnes Issues #1-8*. Stories that are the most mimetic may employ metaphors like the animal faces in Speigelman's *Maus*, or the conversations with God in Satrapi's *Persepolis* of 2003. However, those initially defined as fantasy, including the stories of Kirkman, James O'Barr's *The Crow*, and especially Gaiman's *Sandman* help the reader to imagine more and better glimpse the hidden depths of emotions, especially loss and pain, and thereby enrich their appreciation of life.

Works Cited

Broderick, Damien. "New Wave and backlash: 1960-1980." *The Cambridge Companion to Science Fiction*. Eds. Edward James and Farah Mendlesohn. Cambridge: Cambridge U P, 2003: 48–63.

Campbell, Joseph. *The Hero with a Thousand Faces*. 1949. Princeton: Princeton University Press, 1972.

Cawelti, John G. *Adventure, Mystery, and Romance: Formula Stories as Art and Popular Culture*. Chicago: University of Chicago Press, 1976.

Frye, Northrop. *Anatomy of Criticism: Four Essays*. 1957. Princeton: Princeton University Press, 1990.

Gresh, Lois and Robert Weinberg. *The Science of Superheroes*. Hoboken, NJ: John Wiley & Sons, 2002.

Kakalios, James. *The Physics of Superheroes*. New York: Gotham Books/ Penguin Group, 2006.

McCloud, Scott. *Reinventing Comics: How Imagination and Technology Are Revolutionizing an Art Form*. New York: Perennial, 2000.

_____. *Understanding Comics: The Invisible Art*. New York: Harper Perennial, 1993.

Nightingale, Andrea. "Mimesis: Ancient Greek Literary Theory." *Literary Theory and Criticism: An Oxford Guide*. Ed. Patricia Waugh. Oxford: Oxford University Press, 2006. 37–47.

Rauch, Stephen. *Neil Gaiman's* The Sandman *and Joseph Campbell: In Search of Modern Myth*. Holicong, PA: Wildside Press, 2003.

Reynolds, Richard. *Super Heroes: A Modern Mythology*. Jackson: U of Mississippi P, 1992.

Sabin, Roger. *Comics, Comix & Graphic Novels: A History of Comic Art*. 1996. London: Phaidon Press, 2010.

Savage, William W., Jr. *Comic Books in America, 1945–1954*. Norman: University of Oklahoma Press, 1990.

Walker, Karen. "The Life and Death (and Life and Death) of Adam Warlock." *Back Issue* 1.34 (June 2009): 3–13.

Wright, Bradford W. *Comic Book Nation: The Transformation of Youth Culture in America*. Baltimore: Johns Hopkins University Press, 2003.

CRITICAL
READINGS

Will Eisner's *A Contract with God*

Daniel D. Clark

It would be difficult to overestimate the influence Will Eisner has had on the development of the graphic novel. Born in New York City on March 6, 1917 to Samuel and Fannie Eisner, both Jewish immigrants, Eisner experienced a childhood marked by poverty and constant relocations (Shumacher 2–5). Samuel, a dreamer and an untrained but naturally gifted artist, found unsteady work painting backgrounds for vaudeville stages, selling used furniture, and even manufacturing fur coats, but none of these sporadic jobs provided sufficiently for the Eisners (5). Fannie had been orphaned as a child and raised by her step-sister, who kept Fannie so busy with household chores that Fannie never learned to read or write, but she did learn to be pragmatic, accepting the harsher realities of life and insisting that Will pursue an occupation that would guarantee steady work. Eisner credited his father with inspiring him to dream and his mother for giving him a clear sense of the practical (Hajdu 16).

Eisner knew at an early age that he wanted to draw comics. "The comic strips in the newspapers of the time were everything to me. . . . They made me want to become an artist . . ." (Hajdu 16). On Saturday evenings at home, Eisner and his younger brother would practice redrawing newspaper comic strips. As Eisner's talents became apparent, Fannie, having seen her talented husband fail to make a living with his art, attempted, unsuccessfully, to steer her son toward more practical pursuits (Schumacher 14–15). Sam, for his part, encouraged Will's artistic bent by drawing with him or taking him to the Metropolitan Museum of Art to study paintings up close (13). Will continued to hone his craft in high school, drawing illustrations and a comic strip for his school's newspaper. He further developed his skills by taking classes with the Art Students League of New York.

When he was nineteen, Eisner met with Jerry Iger to discuss forming a studio that would publish original comics. At the time, the comics industry was exploding, and Eisner sensed an opportunity to reach his dream. In early 1937, the Eisner and Iger Studio opened for business and expanded quickly, adding additional artists. From the very beginning, Eisner took his craft seriously. One artist, Bill Bossert, who worked with Eisner in the early days of Eisner and Iger, noted that Eisner "never looked down on comics. Of course, most people did, and I did, too. It seemed a little weird to me that he wanted us to put so much effort into comic books" (Hajdu 25). Though the studio met with success, Eisner was growing dissatisfied with creating comics that he felt were bland and monotonous, and he wanted to "transcend the juvenilia" of most comic books (Hajdu 38). By 1940, Eisner had sold his share of the studio and began publishing *The Spirit* comic strip, to which he had been given full artistic freedom.

Eisner was an early advocate of comics reaching beyond popular children's entertainment. "I felt comic books were underrated—I felt they had untapped potential, at that time. I thought that most of the guys in comics underestimated their readers (Hajdu 38). "[W]hen I made the decision to do the Spirit, I thought that comic books could be an art form, a literary art form" (Hajdu 39). As early as the 1940s, Eisner argued for the legitimacy of comics as a medium to convey mature and complex stories and that the comics had far more potential than even those in the industry realized. It would be three decades later, when Eisner first published *A Contract with God*, that he would fully test his belief.

A Contract with God, first published in 1978, became a foundational work in the medium of comics and is often seen as "the first definitive graphic novel . . . that strives to be literature" (Duncan and Smith 16). Forming a type of cycle narrative, its four stories are connected not by a cohesive plot or a single protagonist, but rather by the stories' thematic concerns and shared setting of a fictional Bronx neighborhood on Dropsie Avenue (Royal 151). The stories present grim, if at times melodramatic, tales of members of a mostly immigrant community attempting to overcome the bitter economic and social realities of their lives during the Great Depression. Eisner's inventive composition, his page layouts, line work, perspective, and use of shadow and light reinforce and amplify the works' themes and somber tones. In the preface to the original edition of A *Contract with God*, Eisner notes,

> [E]ach story was written without regard to space, and each was allowed to develop its format from itself; that is, to evolve from the narration. The normal frames (or panels) associated with sequential (comic book) art are allowed to take on their own integrity. For example, in many cases an entire page is set out as a panel. The text and the balloons are interlocked with the art. I see all these as threads of a single fabric and exploit them as a language. If I have been successful at this, there will be no interruption in the flow of the narrative because the picture and the text are so totally dependent on each other as to be inseparable for even a moment (Eisner xix).

The title story, "A Contract with God," presents Frimme Hersh, who turns his back on God after the death of his young adopted daughter, believing God has violated their shared contract. In "The Street Singer," Eddie, an unemployed accountant, is reduced to singing for loose change, but seems to catch a break as a former opera diva wants him to become her protégé. "The Super" presents Scruggs, a bully of a tenement superintendent, who is brought to ruin by a manipulative, mature-beyond-her-age ten-year-old, named Rosie. In the final story, "Cookalein," various members of the neighborhood head to the Catskills for an inexpensive holiday; most are looking for a respite from their lives in the city, while others are looking to make a more permanent change of station.

These stories creatively present Eisner's recollections from his youth and portray the various hardships faced by immigrant communities living in the Bronx during the Great Depression. Eisner insisted that he was doing little more than "reportage," but his empathetic renderings of suffering belie his humanistic concerns ("Spirit" 207). "Living through the Depression has made me sensitive . . . sensitive to the human struggle for survival," a topic central in all four stories in *A Contract with God* ("Spirit" 208). Eisner's growing up in the tenements, enduring a desperate poverty, experiencing prejudice and ethnic bullying form the foundations of these stories, and much of this work is autobiographical. "This is an area that I knew from my youth, and I was able to talk about it with some authority. A lot of it is autobiographical, a lot of it is experiences that I had, that I saw other people have" ("Will Eisner" 94).

In all four of these narratives, Eisner displays the futility and impotence of human desire and the ephemeral nature of happiness. The characters strive for fulfillment, for self-improvement, and fail. Some are brought low because of their own naiveté; others fail because of their misguided, selfish ambitions; still others stumble as a result of their own prejudices and inability to embrace community. Eisner has noted how the Great Depression taught unmistakable lessons about "how little control we have over human destiny—despite our technology and innovation" (Roth 467). And yet, Eisner's narratives do not surrender completely to despair. Within the bleakness exists a community that, though enduring poverty, is still capable of acts of humaneness—a bowl of soup offered to the mourning, coins given in exchange for a moment of diversion, a community rushing to protect one of its own. In these small acts, Eisner suggests a better way for a community to live.

One of Eisner's great strengths as an artist was his ability to magnify the mood of his narratives with his drawings. This ability is certainly displayed in "A Contract with God." The opening image of the narrative, an establishing panel, presents row upon row of nearly identical five-story tenement buildings lit from within, shadowy and dirty from the front. The narrow alleys seem barely wide enough for a person to traverse. The fire escapes, trash cans, and laundry hung between the buildings suggest the confinement and lack of upward mobility the tenants endure. Behind the buildings, far away, stand the glamorous skyscrapers of the big city, glumly masked in a light haze. These images emphasize the otherworldliness of lives lived in penthouses and the great gulf fixed between rich and poor.

For Eisner, "A Contract with God" was deeply personal and an outworking of his own personal tragedy. Eisner and his wife Ann had two children, John and Alice. Eisner was particularly close to his children and worked to give them a happier and more secure childhood than he himself had experienced. Eisner took interest in his children's school activities, knew their friends, and would often write his children individual letters when he was traveling (Andelman 128–30). He painted cartoons on the walls of the children's rooms and brought home an old rowboat and filled it with sand for the children to play in (Schumacher 156). Alice was particularly skilled in having her way, as her father would all too easily give in to her requests. This seemingly cheerful family life would crumble when Alice was diagnosed with terminal leukemia. Alice died a year later, in 1970, at the age of sixteen, leaving Eisner grieving and deeply bitter at God. After her death, Eisner refused to talk about Alice, and only years later did he publically address her loss.

In "A Contract with God," Eisner works out his own anger and his sense of God's personal betrayal. The protagonist of the story, Frimme Hersh, like Eisner, feels he has done his best to love and provide for his child, feels he has lived a moral life, demonstrating generosity to others, and feels exceptionally violated for having his child plucked from the earth. In the preface of *The Contract with God Trilogy*, Eisner writes, "[Frimme's] argument with God was also mine. I exorcised my rage at a deity that I believed violated my faith and deprived my lovely 16-year-old child of her life at the very flowering of it" (xvi). Hersh, as a child, had written his contract with God on the back of a small stone that he always carried in his pocket. Hersh had abided by this agreement and had lived a life full of good fortune, but with the death of his daughter, he believes God has violated this pact. He takes the stone, spits on it, and heaves it out his upper floor window.

Again, the images Eisner creates intensify the sense of Hersh's agony. The opening panels present Hersh walking the flooded city streets through a heavy downpour, a common visual motif used by Eisner that Harvey Kurtzman facetiously called (and which now is commonly known as) the *Eisner spritz*. The water is as burdensome as it is ubiquitous. It streams from the street lamps, from the steps of the tenement, from the bill of Hersh's hat, and down the back of his coat. The water itself seems to obstruct his way as he climbs the front steps of the building hunched over from the weight of the water. Once inside, the water continues to pour from his coat; with each step, he leaves a puddle on the wooden floor. As he enters his room, he places his dripping hat on a hook and removes his coat, while water pools at his feet. This water imagery is juxtaposed with a conspicuous tear flowing from Hersh's eye and emphasizes the magnitude of Hersh's sorrow.

Hersh, angry and embittered, seeks retribution, not so much by abandoning his belief in God, but by intentionally turning his back on the principles of the original contract. Instead of helping others, he seeks personal gain. He uses his synagogue's bonds, which are in his care, as collateral for a loan to purchase the tenement he lives in; he then raises the rents, without regard for his neighbors' ability to pay, and acquires a *shikseh*, a Gentile mistress. Over time, Hersh gains wealth, but he cannot fully escape his faith or conscience. Even after the death of his adopted daughter, Hersh has observed the *shiva* (the seven days of mourning). He remains embittered towards God for not honoring his contract, but he eventually reaches his moment of crisis, when his mistress suggests that she will become Jewish if it will make him happy. At that moment, the futility of his bitterness and pursuit of wealth becomes apparent, and he fixates on developing a new contract with God. The elders of his synagogue are quick to forgive him when he returns the bonds with interest. Hersh's only request is that they write him a new contract with God, one that cannot be broken. Contract in hand, Hersh makes plans to again take up his good deeds, only to be killed by a heart attack.

Again, Eisner presents images that work to heighten the intensity of Hersh's sorrow and suffering. Eisner's dark images of Hersh's violent confrontation with God contain subtle elements that lead to an ambiguity of meaning. As Hersh rages against God, his fists clenched, his eyes looking heavenward, his anger seems to be met in kind as lightning flashes, and the window shade flaps sideways in the wind. After spitting on the stone contract, Hersh throws it out the window. Immediately below this image, Eisner presents three elongated, parallel panels, the first of which shows that the small tablet has come to rest in the alleyway next to a garbage can. In the next panel, teardrop-shaped rain begins to fall, and in the third, the rain is so heavy as to obscure both tablet and garbage can. In addition to the *Eisner spritz* suggesting Hersh's anguish, it may also suggest a divine sorrow as Hersh, unlike the biblical Job, has severed his relationship in his time of trouble.

Eisner also uses shading and shadows to create mood. The background and edges of most of the shadowy panels are not shaded, but in key panels, Eisner floods the background and edges with darkness suggesting Hersh's inner gloom. When Hersh meets with his banker, putting up his synagogue's bonds as his own collateral, Hersh and the banker are brightly lit but surrounded by darkness. Again, when Hersh's mistress presses him to sell his tenements and jokingly offers to become Jewish, the background is nearly completely dark. His unknowing tormentor exposes the void that his life has become. Eisner covers Hersh's face in shadow, as he must steady himself against a window.

Eisner raises some particularly theological questions in "A Contract with God." Is it possible for humanity to establish a relationship with God? Is it presumptuous for a person to create an agreement by which God must abide? Is God a vitriolic being who cares little about the desperation of humanity? Is God a being who disregards the good works of individuals? Is belief in God simply a wasted effort? In an epilogue to the story, Eisner has a young, kind-hearted Hassidic boy find the discarded stone contract and make it his own by signing his name to the bottom of it. The boy sits in a similar pose as that of the young Frimme Hersh, when he first carved out the contract. Whatever the answer to these questions, Eisner suggests that the cycle of Hersh's life will be repeated.

In "The Street Singer" Eisner turns his gaze upon the indignity, anger, and violence born out of the Great Depression. Eddie, an unemployed accountant, becomes a metaphor for the loss of dignity and independence shared by many during the 1930s, as he scrounges for whatever coins he can collect by singing in the alleyways between the tenements. In one of the first images of the story, Eddie is seen from high above looking up, arm outstretched, hat on ground, singing. Eisner's use of perspective in this full-page panel makes Eddie appear small, trapped between three high walls with laundry fluttering overhead. The dirty alleyway is filled with garbage cans and loose debris. Taken together, these images suggest Eddie's relative insignificance and his desperation.

As Eddie sings, an older woman appears at a third floor window and drops a note asking him to come up to her apartment. As soon as Eddie enters her tenement apartment, she identifies herself as former diva Marta Maria. She flatters him about his voice and confidently promises to make him a famous baritone. His impotence before her is apparent. He has little opportunity to speak, but does ask for some food. Marta's confidence is juxtaposed with Eddie's passivity. She gives him food; he eats. She talks; he listens. She leads him to a couch; he reclines. She initiates sex; he responds. She hands him money; he accepts. Eddie is effectively emasculated in the presence of Marta's power.

Marta, however, is also desperate, desperate to reclaim her celebrity. Like many during this era, she works hard to maintain appearances. She uses her stage name rather than her real name, Sylvia Speegel. She doesn't bother finding out Eddie's real name and assigns him the stage name Ronald Barry. Even the fruit she keeps in a bowl is made out of wax. Giving Eddie some money, Sylvia encourages him to purchase a new suit, noting, "In this business, you must look prosperous" (Tenement 78). Eisner points to the futility of these pretentions as no amount of make-up or show can alter the reality of the characters' lives. Sylvia, despite her bluster, is ultimately reduced to begging her former agent to book Eddie to sing at a wedding or bar mitzvah, revealing her own desperation and powerlessness to escape her current prison.

Eisner reinforces the dehumanizing effects of poverty with images suggesting Eddie's debasement. Eisner presents Eddie descending a series of steps through a back alley and then walking over litter-covered ground to reach his own tenement apartment. His apartment, unlike Sylvia's, is nearly bare, furnished only with a small table, a single chair, and what looks to be a seat from a car. The walls of the apartment are cracked; a single light bulb hangs from a wire, and a small radiator is attached to the far wall. Eddie's pent up humiliation works itself out violently as his pregnant wife begins to berate him, while holding their wailing infant. Eddie initially remains nearly silent before a woman telling him what he should do. Eddie can only tell her repeatedly to shut up until he grabs and tosses their baby across the room. He then begins punching his wife and only stops when she hits him in the head with one of his liquor bottles.

Eisner doesn't shy away from the gritty realism with which these scenes play out. He knew from his own childhood experiences the degradations of poverty and again addresses the theme of the frailty of human ambition. Eisner ends the story with yet another bitter irony, as Eddie realizes he has forgotten where the diva lives and loses hope of ever finding her again. Eddie is far from a sympathetic character, but he represents many a person made impotent by the Great Depression.

In "The Super," Eisner presents the destruction of its male protagonist, who falls prey to his own moral weaknesses and his inability to embrace his community. Mr. Scruggs, a hulking German immigrant and the building superintendent is openly condescending toward the Jewish tenants, whom he thinks complain too much. Eisner accentuates his menacing presence by drawing a close-up of his furloughed brow with spit coming out of his mouth after he confronts a tenant who asks when he would repair the steps. This frightening image is mitigated somewhat by the text, which sympathizes with Scruggs' thankless position. An overbearing German in charge of an apartment building inhabited mainly by Jews during the 1930s may subtly suggest the oppression Jews in Germany were facing at that time under the Nazis. Scruggs himself alludes to a rising Germany when he contrasts his treatment with how supers are treated in Germany and then seems to make a veiled threat about order and discipline coming to America someday. However, as in "The Street Singer," the protagonist seems powerless before the power of a woman. Here, though, Scruggs is felled by a very sexually aware ten-year-old girl, Rosie Farfell. Rosie walks into Scruggs' room, locks the door behind her, and asks for a nickel if she lifts her skirt. After doing so, she poisons Scrugg's dog and steals his money box, but plays the victim after she is caught; the residents of the tenement rise up against Scruggs. Eisner captures the climax of the story in a single panel framed from a low angle; the tall buildings seem to lean in oppressively as Scruggs realizes the impossibility of his situation and walks away, a look of terror on his face. Eisner has noted his "perspective was learned looking out a window of a five-story tenement. Everything you see in the city as a little boy is in sharp perspective, going up or down" ("Will Eisner Interview" 68). Here, Eisner's use of perspective indicates, once again, the crushing impotence of a man who knows he has been destroyed.

The question arises though, who is the greater villain? Scruggs, the isolated child molester, or Rosie, who seemingly without conscience or fear propositions Scruggs, kills his dog, and lastly, after Scruggs commits suicide, sits on the steps of the tenement and sings while she counts the money she has stolen. It's just such depictions that have made a number of critics accuse Eisner of crating sexist portrayals of female characters (73). Eisner argues that, in this case, the pedophilia was secondary to his main narrative concern, that being Scruggs' relationship with the residents of the tenement (71). Ultimately, Eisner suggests it is Scruggs' alienation from his community, his constant belittling of the residents, and his inability to accept difference that leads to his downfall.

"Cookalein" presents two parallel narratives and may be the most openly autobiographical of the stories in *A Contract with God*. During the Depression, many farmers in the Catskills would rent out rooms and small cottages on their properties during the summers, in order to provide their families with additional income. The guests would have access to the kitchen in the main house and would often be responsible for making their own meals. A cookalein, literally "cook alone," was an inexpensive alternative to more expensive resorts and would draw urban visitors, who sought respite from the city.

In "Cookalein," Eisner again captures the sense of human desperation as two characters, Goldie and Benny, both part of the lower working class, hope to improve their economic state by finding a wealthy mate during their stay. Both play the role of someone above their station: Goldie spends her entire savings buying two famous-labeled dresses, while Benny rents a car. Instead of finding wealthy suitors, they find each other. Upon discovering that Goldie is as poor as he, Benny attempts to rape Goldie. Eisner uses the attempted rape symbolically to mock the naiveté and selfish motives of the two as Benny is unable to make penetration and Goldie doesn't realize she has actually avoided being physically raped. Benny again suggests the man made impotent by his circumstances, while Goldie suggests the foolishness of naïve optimism in simplistic solutions.

The second narrative is, in part, an autobiographical coming-of-age story for a thinly disguised fifteen-year-old Will Eisner. The parallels between Willie and Eisner are many: the names of Willie's parents—Sam and Fannie—the fact that Willie's father works, somewhat unsuccessfully, in the fur business, his practical-minded mother working from home, a younger brother named Petey. "Every one of the people in those stories is either me or someone I knew, or parts of them and me . . . ("Interview" 71). Eisner notes that when he was young, he did go to a cookalein and that he either saw or experienced many of the events presented (71). In the story, Willie is seduced in a hayloft by a sexually voracious married woman. The two are caught together by the woman's husband, who hits her before the two have sex in front of a horrified Willie. Willie has thus been violently cast into the ugly world of adulthood. As if to emphasize this point, the last panel of the original narrative shows a deeply reflective Willie standing on the fire escape looking down on the tenements, his mother telling him that he will now have to be the man of the house.

Eisner has often been called the godfather of comics. He saw and championed the literary potential of the medium to address adult concerns when few others did. Author John Updike said of Eisner's *The Spirit*:

> After the relatively innocent good-against-evil adventures of Superman, Batman, and Plastic Man, Will Eisner's the Spirit made an alarming and indelible impression. . . . The vertiginous perspectives, the long shadows, the vivid pools of blood, the artist's blithe violation of the tidy limits of the panels, and curious moral neutrality of the

noir hero—all this informed, for me, an unsettling transition into what I now realize was the adult world. (Hajdu 50)

Eisner's groundbreaking work has influenced the medium and pushed it toward an ever-expanding creativity and maturity. Eisner's *A Contract with God* challenged the boundaries of what comics could be and took an early step in comics being treated as a serious literary art form.

Works Cited

Duncan, Randy and Matthew J. Smith. *The Power of Comics: History, Form, and Culture*. New York: Continuum, 2009.

Eisner, Will. *A Contract with God and Other Tenement Stories*. 1978. New York: W.W. Norton, 2006.

_____. *The Contract with God Trilogy: Life of Dropsie Avenue*. New York: W.W. Norton, 2006.

Fingeroth, Danny. "The Spirit of Comics: The Will Eisner Interview." *Will Eisner: Conversations*. Ed. Thomas M. Inge. Jackson, MS: U of Mississippi P, 2011. 205–219.

Hajdu, David. *The Ten-cent Plague: The Great Comic Book Scare and How It Changed America*. New York: Farrar, Straus, and Giroux, 2008.

Inge, M. Thomas, ed. *Will Eisner: Conversations*. Jackson, MS: University of Mississippi Press, 2011.

Roth, Laurence. "Drawing Contracts: Will Eisner's Legacy." *The Jewish Quarterly Review* 97.3 (2007): 463–484.

Royal, Derek Parker. "Sequential Sketches of Ethnic Identity: Will Eisner's *A Contract with God* as Graphic Cycle." *College Literature* 38.1 (2011): 150–167.

Schumacher, Michael. *Will Eisner: A Dreamer's Life in Comics*. New York: Bloomsbury, 2010.

Yronwode, Cat. "Will Eisner Interview." *Will Eisner: Conversations*. Ed. Thomas M. Inge. Jackson, MS: U of Mississippi P, 2011. 47–78.

Art Spiegelman's *Maus: A Survivor's Tale*_____

Brian Cogan

Maus is a Pulitzer Prize–winning, two-volume autobiographical graphic novel by acclaimed comics artist Art Spiegelman. The incredibly complex and compelling work is essentially both a graphic description of Spiegelman's parents' survival of the Holocaust (as related by Vladek, Spiegelman's father), as well as an examination of the tortured and guilt-wracked relationship between father and son decades after the Holocaust. *Maus* had begun as a series of short comics that Spiegelman had published sporadically since as early as 1972, and almost all the material from the first volume was derived from chapters in *Raw* magazine, an influential comics anthology edited by Spiegelman and his wife Françoise Mouly.

The first volume (Spiegelman was working on the second volume of *Maus* at the same time) was initially rejected by numerous publishers, including St. Martin's Press; Penguin Books; Alfred A. Knopf; and Farrar, Straus and Giroux) before the first volume was published by Pantheon Books in 1986, followed by the second volume in 1991. The two-volume set was awarded a special Pulitzer Prize in 1992. The committee had trouble deciding if the work (all the characters in the book are depicted as animals) was fiction or nonfiction and gave it a "special" prize as a way of avoiding controversy.

Maus is exceptionally nuanced and detailed and, to some critics, extremely controversial for two main reasons. The first is that it is a graphic novel and perhaps the first serious and widely-known example of that medium to take the Holocaust as its main theme. The second major controversy surrounding *Maus* is how it depicts history. Spiegelman's father, Vladek, the main focus of the story, as well as his wife, Anja, and the other Jewish characters of the recollection are depicted as cartoon mice, persecuted by cartoon Nazi cats. (Other characters are depicted as animals as well, including the Poles as pigs and the Americans as dogs, a riff on the description of

American soldiers during World War II as "dog faces.") While some critics were appalled by the seeming trivialization of one of the most significant and horrific parts of human history, others praised *Maus* as a masterpiece and an example of the graphic novel's potential as a medium.

Many agreed that Spiegelman's work was groundbreaking not only in terms of subject matter and style, but also because it helped allow a new form of literary autobiography via the medium of the graphic novel. As one critic wrote, Spiegelman's "unique approach to collective autobiography would be the most influential in shaping the reception of the form in the decades to come" (Versaci 137). *Maus* is undoubtedly one of the most important graphic novels of the twentieth century and a landmark in graphic storytelling.

History

Art Spiegelman was born on February 15 to Vladek and Anja Spiegelman, both Holocaust survivors, whose first son Richelieu was killed during the war. After living for several years in Stockholm, the family immigrated to the United States in 1951, living in various locations until settling in Rego Park (Queens), New York in 1955. Vladek Spiegelman worked as a diamond importer and Art Spiegelman was largely raised by his troubled mother Anja, who committed suicide in 1968. Spiegelman was also hospitalized for depression that same year.

From an early age, Spiegelman showed an aptitude for art. He was a child prodigy, and as Jonathan Safran Foer pointed out, "By the age of fifteen, Spiegelman was already the publisher of his own magazine, charmingly titled *Blasé*" (Safran Foer 255). Spiegelman was also influenced by the underground comics that started to become more widely known in the early 1960s, and he began to work in that genre, influenced by long-time friend and comics innovator, R. Crumb. To support himself as an artist, he worked for the Topps chewing gum company, where he created the popular "Wacky Packs" and "Garbage Pail Kids" sets of stickers. While working as a comic book writer and artist, he also founded the influential comics anthologies *Arcade* and *Raw*.

Throughout this period, Spiegelman continued to publish his own work. In 1972, in the one and only issue of *Funny Animals*, Spiegelman published his first recollection of his father's experiences during the Holocaust. As Spiegelman later noted, the original three-page *Maus* comic from 1972 was not based on lengthy interviews with Vladek or his efforts to try and find out more about his father's experience, but based only on memory and an awareness that the Holocaust was inextricably tied into his family's identity. As Spiegelman noted later, the original three-page *Maus* was "based on what I knew; before I knew anything, one of those free-floating shards of anecdote I'd picked up" (Spiegelman, *MetaMaus* 22). The importance of the original short piece cannot be underestimated in terms of its influence on both *Maus* and the medium of the graphic novel that followed. As Rocco Versaci notes, *Maus* "began to take shape in the first (and only) issue of *Funny Animals* (1972)," and was "the start of Spiegelman's interest in his fathers' experiences during the Holocaust, but also led to the meticulous research that informs the creation of *Maus* over the next two decades" (137). The piece is also notable in the fact that, as early as 1972, Spiegelman was already using the metaphor of the Jews as mice and the Nazis as cats to represent history. In the late seventies, Spiegelman's interest in his father's stories became the germ of a much more ambitious project, one that would capture the story of his parents' survival during the Holocaust, but depicted in comic book form. Spiegelman started seriously researching the history of the Holocaust and began taping and transcribing interviews with Vladek that later became the bulk of the story of *Maus*.

During his research, Spiegelman began to publish the original six chapters of *Maus* in *RAW*, and the first volume was finally collected as a book by Pantheon in 1986. It went on to be translated into eighteen languages and receive a National Book Critics Circle nomination. Five years later, Pantheon published the remaining chapters as *Maus II*, which met with great critical successes (Safran Foer 260).

Key Themes

Maus is innovative not just in terms of the story, but also in terms of Spiegelman's creative use of the medium. While Spiegelman's artistic style is deceptively simplistic in some cases, the evocative and simplistic "mouse faces" draw the reader's attention to the seriousness of the story. As Thomas Doherty notes, "The pictures lack detail, but not depth, the low definition medium enhancing the deep involvement of the reader" (77). While photos or other visual depictions of the Holocaust can be off-putting enough to stop a reader from continuing reading, *Maus* draws the reader in and gives them enough impetus to continue reading, no matter how harrowing Vladek's tale becomes.

However, the storytelling of *Maus* is also a crucial part of Vladek's story. While *Maus* is a true story of both Spiegelman's parents, told through Vladek's perspective, it is not always chronological. It weaves its way back and forth between the present conversations between Art and Vladek, Vladek's recollections of his survival, and his attempts to keep himself and his wife alive, both when they were together and later, when they were separated at Auschwitz. However, the book emphasizes not only Vladek (and Art's) story, but also returns to reoccurring themes that help propel the narrative. One of the key themes has to do with how a desperate but pragmatic Vladek improvises and adapts consistently in the name of survival.

It may well be that Vladek is an annoying and sometimes ruthless curmudgeon, but it is also emphasized that his ruthlessness and ability to consistently adapt and improvise is what keeps him and Anja alive for the duration of the war. From before the war to his later conversations about his history with Art, Vladek consistently shows his innate ability to seize chances that others around him fail to see, and this is one of the main reasons he is able to survive. This isn't to say that he is more noble or courageous than any of the other concentration camp prisoners, but it does imply that he learned early on that adaptation was paramount to survival.

This adaptability is illustrated early on in *Maus*, even before Vladek's family is aware of the plans of Nazi Germany. As a Polish citizen, Vladek is subject to the draft, where he would have been forced into the army and into especially grave peril as a Jew. Vladek learns an important lesson from his equally pragmatic father, who goes to great lengths to keep his vulnerable son out of harm's way. Vladek's father—in perhaps an inadvertent foreshadowing of what Vladek experiences later in the camps—starves him, deprives him of sleep, and dehydrates him in order for Vladek to appear frail and sickly and thereby successfully avoid, for a while, being drafted into the Polish army. As Vladek recalls, "For three months I ate only salted herring and no water to lose weight. And for a few days before the exam, no food and no sleep" (Spiegelman, *Maus I* 46). An increasingly skeletal Vladek refuses to go through the same ordeal the following year and finally ends up in the army. There, he is captured and eventually sent to the first of many prison camps that will dominate the next six years of his life. The lesson Vladek learns along the way is that if a system is unjust, it is morally acceptable to try and game the system in order to survive.

After surviving military service and a relatively benign (compared to the future horrors of the concentration camps) imprisonment, Vladek returns to his family and his new bride, where conditions are gradually worsening. He is able to use his position and friendships with various officials to gather extra rations of food and clothing for his extended family, but eventually, most of his and Anja's relatives are rounded up and killed. Through connections, bribery, and his own innate cunning, Vladek manages to keep himself and Anja alive, albeit narrowly.

After learning that their only son at the time, Richelieu, has been killed while hiding with a family friend, Anja despairs of their survival and tells Vladek that she, too, wants to die. Vladek's response, over a four-panel sequence, is as follows: "No, Darling, to die it's easy… But you have to struggle for life! Until the last moments we must struggle together! I need you! And you'll see together that we'll survive." (Spiegelman, *Maus I* 122).

One of Vladek's key qualities is precisely his dedication to survival by all means necessary, as demonstrated throughout the story. At first, Vladek survives owing mostly to his ability to speak English. When a Kapo at the camp wants to practice his own English, he relies on Vladek to help him. Vladek notes, "for Polish, I spoke good English" (Spiegelman, *Maus II* 30). Despite the Kapo's cruelty, he needs Vladek enough to keep him off the work gangs that would have killed him, and he even gives him extra rations of food.

In consistently finding new ways to escape the starvation rations and back-breaking labor designed to wear the prisoners out before their inevitable execution, Spiegelman illustrates Vladek's ability to find jobs that he could use to keep himself alive, regardless of whether he initially knows any of them. In one particularly vivid piece of graphic storytelling, Spiegelman illustrates his father's clever shoe repair technique that he borrowed from an old book on shoe making and repair. Through Spiegelman's matter-of-fact illustrations, Vladek's improbable survival plans come across not so much as clever attempts to outwit the inevitable fate but as pragmatic and logical steps taken to survive. Although Vladek is self-sufficient, he is also smart enough to realize when he needs help. When a particularly odious SS officer tells him to repair a badly damaged new boot and to make it look as good as new with the implied consequences that he will be executed if he does not accomplish this within a day, Vladek finds a more accomplished shoemaker in the camp and trades him a day's ration of food to fix the boot to the SS officer's satisfaction.

The horrors of the day-to-day life in the camps are clearly shown in this vignette, as the "reward" for fixing a boot is a sausage—a rare commodity in a place designed to wear down the prisoners through starvation rations. Vladek's description of the scene to Art is particularly telling: "You know what this was, a whole sausage? You can't imagine! I cut it with a shoe knife and ate it so fast I was a little sick after." (Spiegelman, *Maus II* 61).

Even when faced with the overwhelming horror of a "death train" packed with fellow prisoners, who are left alone on the train for over a week to die, Vladek realizes that the two hooks at the top of the cattle car could be used to hold a blanket. So he elevates himself over the other prisoners by relying on those two hooks. As the other men die pitifully below him, Vladek is able to survive not only by eating the snow he can reach from his position, but also for bartering with the prisoners for sugar in order to sustain him through the starvation. As Vladek recounts, "This saved me. Maybe 25 people came out from this car of 200" (Spiegelman, *Maus II* 85).

While imprisoned under horrific conditions and under constant threat of death day in and day out, Vladek learns that everything can be useful, or possibly could be traded for something useful later. This mentality helps him when he seeks work after the war in a department store. He is hired because he is savvy enough to realize that goods that had no use in one country might be scarce in another. The unfortunate side effect of this is that the older Vladek is also somewhat of a hoarder, picking up wires and other paraphernalia that might be possibly of use someday. Ironically, indeed, the very qualities that kept Vladek alive throughout the Holocaust are detrimental to his relationship with his suicidal wife, his estranged son, and his second wife, Mala, who is consistently angered by Vladek's miserly ways and constant criticism.

Another key theme in *Maus* is the uneasy relationship between Art and Vladek. Although they are related, Art is disgusted by Vladek's racism, verbal abuse of his second wife Mala, and inappropriate miserly ways. Vladek and Art's constant struggle to find common ground and Art's attempt to understand the enormity of the Holocaust are particularly highlighted in *Maus, Volume II.* While in some ways it seems as though a Holocaust survivor should be allowed some leeway, Art refuses to budge, perhaps haunted by the fact that he never could reconcile with his mother Anja, herself a survivor who committed suicide.

Art is also ambivalent about not only his relationship with his father, but also to history and his own Jewish identity. While the drawings of Vladek and the other older Jewish survivors in the Catskills—where Art, Françoise, and Vladek go on vacation—are stylized the same, Art is shown wearing a mouse mask, tied on by string in the back. As Versaci has noted previously, this literal "mouse disguise" metaphor has its roots as far back as the first three-page iteration of *Maus* in 1972:

This story was also the first to feature Spiegelman's analogy of the Jewish victims of the Nazis as mice, although at that point he was drawing the characters in a more realistic style, instead of the stylized mask like (or sometimes in his own case, masked) figures who populate the later more thought out versions of the story. In Spiegelman's case, he is not the anthropomorphosized mouse of the central story as related by Vladek, but an observer and as a symbolic outsider who cannot experience the reality of what it is to be a Holocaust survivor, Spiegelman can only approximate the authenticity that Vladek and other survivors naturally posses (137).

This problematic relationship with Art's father and with history grounds the book not just in the unimaginable—that is, the horrors of the Holocaust—but also in the banal, everyday bickering of a long-estranged father/son relationship. Vladek, while an astoundingly tenacious and resourceful survivor, is perhaps moved by his inherent pragmatism (and survivor's guilt) to reject some of the familiar standards of family relationships. As Thomas Doherty noted, "Artie's father forthrightly defies one stereotype: the stereotype of the Holocaust survivor. Neither saintly sufferer nor guilt ravaged witness; he is most appealing at his most annoying. Vladek seems pretty much the same irascible SOB before Auschwitz as after" (Doherty 81).

What is clear from the start of *Maus* is how estranged Art and Vladek are as son and father. Neither is able to comment on the fact that, although Vladek was able to keep his wife (and Art's mother) Anja alive during the Holocaust, neither of them was able to save her from herself afterwards. One key aspect of *Maus* that critics often neglect to recognize is that the graphic novel is not only the story of the Holocaust and of survival, but also the story of how *all* relationships are destroyed by the horrors that human beings inflict on one another. Art is Vladek's son, yet he cannot draw himself as a "mouse," as he cannot connect to the man his father had to become in order to survive the events he lived through. In some ways, what is most challenging about *Maus* is "Spiegelman's complex approach to narrative address, to time and framing, to the ways in which he simultaneously validates his father's memories and firsthand experience as authentic, even as he recounts the costs and the fictions—for both father and son—required to record those memories" (Versaci 138).

Perhaps in many ways, *Maus* is the result not just of Vladek's ability to survive, but the way in which Art can use his ability to draw and his gift for storytelling to allow Vladek to tell his story. Art is able to use his own gift—his artistic genius—in order to render Vladek's memories as "consumable" to the general public, but at a cost—that of the relationship between Art and Vladek. But in terms of his success, Art can only feel guilt that he has become a success by selling his father's story. This is why he is wracked with anguish that he has symbolically commoditized the story that Vladek lived through. And, as one critic noted, "Spiegelman frankly realizes the inevitable commodification of culture, even Holocaust culture" (Rothberg 670).

Art uses the "mouse/Maus" metaphor in order to make the unspeakable real for those who did not live through the horrors that Vladek endured. Spiegelman's mice are both a commentary on the masks we use to avoid the horrors of the everyday world, and the especially significant horrors of his own family's history. As *Maus* both disarms and engages the reader, the unspeakable becomes *tellable* through the medium of the graphic novel. As Thomas Doherty notes, "The cartoon medium possesses a graphic quality well-suited to a confrontation with Nazism and the Holocaust" (71), in that it both displaces and intensifies the experience for the reader, even if it cannot heal the wounds of either Art or Vladek. As Versaci notes further, "Graphic autobiography explicitly does not release the autobiographer from the 'unhealed wounds' of the past trauma…" (139). It does not matter that Spiegelman is attempting to tell a story that does not fit in with the usual depiction of the Holocaust survivor, as Vladek cannot become anything but the irascible old man he is from the start. As another critic noted, "Spiegelman transgresses the sacredness of Auschwitz by depicting in comic strip images his father's suffering and by refusing to sentimentalize the survivor" (Rothberg 665).

Overall, the importance of *Maus* is its creator's ability to tell a tale that cannot be told the same way through another medium. As Doherty explains, "Maus redrew the conceptual themes of depictions of the Holocaust on popular art" and "offered a media-wise vision whose rough images put traumatic history into sharp focus" (70). Even the "comic" mice of *Maus*—the "not so funny" funny animals—are a tribute to the resilience of Jewish culture, as well as a way of mocking the stereotype of the Jews as passive victims. In attempting a story on such an epic scale, *Maus*, as a whole, works through "the desacralizing and secularization of Jewish experience" (Rothberg 682). Put simply, *Maus* is not just an epic retelling of one survivor's story, but a commentary on the nature of history and of the Holocaust.

Criticism and awards

As a result of Spiegelman's dedication and vision, *Maus* was an immense success at the time it was published, albeit a controversial one. Many critics—confused or perhaps incredulous at the depiction of the main characters as animals—were not sure how to categorize it. Was it a faithful, if novel, recounting of a survivor's experience? Or was it a fanciful and fictionalized cartoon version of history? At the time of the graphic Novel's publication, many were divided as to how to examine it. In 1992, the Pulitzer Prize committee awarded *Maus* a "special" Pulitzer Prize, as they, like the *New York Times* bestseller list before them, were confused about how best to identify the work. Was it simply a lengthy "comic book?" A work of straight-ahead history? Or a mixture of fact and fiction? The Pulitzer Prize committee members were, as Doherty wrote, "befuddled by a project whose medium they could not quite categorize" (69).

At this point, serious, mainstream graphic novels were not as prevalent as they are today, and the success of *Maus* went a long way in explaining why graphic novels should be taken seriously and regarded as works of high art. However, back in 1991, this was less clear. In November 1991, *The New York Times Book Review* section put *Maus* on their fiction bestseller list. The framing device of using mice to stand in for the book's Jewish characters was apparently enough for the *Times* to consider the book wholesale as low-brow, comic book fiction.

After an impassioned letter by Spiegelman, the *Times* changed their mind and put it on the nonfiction list, but apparently not before one enraged editor was said to have remarked, "Let's go to Spiegelman's house and if a giant mouse answers the door, we'll move it to the non-fiction side of the list!" (Spiegelman, *Metamaus* 150). Spiegelman himself acknowledged any representation of both history and memory as potentially difficult. *Maus*, while meticulously researched by Spiegelman, is largely a recounting of Vladek's memories, filtered through three decades of time, and Art's subjective representation of the problematic relationship between Vladek and his son. As Spiegelman wrote, "reality is too complex to be threaded out into the narrow channels and confines of narrative," and *Maus*, like memoir, biography, and history, is streamlined and, at least on that level, a work of fiction. But Spiegelman is also careful to clarify that, after all, it was still "unsettling, after having gone to such lengths to get the facts and details right" (Spiegelman, *Metamaus* 150).

Conclusion

Although controversial at first, *Maus* is now ranked both by critics and by public acclaim—including overall sales, use in schools and universities as a teaching tool, and cultural resonance—as one of the greatest graphic novels of the twentieth century. Although journalists questioned Spiegelman for years about why he used mice, Spiegelman relentlessly defended his vision and storytelling techniques. Spiegelman, in his meticulous research into the Holocaust, realized the depiction of Jews as mice, literally vermin, came originally from despicable Nazi propaganda. As he noted, "the idea of Jews as toxic, as disease carriers, as dangerous subhuman creatures, was a necessary prerequisite for killing my family" (Spiegelman, *Metamaus* 115).

While in hindsight, it seems obvious that using caricatures of animals and the analogy of cats hunting down mice is a legitimate way of retelling a survivor's history, it was not as obvious when *Maus* was first published. It would take several years before *Maus* became truly appreciated by the public as a landmark in the graphic novel genre and a praiseworthy representation of the complex relationship between Holocaust survivors and their children. Jonathan Safran Foer sums it up by stating that:

> *Maus* is not the product of the Holocaust. It's in defiance of it. It's easy to assume that artists have always been taking such creative liberties with World War II. But, no one was doing what Spiegelman was doing before him. No one was handling history like that and no one was using comics in that way (262).

In many ways, no one else has ever done what Spiegelman has done: mix history and memoir with the graphic novel medium's storytelling power. *Maus* is, therefore, not only the tale of Spiegelman's family, but a vivid, gripping, and often horrific reminder of the frail line between what makes us human beings and what turns us into feral animals. If "never again" became the mantra of the Jewish people after the Holocaust, then *Maus* is a vivid reminder of how easy it was, and still is, to consider our neighbors as pests that need to be eliminated. *Maus* reminds us of how a story of human survival resonates today as much as it did when Vladek survived the horrors of the Holocaust many decades ago. It also reminds us that for Vladek, Art, and his doomed mother Anja, those same horrors must never be allowed to become forgotten history, but must remain fresh in our minds, so they can never again come to pass.

Works Cited

Doherty, Thomas. "Art Spiegelman's Maus: Graphic Art and the Holocaust." *American Literature* 68.1 (1996): 69–84.

Rothberg, Michael. "'We were talking Jewish: Art Spiegelman's 'Maus' as 'Holocaust' Production." *Contemporary Literature* 35. 4 (Winter 1994): 661–687

Safran Foer, Jonathan. "Art Spiegelman: Breakdownable." *Masters of American Comics*. Eds. John Carlin, Paul Karasik, and Brian Walker. New Haven: Yale University Press, 2005.

Spiegelman, Art. *Maus: A Survivors Tale I: My Father Bleeds History.* New York, Pantheon Books, 1986.

Spiegelman, Art. *Maus: A Survivor's Tale II: And Here My Troubles Began.* New York, Pantheon Books, 1991.

Spiegelman, Art. *MetaMaus: A Look inside a modern classic,* Maus. New York, Pantheon Books, 2011.

Versaci, Rocco. *This Book Contains Graphic Language: Comics as Literature.* New York: Continuum, 2007.

Frank Miller's *Batman*

In the latter years of the twentieth century and in the first two decades of the twenty-first century, American superheroes have become a dominant worldwide cultural mythology. These characters, which originated in comic book stories, have transformed into billion dollar media franchises that are now more often associated with movies, television, and video games than with their comic book roots. Arguably, the most popular and influential superhero of the last forty years is Batman, the costumed crime fighter who first appeared in *Detective Comics #27* (May 1939). The majority of modern audiences are most familiar with the dark and driven Caped Crusader of the Christopher Nolan films. This Batman, which differs greatly from other interpretations of the Dark Knight, can primarily trace his evolution and character development to the 1986 Frank Miller story *Batman: The Dark Knight Returns*. In this tale, a grizzled, older Batman comes out of retirement to once again combat crime and placate his inner demon(s). Miller's Batman is an outsider fighting for understanding and traditional values in a hollow society that has degenerated into a crime-ridden shell of its former self. The Batman of *The Dark Knight Returns* serves as a template not only for most later Caped Crusader stories, but also for many other superhero tales that have appeared in subsequent years. In Frank Miller's *The Dark Knight Returns*, Batman contains numerous innovative understandings of the Caped Crusader, including Batman as the damaged and unstable anti-hero; the desecration of society; and the Dark Knight as a contrast to the traditional, conservative hero that is Superman. All of these elements combine to fashion a formerly unseen Batman, who has become the decades-long standard for how the Dark Knight should both look and act.

Frank Miller's *Batman: The Dark Knight Returns* presents a Caped Crusader who is no longer a hero in the traditional comic book understanding of the concept. This older, weary, beaten-

82   Critical Insights

down Dark Knight is not a rational crime-fighting good guy, but rather an unbalanced individual, who has the almost pathological need to impose order in a society that appears to be descending into chaos. It should be noted that the early 1930s Batman was a rough-and-tumble vigilante, who battered criminals and seemed to worry little about following the law. The original Great Depression Batman was a seemingly mentally-stable man, who made the odd choice of dedicating his life to avenging his parents' deaths by dressing in a bat costume to intimidate criminals. This Batman and the numerous versions that followed appear to be obsessive, but rational individuals, driven to fight crime as costumed superheroes. However, they seem to be lucid and reasonable nonetheless.

While Batman has suffered from mental problems in past stories (most notably the Caped Crusader's breakdown in *Batman #156*), Miller's Dark Knight is the first comic book portrayal in which Batman is inherently unstable. This Batman is not a character that has suffered some recent distress, which has caused him to temporarily lose control of his faculties. Instead, the childhood trauma of seeing his parents' murders have left Miller's Batman mentally deranged in ways that past writers would have perceived as unthinkable. To cope with this horrific event, young Bruce Wayne created an identity based on a child's fantasy of a being strong and punishing the criminals who harmed his family. Wayne disappeared within the Batman construct for years and even chose to believe that a demon-like bat creature had possessed him and forced him to become a vigilante. While Miller's Dark Knight still fights crime and rights wrongs, he is not the Batman of the past. This Batman is a terrifyingly unbalanced megalomaniac, who wants to impose his version of justice on a crumbling society. He is a dark protector for a dark age, but it is unclear if one should regard him as a hero.

Frank Miller's Batman is best described as an anti-hero, who combines the Caped Crusader's basic mythology with a 1970s and 1980s vigilante ethos. While the Great Depression Batman could be described as a vigilante, he was not the overly brutal, anti-social, judge, jury, and executioner that came to define the term in the seventies and eighties. The 1930s and 1940s Batman borrowed many of his traits and tactics from hard boiled detectives, pulp heroes, and the masked mystery men of radio programs, while Miller's Batman uses as templates silver screen characters, like Clint Eastwood's Dirty Harry Callahan and Charles Bronson's Paul Kersey from the film *Death Wish*. These movie anti-heroes are portrayed as good men, whom a decaying society forces to act in vicious and illegal ways. During the late 1970s and early to mid-1980s, the legacies of Watergate and the Vietnam conflict had left the collective American psyche battered. To make matters worse, crime was seemingly rampant and cities, like New York and Los Angeles, appeared to become ungovernable urban wastelands, in which hardworking citizens no longer could feel safe and secure. The era's anti-heroes portrayed the fantasy of decent citizens using any means necessary to take back their streets from the plagues of crime and violence. Many people no longer trusted traditional authority figures, such as politicians, law enforcement officers, and the news media, but instead fanaticized about an incorruptible protector who could be counted on to return American society to its glory days. It is within this context that Miller created his Batman, a long-historicized character, who had imbibed the nation's pain and fear and who would now, in turn, personify the harsh guardian desired by a weary and damaged populace. The Batman portrayed in *The Dark Knight Returns* is a traditional hero modified to meet the needs of a new era. He is a hero for a society that requires he feel as bitter and scared as many Americans already do.

The Dark Knight Returns features a Batman, who embraces and emulates the popular anti-hero concept of the day. Simultaneously, the story is a deconstruction of a costumed crime fighter in an attempt to understand how he would behave in the real world. Miller imagines the kind of person who would prowl the streets at night, dressed as a bat, and his end-product is much different from the Batmen of the past. *The Dark Knight Returns* begins with a Bruce Wayne, who retired his Batman persona ten years before, and who has seemingly been able to move on and leave his superhero days behind. Wayne is intensely unhappy, though; he is a thrill-seeking billionaire with a death wish, who continually fights against his deep-seated need to return to his Batman identity. After the death of the second Robin, Jason Todd, Bruce Wayne swore never to become Batman again, and this oath has left him at odds with himself and his powerful desires. Ultimately, the mentally unstable Wayne breaks his promise and again dons the cowl and cape.

At this point, Miller deviates firmly from traditional Batman lore by stating that the Dark Knight not only fights to avenge his parents' deaths, but also believes he is possessed by a bat demon-like creature he encountered when he was six years old, after falling into what would eventually become the Batcave. Wayne remembers the bat creature, "Gliding with ancient grace...unwilling to retreat as his brothers did...eyes gleaming, untouched by love or joy or sorrow... breath hot with the taste of fallen foes...the stench of dead things, damned things...surely the fiercest survivor—the purest warrior... glaring, hating...claiming me as his own" (19). Notice that all of the bat's traits are ones that Batman values. The bat creature is a strong warrior, who shows no fear and always defeats his enemies. Bruce Wayne believes himself to be a man possessed by a bat and states multiple times, throughout the story, that he is acting on the desires of the bat creature living within. This evolution changes Batman from a standard good-guy hero to an unbalanced sociopath, who fights crime because of an entrenched need to create his own personal version of justice and order. This Batman is no longer a traditional hero, but is either a mentally disturbed vigilante or a demon-possessed psychopath. Both possibilities are far different from the Batman of yore.

No matter how the reader views Batman's sanity, Miller continually presents the Dark Knight as an animalistic force of nature, who constructs his own rules and is not bound by existing social mores or norms. After struggling through the beginning of the story, Bruce Wayne eventually gives into his demon and again becomes Batman. This takes place as a stifling Gotham City heat wave finally breaks and a massive thunderstorm rolls into the city. Much as Shakespeare often employed weather phenomena to represent changes to the natural order in his plays, Miller utilizes lightning and thunder to signal Batman's return to the hero's post.

More importantly, Batman is a natural force in this story, just as the rain cools the city and makes it more livable, the Caped Crusader cleans the streets of criminals and seemingly makes it safer for all. In the tale, a newscaster describes the approaching storm, but he also could be describing Batman as, "...a mean one—and it's headed straight for Gotham. Like the wrath of God it's headed for Gotham" (27). The Dark Knight does not choose to fight crime. He does not do so out of obligation or morality. He does not rationally work to improve the world. He fights crime because he has a deep-rooted need to do so, and he cannot and does not want to control his actions. Batman craves the power, authority, adrenaline, and violence, and without these things, Bruce Wayne's life has no meaning. During his initial outing, Batman notes, "This should be agony. I should be a mass of aching muscle—broken, spent, unable to move. And, were I an older man I surely would...but I'm a man of thirty—of twenty again. The rain on my chest is a baptism—I'm born again" (34). Tellingly, a citizen who witnesses Batman's return describes him as a "wild animal. Growls. Snarls. Werewolf. Surely...Monster! Like with fangs and wings and it can fly—" (34). Even the future Robin, Carrie Kelly, describes him as, "...a man—about—twelve feet tall" (34). While Batman always wanted criminals to fear him, Miller's Batman's very nature is so disturbing that it would be almost impossible not to be afraid.

Just as Batman has changed to become a violent animalistic force so, too, have the not-so-common criminals that he now battles. At the beginning of *The Dark Knight Returns*, Gotham City finds itself plagued by a new breed of villains known as the mutants. This younger generation of lawbreakers is not the evildoer of old, who stole and killed for money and or glory, but rather it is comprised of violent sociopaths, who wish to harm, maim, and kill. Much like Batman, the mutants seemingly have no conscience and instead want to create chaos, as opposed to the order that the Caped Crusader desires. While visiting the Crime Alley corner where his parents were shot, Bruce Wayne reflects on the differences between Joe Chill, the mugger who killed his parents, and the mutants that have followed, "He flinched when he pulled the trigger. He was sick and guilty over what he did. All he wanted was money. I was naïve enough to think him the lowest sort of man. These—These are his children. A purer breed…and this world is theirs" (14).

The mutants are led by a man who appears to be as much animal as human and who frequently appears on television in order to threaten Batman, Commissioner Gordon, various politicians, and members of the general public with rape, murder, and cannibalization. One of his televised diatribes reads:

> We will kill the old man Gordon. His women will weep for him. We will chop him. We will grind him. We will bathe in his blood. I myself will kill the fool Batman. I will rip the meat from his bones and suck them dry. I will eat his heart and drag his body through the street. Don't call us a gang. Don't call us criminals. We are the law. We are the future. Gotham City belongs to the mutants. Soon the world will be ours (61).

The mutants are not the criminals of Batman's youth, they are the embodiment of senseless crime and chaos. They are the outgrowth of a society that has become corrupt and lazy. During one scene in *The Dark Knight Returns*, two mutants appear to rob a woman of her purse, a standard action for a traditional criminal and the type of crime that led to Bruce Wayne's parents' murders. The mutants have no interest in robbing the woman though, but rather, they place a bomb in her handbag and mindlessly kill her, leaving her son an orphan (69). Later in the story, the mutant leader uses his teeth to rip out the throat of Gotham City's mayor to grotesquely kill the public official. The mutant leader murdered the mayor during a peace negotiation and seemingly respected none of society's rules (91). There is no logical reason for the mutants' crimes and no traditional manner of understanding them. Batman's new enemies are amoral, animalistic psychopaths, who want to shape society in their own image, all things that also could be said of the Dark Knight himself.

After returning to his vigilante ways, Batman quickly challenges the mutant to a fight and loses, only surviving because a new self-appointed Robin steps forward to assist him. The Dark Knight makes the mistake of trying to fight the mutant leader in unplanned, traditional hand-to-hand combat, a method that favors the young criminal. However, Batman prepares for the second battle, chooses the venue, and sets the tone and fighting style. The Caped Crusader defeats and humiliates the mutant leader, causing many mutant members to become Dark Knight followers, who fight crime using the name The Son of the Batman. It is telling that the former mutants so effortlessly align with Batman and find it as easy to fight crime as to act criminally. This displays the fine line that divides Batman from the lawbreakers he fights. The mutants act on impulse and crave the thrill of action, violence, and power. They subscribe to no dogma and present no moral context. Instead, they are a force of nature to be harnessed and used for good or evil, depending on who is leading them. Miller uses the former mutants as a metaphor for society's need for Batman's leadership. In this post-Watergate, post-Vietnam era, citizens are mentally and morally adrift and need a strong leader to instruct them on how to act. Commissioner Gordon comments on Gotham City's need for Batman's leadership while talking to his successor, Ellen Yindel. Gordon tells Yindel about how important President Franklin Roosevelt's leadership was after the Japanese bombed Pearl Harbor and drew the United States into World War II. The current commissioner says that he had read rumors that FDR knew about the attack on Hawaii prior to its execution, and the president let it happen because it was good for the country in the long term. Gordon finishes by saying that the allegations against FDR were never substantiated:

> Things like that never are. I couldn't stop thinking how horrible that would be... and how Pearl Harbor was what got us off our duffs in time to stop the Axis. But a lot of innocent men died. But we won the war. It bounced back and forth in my head until I realized I couldn't judge it. It was too big. He was too big (96).

Gordon never mentions Batman by name, but it is clear that the commissioner is referring to the Dark Knight. In the policeman's mind, the masked vigilante is leading a war against crime and the city needs Batman even though his presence has both good and bad consequences. The Dark Knight's leadership can turn criminals into crime fighters and can inspire average citizens to do both common acts of kindness and extraordinary deeds of heroism. As many of the denizens of Gotham City enter into a war against criminals, Gordon (and presumably Miller) believes that Batman is the leader that they need.

The end of *The Dark Knight Returns* demonstrates Batman's leadership abilities and showcases the positive benefits of allowing the Caped Crusader to conduct his war against criminals. After a nuclear device creates an electromagnetic pulse that causes a blackout in Gotham City (and many other places) and renders electronic devices useless, Batman and his gang of crime fighters take to the streets and impose order on the chaos that is certain to reign. The Dark Knight rides a giant black horse and keeps order, provides medical supplies, helps the injured, and inspires ordinary citizens to act as heroes. Batman is the leader that the city needs and because of his efforts, Gotham City is the only major American metropolis that remains calm and orderly during the catastrophe. The Dark Knight's leadership may be too authoritarian and domineering during times of peace and tranquility, but when lawlessness and unrest threatens, Batman's otherwise unappetizing strongman tactics are sorely needed.

Interestingly, in order to create a situation in which Batman can assert his control, Miller returns Gotham City to a nearly quasi-preindustrial state. A literally and figuratively powerless city needs Batman to ride in on horseback and save the day, like an Old West cowboy or an ancient warrior. The Dark Knight's temperament and outlook make him an outsider in a modern society, in which his methods seem dictatorial and arcane. When the supporting social structural that girds Gotham City is damaged, the city has no choice but to turn to Batman and embrace him as a hero once again, the lesson seemingly being that every hero has a time and a place, and while many heroes outlive their usefulness, a few may return to their day in the sun once again.

While Miller regards Batman as a hero, who can and does help society, the author also investigates the role that the Dark Knight has in encouraging criminals and creating villains. The most obvious example of this is Batman's arch nemesis the Joker, the criminal in clown make-up, who has battled the Caped Crusader in comic book stories since the 1940s. Miller's Joker is a psychopathic madman, who relishes murdering innocents and exists to serve as a social counterbalance to Batman. In *The Dark Knight Returns*, the Joker has been in a catatonic state during the ten years Batman has been in retirement and, in essence, has ceased to exist while the Caped Crusader has been gone. Without Batman as an adversary, the Joker has had no reason to exist and his criminal activities have concluded. If Miller's Dark Knight is a force of nature for order, then the Joker is the counterforce for chaos. Soon after Batman returns from retirement, the Joker once again becomes cognitive and quickly goes on a murderous spree that eventually results in a final showdown between him and the Dark Knight. The Joker, and many of the Batman's villains, only exist to fight the Caped Crusader and are the obvious disadvantage of Batman's leadership.

Ironically, Batman's quest for control and order creates much of the turmoil and instability that he battles. The Dark Knight serves as a mirror from which numerous criminals, villains, heroes, and other vigilantes observe grotesque reflections that change Batman's social context. Throughout *The Dark Knight Returns*, Miller lampoons liberals who coddle criminals and blame Batman for society's problems. These left wing citizens claim that the Caped Crusader's violent actions and vigilante ways cause social disorder and create criminals and madmen. While Miller mostly declares these leftish ideas to be nonsensical, he does grant that the Joker would not exist in a world without a Batman. Although Miller seems to contend that Batman's utility outweighs his flaws, the author does not add up the social cost of the mayhem that Batman's dozens of villains have inflicted on Gotham City. The Dark Knight's liberal opponents may be overly lax naval gazers, but they also understand the deeper repercussions of some of Batman's actions and his very existence.

If the Joker serves as the criminal counterbalance to Batman in *The Dark Knight Returns*, then the Caped Crusader's heroic counterweight is Superman. The Man of Steel is the most heroic of superheroes, and his sunny disposition and deep respect for authority serve to contrast with Batman's dark outlook and vigilante ways. In Miller's tale, Superman is an ultra-powerful agent of the state, who works in secret for the U.S. government in general and the President of the United States in particular. The president is a seemingly senile commander-in-chief, who looks like Ronald Reagan and who unsophisticatedly orders the Man of Steel to run errands and complete missions. The Man of Tomorrow is the political and military tool of a weak old man and the crumbling society he serves. Superman possesses godlike powers, but allows himself to become subservient to ordinary humans and doddering politicians. This is in direct contrast to Batman, who has little natural power, but has trained his entire life to become physically and mentally superior, so that he does not have to follow orders from anyone. Superman trusts the political and social order and believes that he best helps society by serving the dominant authority.

Batman, on the other hand, deems himself superior to those around him and believes that he can make society better by forcing it to change, and then he himself leads the change. In the story, the president compares Batman to a high-spirited bronco that needs to be broken in order to prevent the horse/crime fighter from creating social turmoil (84). In this metaphor, Superman is the lawman/ cowboy who must impose his will on the strong-minded animal and force him to abandon his natural state of mind. Batman is once again presented as animalistic and Superman as the dutiful protector and peacekeeper. This is ironic because the mythic cowboy is generally presented as a lone, solitary, anti-social figure who may bring order to lawless regions, but does so on his terms, often in a rough-and-tumble vigilante manner. These traits much better describe Batman than Superman and force the reader to consider the Dark Knight's resemblance to an Old West lawman. Superman is a governmental agent, who follows orders, while Batman is the embodiment of the untethered cowboy/ law bringer.

Miller presents Superman and Batman as heroes who have much different philosophies on how to protect society. The Man of Steel believes that he should remain hidden, in order not to frighten average citizens; Batman wants to frighten everyone, criminals and innocents alike. Strangely, the overly powerful Superman is afraid of average humans, while Batman wants people to fear him. Superman opines, "They'll kill us if they can, Bruce. Every year they grow smaller. Every year they hate us more. We must not remind them that giants walk the earth" (129–130). The Man of Steel later reflects on the differences between the two crime fighters:

> You were the one they used against us, Bruce. The one who played it rough. When the noise started from parents' groups and the sub-committee called us in for questioning—you were the one who laughed... that scary laugh of yours... "Sure we're criminals," you said. "We've always been criminals. We have to be criminals." (135)

Later, during the pair's epic battle, Batman counters, "Yes—You always say yes—to anyone with a badge—or a flag" (190). The Dark Knight later adds, "You sold us out, Clark. You gave them—the power—that should have been ours. Just like your parents taught you to. My parents taught me a different lesson... lying in the street—shaking in deep shock—dying for no reason at all—they showed me that the world only make sense when you force it to..." (192).

Superman was raised by a peaceful Midwestern couple, who taught him to value and respect authority. Batman lived in a large urban area and witnessed the crime and violence that took his parents' lives. Superman believes that he must work within the boundaries of the existing social order, while Batman wants to recreate and lead society. This difference is the core of Frank Miller's Batman, a ruthlessly driven vigilante who needs to impose his will on those around him. He is no longer a comic book good guy, but rather a seemingly insane strongman, whom the world might need more than ever.

Frank Miller's Batman is a creature of darkness, who wishes to impose his morals and values on those around him. The contrasts between Batman and Superman, the Joker, the mutants, and other characters showcase the Dark Knight's strengths and limitations and display what is both heroic and horrifying about the character. The Caped Crusader's anti-hero identity is the essence of *The Dark Knight*

Returns, and it is a break from traditional views of the character. The anti-hero Dark Knight represents a new interpretation of a character that had already been envisioned in dozens of ways during his prior almost fifty years of existence. This Batman is a nearly sociopathic vigilante who follows his own code, creating both chaos and order in his wake. Frank Miller's *Dark Knight Returns* portrays Batman as the damaged and unstable anti-hero, explores how the Caped Crusader deals with the desecration of society, and focuses on the Dark Knight as a contrast to the traditional conservative hero that is Superman. These elements create a unique view of a traditional hero evolving to survive in a changing society. As the American public adjusted to a frightening time during the nation's history, Batman offered safety and understanding. This new Dark Knight would have been too violent and unpredictable for previous era, but was appropriately reflective of the society that created him.

Work Cited

Miller, Frank. *Batman: The Dark Knight Returns*. New York, NY: DC Comics, 2002.

Alan Moore and Dave Gibbons' *Watchmen*_____

Michael G. Robinson

Arguably one of the most important superhero stories ever created, *Watchmen* casts a long shadow over the genre to this day. A tightly organized and intense narrative, the series shattered expectations about superheroes by casting the archetypes against cold, hard realism. The end result was a popular and controversial cultural phenomenon that affected the tone of an age of comics, inspired a motion picture, and eventually a series of comic book prequel adventures.

Watchmen arrived during an epic time in the comic book industry. As comic book historians Gerard Jones and Will Jacobs described the energy of that year: "To a lot of us who were into comics in 1986, it still feels longer and fuller than all the years since" (296). Released as a twelve-part maxi-series (a format that was still relatively new at the time), *Watchmen* was a big part of a year that also saw major revisions of the entire DC universe, particularly its most popular characters Superman and Batman, as well as an explosion of interest in independent properties. This was a year of challenging the mainstream and its central concepts of the superhero genre in a variety of ways. Some creators avoided what had been seen as axiomatic, while others viewed the axioms in new modes.

British writer Alan Moore was already gaining attention from his earlier work on *Swamp Thing* and re-printings of his older writing on *Miracleman*. The writer began to get all sorts of offers, the most important of which, for this story, involved the Charlton characters. While the company had some beloved characters in its stables, it was never able to match the success of Marvel or DC Comics. In 1977, Charlton Comics went out of business (194), leaving their superheroes without a regularly published home. After acquiring rights to the characters, DC Comics wanted to do something spectacular with them by entrusting their care to a new star. "Fans could dream, but barely imagine, what Alan Moore would do with

Captain Atom, the Question, and Blue Beetle" (285). Working with artist Dave Gibbons, Moore began to construct a story around the characters. However, when editors learned the nature of the tale, they began to worry about the Charlton characters. They decided to take the characters back from Moore and Gibbons, "fearing that their apocalyptic reworking would make the characters unmarketable in the mainstream" (306). To keep their story working, Moore and Gibbons translated those characters into new, more extreme identities that would not risk DC Comics' investment.

The result was comic book magic. As described by Les Daniels in his official history of DC Comics:

> ... in 1986 everyone was watching *Watchmen*, which won enthusiastic notices in publications from the *Nation* to *Newsweek*, from *Time* to *Rolling Stone*. A comic book that seemed to transcend the form, *Watchmen* remains a landmark and made celebrities out of writer Alan Moore and artist Dave Gibbons (196).

Slightly less celebratory, Jones and Jacobs recognize that *Watchmen* was not as commercially successful as other tales in that eventful year of 1986, but they still note the importance of the series:

> ...no one connected to organized fandom dared miss an issue. For its first six issues, it systematically inverted everything fans had ever thought or felt about their heroes (Sept 1986–Feb 1987). Moore and Gibbon's exposure of the antisocial, fascist, and psychologically diseased implications of superheroes was chilling, especially to adult readers still fascinated by superheroes but no longer quite comfortable with the fascination (308).

Watchmen is told in a free-flowing way, working the narrative out through jumps in time and space, often inspired by connections between visual icons or dialogue and occasionally provided through inventive textual material at the end of issues. The nature of this academic summary will, sadly, not do these transitions justice. Reading *Watchmen* is like experiencing memory, where time folds fluidly by triggers of reminiscence and nostalgia.

Set across the backdrop of an alternate Earth, *Watchmen* develops somewhere in a fictional space between the familiar, brightly colored, action-centric universe of the mainstream superhero and the even more familiar world of our own reality. Events in this world parallel the history of the comic book superheroes, but unlike traditional superhero stories, these events are perpetually played out across a contemporary real world context. In our real history, the 1980s were a time of increased tension between the United States and the Union of Soviet Socialist Republics. The anxiety of mutually assured destruction from nuclear war is even greater in this series.

In *Watchmen*, costumed mystery men and women first appear in the late 1930s, but after World War II, the patriotic appeal of these Minutemen is tarnished in the suspicious atmosphere of the early Cold War 1950s. In a moment paralleling the arrival of science-based superheroes in our Silver Age of Comics in the 1960s, this alternate world greets the arrival of its first true super-being. Possessing awesome powers over energy, matter, and time after an accident in quantum mechanics research, Doctor Manhattan tips the balance of the Cold War in favor of the Americans, generating a dramatic departure from the history of our own world. While this creates a new American advantage in this fictional Cold War world, it does not create peace for citizens or for the superheroes themselves. Increasingly unable to tackle the more complex criminal and social problems of the 1970s, superheroes are ultimately outlawed by the Keene Act. Most superheroes disappear, with only a few functioning either as outlaws or as sanctioned agents of the government.

The story begins in 1985, with a murder by defenestration. Investigating the crime is Rorschach, the brutally violent, unbalanced mystery man still operating as an outlaw. Rorschach soon discovers the victim is the Comedian, a cynical, hard-boiled government agent and former member of the Minutemen. This investigation prompts Rorschach to reconnect with the other key characters in the story. The aforementioned Doctor Manhattan now seems to be losing his humanity to the god-like perspective his seemingly unlimited super-scientific powers offer. His lover, Silk Spectre, feels trapped both by their relationship and by the career of her mother, the original

Silk Spectre from the Minutemen. Gadget-loving mystery man Nite Owl, now out of shape and impotent, finds human connection mostly in tending to the aging hero who gave him his name. Only Ozymandias, the so-called world's smartest man, seems content now that his superheroic career has been abandoned in favor of running a successful corporate empire.

Rorschach's relentless investigation turns up the early levels of a massive conspiracy, triggering a spiral of narratives and flashbacks. These work in, around, and through the main characters, fleshing out superheroes from the past and even involving ordinary people as characters. An attempt on Ozymandias' life stirs concerns of a mask killer. Rorschach is captured and imprisoned. Doctor Manhattan temporarily leaves Earth, prompting a dramatic escalation in the nuclear standoff between the Americans and the Soviets. Ultimately, Nite Owl and Silk Spectre are pulled back into the world of the superhero as they are drawn emotionally together for the first time, their costumes providing a fetishized cure for Nite Owl's sexual frustrations.

By the end of the story, Rorschach and Nite Owl have come to the disturbing conclusion that Ozymandias killed the Comedian to cover up the true goal of his conspiracy. Reasoning that only the world's smartest man can save world from certain nuclear annihilation, Ozymandias has used his great resources to fabricate a giant alien. By teleporting the fake alien into the heart of New York City, Ozymandias has killed millions to save billions. He sees his ends justifying his means, as this extraterrestrial invasion scenario averts imminent nuclear conflict by creating a common cause for the world to unite against. Too late to prevent the attack and convinced of the danger of exposing the crime, Nite Owl, Silk Spectre, and Doctor Manhattan agree to a cover up. Only Rorschach, with his unyielding sense of morality, argues against the decision. He is disintegrated by Doctor Manhattan before the super-human, bored with mere humanity, departs for other galaxies.

In hitting these plot points, this summary somewhat artificially pulled out other narratives running in the comic. There are a number of ordinary people who serve as secondary characters and whose lives are all impacted by the main characters. At the end of *Watchmen*, all of these ordinary people find their lives intersecting at the same city street corner, where tragically they all die in the fake alien attack. There is also *The Tales of the Black Freighter*, a comic within a comic that is read by a young boy, who hangs around a newsstand in the story. Speculating that the superhero genre would not catch hold in a world where superheroes are real, *Tales* posits that the pirate genre would dominate the medium. *Tales* is the story of a man who commits heinous and horrible acts to escape an island, in order to provide a warning to his homeport of an imminent attack by the supernatural and evil pirate ship, The Black Freighter. The story within a story serves as a commentary on the superheroes in the main narrative and on Ozymandias in particular. By making inhuman choices in the name of good, the protagonist of *Tales* has become too monstrous to be with the people he sought to protect. By focusing on the main superheroic characters, this summary has also left out detail on the lives of the Minutemen. This first generation of superheroes are seen in flashback and also recounted in some of the textual material that appears at the end of each issue.

Writing is, of course, only half the equation of comics. Much of the power of *Watchmen* is also due to the extraordinary artistic style of Dave Gibbons. In a structure that was unusual for the time, each page of the series is based on a standard format of nine panels per page. These panels are arranged in three rows and three columns. Many pages use all nine panels of this grid. For dramatic effect, some panels on some pages may become larger, occupying any number of grids. So, for example, the very first appearance in the entire series by Doctor Manhattan takes up six panels, occupying the left and middle columns of the page. The image shows the relative size of the colossal, nude Doctor Manhattan by demonstrating that Rorschach stands only as high as Manhattan's gigantic calf. The effect of using six panels further highlights Doctor Manhattan's immense debut. In comic book art, a "splash page" is when a single panel or image occupies the entire page. Most comics in the 1980s used splash pages to open stories and add emphasis. *Watchmen* rarely surrenders all nine grid squares to a single image. In fact, the only splash pages in the entire series occur in the first six pages of the final issue. These images linger on the devastation of New York City.

The nine-panel system is not cramped. Along with colorist John Higgins, Gibbons is able to include an impressive amount of rich detail in each of these small panels. Rereading this comic will often allow the reader to discover some element and to suddenly realize that element has been playing out as a motif throughout the work. Perhaps the most famous image is the happy face with a red mark. The image opens and closes the entire story. The first use is an iconic pin worn by the Comedian, now bloodstained in the streets following his deadly fall. The final shot is a happy-face t-shirt streaked with ketchup. Pyramids also abound as visual motifs in *Watchmen*. They symbolize Ozymandias' elaborate scheme designed to leave him the last person alive and, in essence, "on top." It is he who knows of the true conspiracy.

Repeated images and design also herald moments of flashback as a character remembers an important event. The same event is also shown at different times from the subjective perspectives of other characters: a failed attempt by the Minutemen's Captain Metropolis to recreate his superhero team in the 1960s serves, at different points in the tale, as a demonstration of the Comedian's cynicism; the first flirtations between Doctor Manhattan and Silk Spectre; and the moment in which Ozymandias realizes that traditional superheroics will not save the world. The series also avoids the traditional use of the yellow narrative box, in which an omniscient narrator reveals information. When used, boxes represent the subjective voice or thoughts of characters. The faces of Gibbons' characters are expressive. His images are frequently moody or dark. However, Gibbons can also provide the good, solid moments of action that always happen in the superhero genre.

The end materials of each chapter also offer distinctive visual elements for comics at the time. Each issue ends with a combined piece of text and visual material. These serve to flesh out the narrative details of this particular world. The first two issues end as selections from *Under the Hood*, a biography by Hollis Mason, the Minuteman's original Nite Owl. These sections reveal much about the early days of those superheroes. Other end materials feature items such as Rorschach's psychiatric report, a *Rolling Stone* interview with Ozymandias, and an ornithological article by Nite Owl.

Thematically, *Watchmen* is about breaking down the traditional archetypes of comic book superheroes. The final page of the collected trade paperback ends the series with Juvenal's famous quote: "Quis custodiet ipsos custodies" (Who watches the Watchmen?). In their earliest incarnations in our real history, superheroes enjoyed a certain moral virtue. DC Comics characters, like Superman or the Flash, faced danger with a smile and a blast of brightly colored heroics. Even their grimmest characters, like Batman, had moral certainty. Later, in the 1960s, Marvel Comics complicated the formula a bit, adding tragic figures, like Spider-Man, the Thing, or the Uncanny X-Men. These characters battled through their problems, redeeming their flaws in the defeat of villainy. *Watchmen* essentially argues that in the cold light of reality, all superhero characters are intensely flawed.

To put it simply, every main character in *Watchmen* is a psychological mess and none of them seem to realize it. Nite Owl struggles with a sense of purpose. Consumed by nostalgia and impotency, his life became empty the moment he gave up his superhero career. In the early parts of the story, the American government clearly sees Silk Spectre as just someone to keep Doctor Manhattan satisfied. She struggles against the superheroic role crafted for her by her domineering mother. Yet when Silk Spectre rebels against the role of girlfriend and daughter, she cannot define herself and ends up in a relationship with Nite Owl. She must also come to terms with her realization that the Comedian is her father. While these characters are merely neurotic, the others are potentially psychotic.

The interwoven back-stories of the comic reveal an appalling list of brutal atrocities committed by the Comedian. He sexually assaults the original Silk Spectre. He casually abandons a woman he got pregnant in Vietnam, murdering her after she attacks him and scars his face. It's strongly implied that he assassinated President John F. Kennedy and got rid of Watergate investigators Woodward and Bernstein at the behest of Nixon. While he wears a patriotic garb and serves his country, the Comedian has no moral compass. In fact, he cynically believes there is no meaning at all. In that way, life is a joke that only he understands.

Rorschach has snapped. His childhood corrupted by the neglect of his mother, a prostitute, Rorschach initially stepped into his heroic role when inspired by the tragedy of Kitty Genovese. However, a case in which a pedophile murdered and fed a young girl to his dogs caused Rorschach to break. He lives in a world of paranoia and brutality, certain of his own moral judgments and his ability to deliver justice for a system that he knows does not work.

Doctor Manhattan has disassociated. His ability to see time in its absolute state, a series of events already determined and unalterable, and his powers to affect all matter have robbed him of his connection to humanity. His relationship with Silk Spectre is quite often depicted as him just going through the motions, feigning some emotional response simply to please her or out of habit. Doctor Manhattan has the greatest power of any being in the universe to act, but he rarely does, since he is consumed instead by scientific interests and discoveries he struggles to express to others.

And then there is Ozymandias, a character who is fashioned as a hero, but who acts as a villain. Byzantine conspiracies and homicidal cover-ups are usually the modus operandi of the great archenemies from comics. In fact, the main thing that distinguishes Ozymandias' operation from the schemes of legendary villains like Lex Luthor or Doctor Doom is that Ozymandias' plan actually succeeds. For him, the cost in millions of lives is slight when compared to the population of billions whom Ozymandias believes that he has saved. Yet when the reader recognizes the corpses of minor characters seen throughout the story, the horrific cost of this utilitarian logic is exposed. Ozymandias' self-assurance and drive reveals itself as narcissism and sociopathic thinking.

All of these problems are essentially pressure cooked through the thematic anxiety of atomic war and the threat of mutually assured destruction. In our own world, the anxieties over a nuclear showdown were heightened in the 1980s. This last worrying gasp of the Cold War had a ripple effect throughout popular culture and many entertainment forms were set against the backdrop of imminent apocalyptic or post-apocalyptic scenarios. Moore had already demonstrated an interest in these themes in *V for Vendetta*, a series started before *Watchmen* that was cancelled before its completion (but finished later after *Watchmen*'s success added to the writer's reputation). In that story, England prevails as a fascist state after the U.S. and U.S.S.R. destroys much of the world in nuclear war. In *Watchmen*, the sense of being trapped in the conflict between powerful state actors plays out on both a national and personal level. All characters in the series are impacted by the threat of impending nuclear annihilation. This sense is heightened on a symbolic level by the constant appearance of the nuclear doomsday clock. Watches and clockwork are another repeated visual motif in the series, but the nuclear clock is particularly relentless as its minute hand pushes on towards the midnight that marks doomsday.

As flawed as these characters are and as tense as the nuclear standoff around their lives becomes, these characters are compelling. *Watchmen* explodes the genre, but not at the cost of relatable characters who interest readers. There is an appeal to the growing romance between Nite Owl and Silk Spectre, a sense that this is the genuine connection neither of them has achieved before. Nite Owl also has an admirable devotion to Rorschach, struggling to maintain their friendship in the wake of Rorschach's emotional issues. The Comedian has done horrible things, but he also sees through much of the phoniness of life in an enviable way. Doctor Manhattan's powers have set him apart from others, but readers also see a kind of elegant poetry in his understanding of time and his quest to understand how the universe works. Ozymandias is driven and narcissistic, but he does indeed save the world. As a symbol of everything that is dangerous and disturbed about costumed vigilantes out for revenge that so dominate the superhero genre, Rorschach should horrify us. Curiously, he became the standout star of the series. There is something undeniably cool about this engine of vengeance.

Watchmen is an extraordinarily rich and dense text. Richard Reynolds writes: "*Watchmen* is at bottom about the inventions and fictions employed by everybody either to achieve power and control or simply to get through their daily lives" (114). In his concluding comments on the comic, Reynolds explains:

> *Watchmen*'s so-called 'postmodernism' largely comprises this process of stripping away the accumulation of 50 years of continuity. In so doing, Moore and Gibbons have produced a text with transcends the accumulated myths through which superhero texts are read— they have, so to speak, stretched the boundaries of the genre. . . The extent of the text's ironic self awareness of the genre's history, and the technique by which stock superhero types such as Nite Owl and the Comedian are interrogated to the point where their mythology collapses into new levels of literal meaning, all mark out *Watchmen* either as the last key superhero text, or the first in a new maturity of the genre (117).

Geoff Klock places the series as one of two key pillars supporting the opening of what he sees as the third great age in comic book superhero history, the age of the revisionary superhero narrative:

> *Batman: The Dark Knight Returns* and *Watchmen* return superheroes to their pulp roots, to darkness and ambiguity; and while the second phase of the revisionary superhero narrative will find this atmosphere too dark, never again will the superhero narrative be able to return to the simplicity from which it came without coming to terms with *Watchmen* and *The Dark Knight Returns* (76).

As a comic book, *Watchmen* has always been marked by its difference, its curious novelty in taking the very old and making something new.

Not surprisingly, this complexity has provoked negative criticism as well. While comic book author Grant Morrison also celebrates the importance of the series, he finds a narrative breaking point: "Ultimately, in order for *Watchmen*'s plot to ring true, we were required to entertain the belief that the world's smartest man would do the world's stupidest thing after thinking about it all his life" (205). Ozymandias' plot is pragmatic and utilitarian, but his

---

logic is also horrific and sociopathic. Making superheroes real in this way robs the genre of some of its magic and wonder.

Interestingly, Alan Moore himself has been critical of the reception of his work. From Moore's perspective, the profound thematic impact of *Watchmen* on the superhero genre itself was something of a mistranslation by fans and by other industry professionals. This trend is particularly well represented in the case of Rorschach, the brutal, psychotic vigilante. Quoted by Les Daniels, Moore explains that his intention with Rorschach was to make him the least likeable character:

> Rorschach was to a degree intended to be a comment upon the vigilante superhero, because I have problems with that notion. I wanted to try and show readers that the obsessed vigilante would not necessarily be a playboy living in a giant Batcave under a mansion. He'd probably be a very lonely and almost dysfunctional guy in some ways (196).

Of course, fans often embrace Rorschach as the most popular character in the story.

This suggests a larger problem for Moore, with the way the story impacted the comics business. In popular culture, success breeds imitation. Post-*Watchmen*, superhero comics took a dark thematic turn. As Moore notes in a 2001 interview by Tasha Robinson:

> Perhaps it happens in any medium, where anything of any kind of great proportion, no matter how good it is, will have an adverse effect upon the medium itself. I think that what a lot of people saw when they read *Watchmen* was a high degree of violence, a bleaker and more pessimistic political perspective, perhaps a bit more sex, more swearing. And to some degree there has been, in the 15 years since *Watchmen*, an awful lot of the comics field devoted to these very grim, pessimistic, nasty violent stories which kind of use *Watchmen* to validate what are, in effect, often just some very nasty stories that don't have a lot to recommend them (5–6).

In essence, *Watchmen*'s impact on the superhero genre was a misappropriation of style that suggests, to Moore at least, a lack of understanding of the work's deconstructive intent for the genre.

Curiously, *Watchmen* also stood inviolate in popular culture for many years. Successful superhero properties are often strip-mined by their parent companies. Any possible angle for further continuation of stories in prequels, sequels, and imaginary tales are explored and executed. Yet strangely, this did not happen for the series. In a curious way, the editor's original fears about what would happen to the Charlton characters came true. *Watchmen* had a powerful sense of finality. Fans raised up the series as the epitome of excellence, so meddling came to take on a feeling of blasphemy. Of course, DC Comics still tried. One reason for a lack of further projects was the eroding relationship between the company and Alan Moore. That deterioration is no doubt worthy of a separate article as the writer and the publisher fell out over a series of projects.

Another reason that inhibited exploitation was the complexity of the original series. As David Hughes describes in more detail in his book, *The Greatest Sci-Fi Movies Never Made*, attempts to bring the series to the motion picture screen began as early as 1987. Writers and directors struggled with the plausibility of the fake alien attack at the end of the series. More importantly for the studios, there seemed to be no way to tell this complicated story for a reasonable budget.

While superhero after superhero leaped onto the big screen, *Watchmen* did not arrive until 2009. Directed by Zach Snyder, the moody film attempted to bring much of the now iconic series to life on the screen. Moore refused a credit in the movie, and his name does not appear in the movie at all. The film itself is long (two hours and forty-three minutes) because it does attempt to pack in much of the detail from the series. An innovative opening credits sequence relates the narrative background of the lives of these superheroes set to Bob Dylan's song "The Times They Are A-Changin." However, most of the time, detail bogs the film down, and its narrative is frankly best understood after reading the comic. The movie also altered the ending of the film. In this new version, Ozymandias makes it appear that Doctor Manhattan is the aggressor by mimicking Manhattan's energy signature in a destructive attack against major cities around the globe. As reported by *Box Office Mojo*, the movie made slightly over $185 million worldwide, but this is not particularly impressive, as the film's estimated budget was $130 million. The film, however, did lead to a flurry of licensed merchandise, something unusual in the *Watchmen* story. Although before the film, there had been T-shirts of the iconic blood-streaked happy face and some items for the DC Heroes Role-Playing Game, there had not been many associated products. After the movie, however, there were action figures, video games, and even a set of figures for HeroClix, a collectible tabletop combat game.

In 2012, DC Comics did the unthinkable, developing a series of new stories under the banner title of *Before Watchmen*. Neither Gibbons nor Moore were involved, as the relationship between DC Comics and Moore had become notably poisonous. Nine different mini-series were created by contemporary writers and artists. The characters featured were: the Minutemen, Silk Spectre, Comedian, Nite Owl, Ozymandias, Rorschach, Doctor Manhattan, Moloch (a villain in the original series), and Dollar Bill (a Minutemen member, who famously died in the original series when his cape became stuck in a revolving door). While the Minutemen series offered an intriguing adventure for the original heroes, most of the stories are not particularly compelling enough to have warranted these prequels.

Decades after its first publication, *Watchmen* still excites readers and interests academics. There was never much truth to the stereotype that comic books were just for kids, but *Watchmen* rightfully put that tired cliché into its grave. The series' dense narrative and rich visual style offers rewards with every re-reading. The complex psychology of its main characters and the morality of their actions offer room for continuous debate. While the series shattered conventional ideas and broke the old rules about the superhero genre, the genre did not die. Instead, *Watchmen* set a new and very high standard for what a superhero story could be.

Works Cited

Daniels, Les. *DC Comics: Sixty Years of the World's Favorite Comic Book Heroes*. New York: Bullfinch Press, 1995.

Hughes, David. *The Greatest Sci-Fi Movies Never Made*. Rev. ed. London: Titan Books, 2008.

Jensen, Jeff. "Crazy Sexy Cruel." *Entertainment Weekly* 25 July 2008: 22–27.

Jones, Gerard and Will Jacobs. *The Comic Book Heroes*. Rocklin, CA: Prima Publishing, 1997.

Klock, Geoff. *How To Read Superhero Comics and Why*. New York: Continuum, 2002.

Moore, Alan, Dave Gibbons, and John Higgins. *Watchmen*. New York: DC Comics, 1987.

Moore, Alan, David Lloyd, Steve Whitaker, and Siobahn Dodds. *V for Vendetta*. New York: DC Comics, 1989.

Morrison, Grant. *Supergods*. New York: Spiegel & Grau, 2011.

Reynolds, Richard. *Superheroes: A Modern Mythology*. Jackson, MS: University of Mississippi Press, 1992.

Robinson, Tasha. "Author Alan Moore." *The Onion AV Club*. 24 October 2001. Web. 20 October 2013. <http://www.avclub.com/article/alan-moore-13740>.

"Watchmen." *Box Office Mojo*. IMDb. n.d. Web. 20 October 2013. <http://www.boxofficemojo.com/movies/?id=watchmen.htm>.

Alan Moore and David Lloyd's *V for Vendetta*

Cathy Leogrande

It is sometimes difficult to believe that Alan Moore and David Lloyd conceived and produced their graphic novel *V for Vendetta* in the 1980s. The tale of a post-nuclear England, in which fascism rules, and people become passive because of their fear seems too close to many aspects of post-9/11 America. Groups with competing political views have used the term "terrorism" to paint their enemies as monsters. A closer look at the themes in this story can provide more complexity to issues of politics, government, and the tension between individual freedoms and need for security.

The Look and Feel of the Novel

In *V for Vendetta*, Moore and Lloyd developed a style in which every aspect of the creative process was a component of the overall literary work. Readers are immediately struck by the unique appearance and tone. Moore explained this process in his essay "Behind the Painted Smile," which originally appeared in 1983 and is now part of the trade. He described how the story and characters developed over time as a collaboration between author and illustrator. Moore had the makings of the narrative idea, but both men shared in the characters' births and the nuances of the overall work. Their combination of images and text created a dark and constrained world, possible after a catastrophic nuclear war. A number of factors added to the sense of hopelessness and despair. The original series was in black-and-white, which evoked the theme of fascism and suggested a country in which dark and evil men and women have exerted control. Graphic Novel Blogger Andrew Edwards has said of the imagery:

> The monochrome scheme perfectly complements the dark tone of the series, and the colorization of the series for publication in the United States could have destroyed the tone of the book. Instead, Lloyd,

with the help of colorist Siobhan Dodds, complements his original approach through the skilled addition of muted pastel shades, which enhances the book's attractiveness and adds to the bleached, washed-out atmosphere of the near-future totalitarian state (616).

The minimalist drawings provide facial emotions and events, with few lines. Emotions, such as fear, worry, and sadness, are obvious through the subtle use of line and shading on characters' faces, without additional words or effects to create meaning.

Lloyd suggested that Moore eliminate thought balloons and sound effects. Moore said that both "terrified" and "fascinated" him (Moore and Lloyd 275). Moore described the result: "All of a sudden it made everything much more real and documentary. The less that you relied upon captions and thought balloons, the more compellingly real the dialogue and pictures became" (Moore and Baker 27–28). Secondary characters became more fully developed in order to bring out additional shades of the story, without verbalized thoughts. A new style emerged, one which made both images and text equally critical components. Moore reflected:

> ...with *V for Vendetta* I think that was where I started to realize that you could get some incredible effects by putting words and pictures together or leaving the words out for a while. I started to realize what you could do with comic storytelling and the kind of — yeah, the layering, the levels of meaning that you could attach to the story. I think that certainly *V for Vendetta* was one of the first real major breakthroughs I made in terms of my own personal style (Kavanagh 4).

The power of the story was enhanced by these techniques; readers were forced to examine pictures and text more closely and think about the plot and characters on a deeper level.

Moore also sought to answer questions about the genesis of ideas by providing the careful reader with myriad symbols to serve as clues or actual references to the sources of the story's origins. In a scavenger-hunt type article, Madelyn Boudreaux annotated over one hundred references within the novel. From books on the shelf and movie posters in the Shadow Gallery (V's home) to quotes from

Shakespeare and popular songs, these add to readers' understanding of the multiple themes. David Lloyd himself commented on the annotations in a letter to Boudreaux: "Interesting and useful to scholars and explorers. Must let you know that all content is not strictly linked to central themes. Works on bookshelves in first Shadow Gallery scene, and posters, etc., are a mixed choice to show V was as much interested in pop culture as the higher arts—an everyman" ("Quotes and Fanmail").

Perhaps the most striking aspect of the story, the appearance of the character V, was more Lloyd than Moore. Moore made a list of concepts he hoped to reflect in the novel, including Orwell, Huxley, Judge Dredd, David Bowie, and Robin Hood (Moore and Lloyd 272). It was Lloyd who then suggested "resurrecting" Guy Fawkes, complete with mask, cape, and hat (274). As he said in a letter to Moore, "He'd look really bizarre and it would give Guy Fawkes the image he's deserved all these years" (274). For Moore, the muse had struck: "All of the various fragments suddenly fell into place, united behind the single image of a Guy Fawkes mask" (Moore and Lloyd 274). This element illustrates the paradoxes within the novel. Guy Fawkes is a failed conspirator in the Gunpowder plot and was executed after attempting to blow up the Houses of Parliament, something V actually does at the beginning of the novel. Readers must repeatedly revise their opinion of V, as he reveals himself to be kind, psychotic, cruel, charismatic, frightening, and vengeful. The mask seems to symbolize the uniqueness of his identity and personality: the smile is a contradiction to the sadness and anger that serve as his motivations.

Major Themes

Alan Moore was not shy about his hopes for this graphic novel. In several venues, he has spoken about the impact of those times on their desire to create a truly British story that reflected a possible future, in which conservative politics morphed into fascism. Central to the story was the main character. As Moore said,

It was playing into the fact that over here in England we've got quite a good tradition of villains and sociopaths as heroes. Like Robin Hood, Guy Fawkes and all the rest of them. And in our fiction, in British children's comics, there were as many sociopathic villains who'd got their own comic strips as there were heroes. Possibly more. The British have always had sympathy with a dashing villain (MacDonald par 2).

It is a credit to Moore and Lloyd, and perhaps a sad statement on Western politics, that themes first explored in the 1980s remain relevant and critical into the twenty-first century.

Government by the People, for the People

Alan Moore has stated that the major theme in *V for Vendetta* is fascism versus anarchy. He first discussed the basis for the novel's political theme in the essay "Behind the Painted Mask," published while the series was still in production (Moore and Lloyd 272). Later, he explained that, in his view, Left Wing and Right Wing are not the polar opposites they appear to be, but "just two ways of ordering an industrial society," one of which is quickly becoming outdated (McDonald par 3). Moore was somewhat disgusted with the idea that, at the time of Ronald Reagan and Margaret Thatcher, people seemed more willing to accept the very kind of government and policies that they had fought against during World War II. In an interview more than twenty years after he conceived the novel, Moore explained,

> It looked like Western society was taking somewhat a turn for the worse. There were ugly fascist stains starting to reassert themselves that we might have thought had been eradicated back in the '30s. But they were reasserting themselves with a different spin. They were talking less about annihilating whichever minority they happened to find disfavor with and talking more about free market forces and market choice and all of these other kind of glib terms, which tended to have the same results as an awful lot of the kind of Fascist causes back in the 1930s but with a bit more spin put upon them. The friendly face of fascism (MacDonald par 1).

Moore's belief was that it was easy to hate fascism when the leaders and followers are monstrous. He discussed the fact that, in *V for Vendetta*, he did not hate any of the characters, even the fascists, and that made them credible and more chilling.

> Whereas in fact fascists are people who work in factories, probably are nice to their kids, it's just that they're fascists. [Laughs]. They're just ordinary. They're the same as everybody else except for the fact that they're fascists (Kavanagh 5).

It is much more difficult to see beneath the smiling face of a benevolent leader who promises a better future than observe discrimination and abuse of power in heavy-handed ways.

Secondary characters add additional depth to the story. Some overtly evil men, like Derek Almond and Bishop Lilliman, exercise power in search of personal pleasure or ambition. Other characters are less black-and-white. Delia Surridge is full of remorse for her part in the experiments at Larkhill, and Eric Finch struggles with and eventually abandons his loyalty to the Norsefire regime. Moore explained:

> I wanted a number of the fascists I portrayed to be real rounded characters. They've got reasons for what they do. They're not necessarily cartoon Nazis. Some of them believe in what they do, some don't believe in it but are doing it any way [*sic*] for practical reasons (MacDonald para 4).

Perhaps Moore's greatest contribution is the character of Adam Susan. Far from a megalomaniac, Susan is a recluse. He has come to embrace fascism after the chaos that followed the nuclear war. He believes in logic and thought over emotion: observe his love for the Fate computer system. He trusts that a singular belief system is England's best hope of survival. He is no Hitler; he is much sadder. He and his men in the Nose, Mouth, Ear, and Finger are examples of the reality of government: a machine that, once established, takes on a life of its own. People become interchangeable parts that maintain the system.

Moore has claimed that, politically, he is an anarchist, but *V for Vendetta* was not developed as a tale about the easy benefits of anarchy. However, in the novel, anarchy does become, "the manifestation of freedom, free will, and individuality, concepts that are set directly against the repression and fascist ideology of the state" (Edwards 616). The complex story provides a number of situations that raise realistic moral dilemmas for readers. Like other dystopian literature, Moore wants the reader to be uncomfortable as he or she recognizes the ways individuals struggle with the difficulties of governing in truly democratic ways. At the end of the novel, Evey comes to understand V's motives and methods and speaks his eulogy:

> You came out of an abattoir unharmed, but not unchanged and saw freedom's necessity, not just for you but for us all. You saw, and seeing, dared to do. How purposeful was your vendetta, how benign, almost like surgery. Your foes assumed you sought revenge upon their flesh, but you did not stop there. You gored their ideology as well. The people stand within the ruins of society, a jail intended to outlive them all. The door is open. They can leave, or fall instead to squabbling and thence new slaveries. The choice is theirs, as ever it must be. I will not lead them, but I'll help them build. Help them create where I'll not help them kill. The age of killers is no more. They have no place within our better world (Moore and Lloyd 260).

Peter Paik wrote about the value of using serious literary works of fiction to help people "come to grips with the unrelenting compulsions and uncontrollable forces that are unleashed in the process whereby one kind of order gives way to another" (1). Paik discussed ways that "speculative content," such as works by Moore and Vonnegut, arouse emotions and strong reactions in ways that real "inexplicable acts of human evil" do not (4). The need for individuals to truly change their point of view and understand the ramifications of that change is difficult to grasp. While Paik discusses the realities of Iran's struggle from dictatorship to democracy, he finds value in stories like Moore's, which bring about a deeper understanding of the political realities. He states:

The ability to inhabit another perspective is crucial to grasping the mechanisms of political change, for what is being transformed is a specific outlook. The science fiction narratives I study are especially productive of this kind of reflection, as they show how an idea or action plays out within a concrete temporal sequence. We are taken from one distinct point to another, as well as shown the consequences of the action that unfold. As such, these texts evoke the experience of unwilled change that ensures the passing of one epoch into something new and different (4).

Ultimately, Moore and Lloyd hope that these are exactly what readers of *V for Vendetta* will experience. The hoped-for result will be thinking, active citizens invested in their world, rather than individuals who buy into a false sense of equality put forth to eliminate disharmony (Hanamy 420).

Terrorism and Protest

In the post-9/11 world, it is sometimes easy to forget that terrorism existed long before the World Trade Centers were attacked. America itself owes its very existence to acts of terrorism. The establishment of colonies by Anglicans, Catholics, and Puritans, who left England for religious freedom, included those who considered themselves allies or enemies of Guy Fawkes. Acts perpetrated on natives indigenous to North America by explorers and settlers easily fit the term terrorism. England also has a history of torture, murder, and espionage stretching for centuries. *V for Vendetta* serves as the basis for a comprehensive discussion on the roots of terrorism and how the acts and the actors become defined by those in power.

Cord Scott provides a historical view of terrorism in comics and the context within which *V for Vendetta* can be situated. From World War II to the Cold War and then the Middle East, comics have tended to reflect a clear distinction between terrorist-style villains and heroes battling for the established state (2–6). Moore broke from that mainstream, primarily American stance, creating V as a terrorist who battles *against* the state. Moore saw into a post-9/11 future, where fear causes individuals to trade freedom for security:

V's acts of terrorism are designed to remind ordinary men and women of what they have lost and to expose the inadequate and dangerous regime with which they have replaced it. Despite the measures of order and control offered by the Norsefire Party following nuclear war, V reminds readers that the human costs of totalitarianism are too high (Edwards 616).

Max Abrams provides a broad examination of terrorists and their motives. His discussion of the strategic model for terrorism generated in the 1980s is a plausible basis for describing V as a terrorist. To some degree, V weighs the costs and options and resorts to acts of violence because he believes political avenues are blocked or useless (Abrams 80–81). When Evey protests, V explains the dichotomy:

> Anarchy wears two faces, both creator and destroyer. Thus destroyers topple empires; make a canvas of clean rubble where creators then can build another world. Rubble, once achieved, makes further ruins' means irrelevant. Away with our explosives, then!
> Away with our destroyers! They have no place within our better world. But let us raise a toast to all our bombers, all our bastards, most unlovely and most unforgivable. Let's drink their health, then meet with them no more (Moore and Lloyd 222).

Some aspects of V's behavior suggest he understands the paradoxes Abrams articulates regarding the use of terrorism. For example, he does not target innocent civilians (83). He is not a political zealot with an extremist point of view, but an individual seeking a fairly mainstream result: self-determination in government (86). He sees these actions as means to an end, but that motive has justified atrocities throughout history.

The idea that V is a terrorist and a villain or antihero is a subject of debate. Readers discuss the line between treason and protest, between defensible subversive rebellion (like those leading to the founding of the United States) and criminal behavior. Can violence ever be carried out for the greater good? This is the question Moore and Lloyd makes Evey, and all readers, face. Moore knows there is no easy answer:

I actually don't think it's right to kill people. So I made it very, very morally ambiguous. And the central question is, is this guy right? Or is he mad? What do you, the reader, think about this? Which struck me as a properly anarchist solution (MacDonald par 5).

With drone strikes and terms like *collateral damage* used to dehumanize civilian casualties, such questions are even more relevant today.

Legal questions can be framed around issues, such as those presented in *V for Vendetta*. Some would suggest that V work through justice systems and seek trials such as those held for Nazi war criminals in Nuremburg or Israel. The field of law has recently begun to examine how cultural stories relate to overall concepts of crime and justice. In their introductory essay to a guest-edited edition of *Law Text Culture*, Luis Gómez Romero and Ian Dahlman, "assert that comics are a locus of emergence of legal meaning that effectively constitutes and shapes law. In other words, comics are operating as relevant cultural sources of law's authority and legitimacy" (6). In a later essay, Cassandra Sharp discusses public perception and acceptance of the vigilante archetype as a response to a quest in an ordinary world that, "does not seem to provide an adequate connection between legal process and justice (356). People cheer the vigilante and boo the terrorist, but the line is often more blurry than sharp.

Moore and Lloyd depicted the media of the 1980s as a powerful arm of the government. The *Voice of Fate* was like a family member to all who listened, and when Lewis Prothero is unable to give his usual broadcast, people are in fear. Government control of the media, ostensibly for security reasons, is something that has become reality. Hidden surveillance cameras and National Security Agency wiretaps have been exposed. Citizens are asked to trade freedom for security and believe what the government propaganda machine tells them. The terms 'treason' and 'violence' have been traded for 'national security' and 'protective action' and continue to be terms used by those with differing agendas to provoke emotional reactions rather than logical responses. The rise of talk radio and "news" broadcasts skewed to one side of the political spectrum seem eerily like the *Voice of Fate* updates, regardless of which ideology is being advanced. Perhaps a V for the twenty-first century will appear.

Within the United States, a backlash has begun against a government that purports to be open and democratic, yet has used legislation, such as the Patriot Act, to violate human rights and erode civil liberties, according to some. Julian Assange and other whistleblowers have acted in ways reminiscent of V to expose to the populace governmental flaws in hopes of bringing about change. With perfect understanding, groups, such as the online, leaderless activist group named Anonymous, have adopted the Guy Fawkes mask as a symbol in their protest activities and material (Chance 18). Members of the Occupy movement, which has spread worldwide to protest unequal distribution of wealth, also use the mask as an identification of protest. This seems to support Paik's notion that literary works resonate with people. According to Tom Lamont, who spoke to Paik by phone:

> Moore seems variously baffled, tickled, roused and quite pleased that his creation has become such a prominent emblem of modern activism. "I suppose when I was writing *V for Vendetta* I would in my secret heart of hearts have thought: wouldn't it be great if these ideas actually made an impact? So when you start to see that idle fantasy intrude on the regular world... It's peculiar. It feels like a character I created 30 years ago has somehow escaped the realm of fiction" (par 4).

Moore claims that his own activism has not gone beyond "a good moan in a local pub," but he is sympathetic to the protesters, their cause, and their methods. He points out that he was struggling to find phrases or terms beginning with the letter 'v' for some of the final chapters.

> He eventually settled on *Vox populi*. "Voice of the people. And I think that if the mask stands for anything, in the current context, that is what it stands for. *This* is the people. That mysterious entity that is evoked so often – this is the people" (Lamont par 19).

Social justice and global activism in V's image—with a smile—seem all that Moore could want.

The Meaning and Impact of Love

In *V for Vendetta*, love is as complex a notion as politics. Readers are often unsure about relationships throughout the novel. Even when connections between people are explained on one level, additional information and back-story can later change perceptions. Moore and Lloyd test people and demonstrate how adversity and events result in different reactions from different individuals. Often, it is the personal relationships that form the basis of these actions.

At the beginning of the novel, affection between V and Evey sets the tone for what follows. Evey has accepted her fate as an orphan and chosen to make money from physical love by attempting to sell herself as a sex partner. However, when Fingermen threaten to rape and kill her, she is saved by V and finds herself drawn to him in a caring way. After remaining in his care at the Shadow Gallery, she asks him why he does not seek her love in a physical way. She hypothesizes that he may be gay and is accepting of that orientation. V treats Evey in a paternalistic way, and many readers, at that point, suspect that he is really her father. It is almost as if the audience finds a relationship between two strangers unusual unless it takes the form of parent-child or lovers.

Moore eventually establishes that V is not Evey's father, and Evey then finds more traditional love with Gordon. However, Gordon is killed. She dreams of her father and of an incestuous encounter with him before she is captured and imprisoned. The letter from Valerie brings Evey into an imaginary, but strong lesbian relationship. Readers are then shocked to learn that V is behind the charade of torture and mind games. The evolution of their relationship tests the limits of what is meant by love. The end of the novel brings a definition of love to a more powerful and deeper degree than that between blood family members or spouses. Evey adopts V's persona and the apprentice becomes the mentor.

When one examines the many layers in just the relationship between Evey and V described above, one is struck by the lack of nuance in the term *love*. So many emotions exist throughout the novel as situations occur, and to encapsulate them with the same term seems limiting. Moore and Lloyd demonstrate, through images and words, how vast the capacity for human interaction can be. The two may disagree and remain distant in some ways; yet their closeness and caring provide a foundation for whatever happens.

Along with the two main characters, others provide a lens for readers to examine relationships. There are two married couples, the Almonds and the Hayers. Both demonstrate lack of intimacy and respect among spouses. Rosemary Almond and Helen Hayer both exemplify unhappy women who use men to provide for them in different ways. Issues of females using manipulation are also explored, while individual strength is shown as a possible and positive female trait. Readers see women as victims, angels, lovers, caregivers, and avengers. Questions of vengeance run throughout the story. Is revenge more justified if the victim is a loved one? At what point is vengeance for its own sake a hollow act? In discussing revenge, Kent Worcester states,

> One of its recurrent motifs is the status and legitimacy of the law, both as text and as embodied in specific occupations and individuals, such as judges, lawyers, and police officers. The genre fixates on our obligations to the law, our relationship to the law, and whether, when, and under what conditions acting outside of the law might be considered acceptable (334).

Did Rosemary Almond act the way she did as a vengeful response to her husband's abuse? Is her background an excuse?

Love outside the norm is also explored. Lewis Prothero has an unnatural attraction to his porcelain dolls. Pedophilia by the bishop brings into question religious abuse. Discrimination and harassment of gays and ethnic cleansing brings into question what constitutes the norm. Adam Susan's love for the Fate computer borders on a fetish. Moore and Lloyd probe the edges of love and ask the reader to go on that journey with them.

Summary

Attentive individuals took note of the unique relationship between Barack Obama and comics during the 2008 election. With his origins questioned, he joked that he was not born in a manger, but sent to Earth from Krypton by his father Jor-El (Welhouse par 3). His Spiderman comics collection and Superman-pose gave birth to a number of comic book crossovers, including a *Final Crisis* edition with a black president, who is also Superman (Hudson par 13). Non-supporters fashioned a parody of Obama's HOPE poster, with a Heath Ledger-like Joker face (Welhouse par 5). Voters cannot help but understand the message:

> In casting himself as a masculine nerd speaking to a media-savvy population, Obama not only navigated a difficult gendered performance, he fictionalized and idealized himself. By connecting his message with Superman's, Obama has become replicated within the pantheon of superheroes (Welhouse par 8).

It is not a coincidence that graphic literature with political messages has become more potent in many ways that mainstream media vehicles. Moore and Lloyd saw the future in 1981.

In times of polarizing viewpoints, a closer reading of Moore and Lloyd's work can remind citizens of the complexity behind decisions. It seems curious that the themes and motifs in *V for Vendetta* remain even more meaningful over the thirty years since it was first published. The thirty-eight-part series continues to poke and prod readers, demanding that they explore the need for thinking and action rather than apathy and comfort.

Works Cited

Abrahms, Max. "What Terrorists Really Want: Terrorist Motives and Counterterrorism Strategy." *International Security* 32.4 (2008): 78–105.

Boudreaux, Madelyn. *An Annotation of Literary, Historic, and Artistic References in Alan Moore's Graphic Novel, V for Vendetta.* 27 Apr. 1994. Web. 04 Oct. 2013. <http://www.enjolrasworld.com/

Annotations/Alan Moore/*V for Vendetta*/*V for Vendetta* Revised -Complete.html>.

Chance, Tyler R. "Super Terror: The Complex Relationship Between Sequential Art and Real World Political Violence." Thesis. Southern Illinois University Carbondale, 2013. Web. 10 Oct. 2013. <http://opensiuc.lib.siu.edu/uhp_theses/358/>.

Edwards, Andrew. "*V for Vendetta*." *Critical Survey of Graphic Novels: Heroes & Superheroes*. Ed. Bart Beaty and Stephen Weiner. Ipswich, MA: Salem, 2012. 614–17.

Gómez Romero, Luis and Ian Dahlman. "Justice Framed: Law in Comics and Graphic Novels." Introduction. *Law Text Culture* 16.1 (2012): 3–32. *Law Text Culture*. University of Wollongong, 1 Jan. 2012. Web. 13 Oct. 2013. <http://ro.uow.edu.au/cgi/viewcontent.cgi?article=1287&context=ltc>.

Hanamy, John. "The Story of Bohemia Or, Why There Is Nothing to Rebel against Anymore." *Law Text Culture* 16.1 (2012): 411–20. *Law Text Culture*. University of Wollongong, 1 Jan. 2012. Web. 12 Oct. 2013. <http://ro.uow.edu.au/cgi/viewcontent.cgi?article=1302&context=ltc>.

Hudson, Laura. "The Best Obama Cameos in Comics." *Comics Alliance*. 29 May 2009. Web. 11 Oct. 2013. <http://comicsalliance.com/the-best-obama-cameos-in-comics/>.

Kavanagh, Barry. "The Alan Moore Interview." *Blather*. 17 Oct. 2000. Web. 012 Oct. 2013. <http://blather.net/articles/amoore/index.html>.

Lamont, Tom. "Alan Moore: Meet the Man behind the Protest Mask." *The Guardian*. 26 Nov. 2011. Web. 13 Oct. 2013. <http://www.theguardian.com/books/2011/nov/27/alan-moore-v-vendetta-mask-protest>.

MacDonald, Heidi. "A For Alan, Pt. 1: The Alan Moore Interview." *The Beat*. Mile High Comics, 15 Mar. 2006. Web. 13 Oct. 2013. <http://web.archive.org/web/20060404210249/http://www.comicon.com/thebeat/2006/03/a_for_alan_pt_1_the_alan_moore.html>.

Moore, Alan and Bill Baker. *Alan Moore on His Work and Career*. New York: Rosen Pub., 2008.

Moore, Alan and David Lloyd. *V for Vendetta*. New York: Vertigo/DC Comics, 2005.

Paik, Peter Y. "Peter Y. Paik On His Book *From Utopia to Apocalypse: Science Fiction and the Politics of Catastrophe*." *Rotokoko*. 22 Mar. 2010. Web. 11 Oct. 2013. <http://rorotoko.com/interview/20100322_paik_peter_on_utopia_apocalypse_science_fiction_politics_catastrop/?page=1>.

Rubin, Daniel I. "'Remember, Remember, the Fifth of November' Using Graphic Novels to Teach Dystopian Literature." *Graphic Novels and Comics in the Classroom: Essays on the Educational Power of Sequential Art*. Ed. Carrye Kay Syma and Robert G. Veiner. Jefferson, NC: McFarland, 2013. 84–90.

Scott, Cord. "From HYDRA to Al-Qaeda: Depictions of Terrorism in Comic Books." *Purdue University E-Pubs*. Purdue University, n.d. Web. 13 Oct. 2013. <http://docs.lib.purdue.edu/cgi/viewcontent.cgi?article=1011&context=revisioning>.

Sharp, Cassandra. "'Riddle Me This…?' Would the World Need Superheroes If the Law Could Actually Deliver 'justice'?" *Law Text Culture* 16.1 (2012): 353–78. *Law Text Culture*. University of Wollongong, 1 Jan. 2012. Web. 12 Oct. 2013. <http://ro.uow.edu.au/cgi/viewcontent.cgi?article=1300&context=ltc>.

Welhouse, Zach. "Son of Jor-El: The Visual Rhetorics of Obama-Superman." *The Comics Grid Blog*. 9 May 2012. Web. 11 Oct. 2013. <http://blog.comicsgrid.com/2012/05/obama-superman/>.

Worcester, Kent. "The Punisher and the Politics of Retributive Justice." *Law Text Culture* 16.1 (2012): 329–52. *Law Text Culture*. University of Wollongong, 1 Jan. 2012. Web. 12 Oct. 2013. <http://ro.uow.edu.au/cgi/viewcontent.cgi?article=1299&context=ltc>.

Neil Gaiman's *Sandman*

Mary Catherine Harper

Dream of the Endless is no superhero. Unlike Superman, Batman, Green Lantern, and other characters found in DC Comics, the character, who is variously called Morpheus, Dream, Kai'ckul, Oneiros, Dream King, Prince of Stories, and Lord L'Zoril, is often confused about his own motives. From the beginning of the Sandman series, collected in the *Prelude & Nocturnes* volume, to his final appearance in the series' last episode, called *The Wake*, Morpheus, the central character of *The Sandman*, reminds us that dreams and dreaming are not really the stuff of superheroes. They are the stuff of humans.

The word "stuff" is apt because the final episode, which is a flashback to the early 1600s, shows Morpheus and William Shakespeare discussing the purpose of Shakespeare's *The Tempest* (*The Wake* 182). One of the most famous lines of Shakespeare comes from that play and is spoken by the magician, Prospero: "We are such stuff as dreams are made on, and our little life is rounded by a sleep" (*Tmp.* 4.1.156–58). Morpheus, like Prospero, shapes dreams, and his plot in *Sandman* sometimes alludes to Shakespearean plays.

Besides being the shaper of dreams, Morpheus also embodies the human dream state. He is an allegorical figure that represents a biological state, as well as the aspirations and hopes of humanity. Allegorical figures tend to be flat, not "round," complex characters. But that is not quite true for Morpheus. *Preludes & Nocturnes* is structured to include complex characters. As Annalisa Castaldo says, the *Sandman* comic series:

> is inherently more meditative and ambiguous than comics, which feature a clear cut good and evil. Even a comic such as *Batman*, with its tormented vigilante hero, presents battle against opponents who want to destroy humanity or take over the world. *Sandman*, on the

other hand, is free to spend entire issues contemplating the nature of reality and responsibility without straightforward villains (99).

Castaldo also asserts that Gaiman felt a "feeling of kinship with Shakespeare," while creating the *Sandman* episodes because both writers "borrowed from sources" that became "obscured" by the creative way they were used (107). This borrowing is one of the types of intertextuality that is sometimes found in literary texts, especially literary texts of the contemporary postmodern period. Costas Constandinides, who works with a wide range of contemporary media, including film adaptations and graphic-text images, describes the intertextual ways in which various media are inserted into each other (3). Like so many contemporary texts today and like Shakespeare's characters coming from other sources, as Castaldo says, Gaiman's character Sandman "was an unpopular DC character from the 30s" (107).

But Gaiman shapes the Sandman character into a complex being, who breaks the "frame" that traditional comics tend to place around superheroes: specifically, the way in which comic books rely on rectangular panels to indicate scenes and the flow of events that make up a plot. When a frame is broken, the panel's image flows past where its frame would go, beyond the "gutter" between frames, and into the space of one or more nearby panels. The form and meaning of the gutter in comics is explained by several literary critics, including Jared Gardner, who discusses the importance of the gutter as a metaphor for "the larger and often less formally explicit gaps that everywhere define how comics tell stories" (xi). The flow of a panel into and beyond a gutter has the effect of stopping the reader, as if it is saying "pay close attention to this out-of-bounds panel." For *Sandman*, the breaking of a frame serves, in part, as a metaphor for Morpheus deviating from the clear set of values and behavioral guidelines of superheroes in other episodic comics.

In other words, motives and behavior are not clear-cut for Morpheus. As the keeper of human dreams, the Lord of the Dreaming suffers the conflicting motives and urges of humans. And he acts on them, sometimes for good. An example of a good act comes early on in *Preludes & Nocturnes*, which begins with Morpheus being captured and detained in a glass cage by a magician names Burgess. After over seventy years in the cage, Morpheus escapes ("Sleep of the Just") and will recover some of his strength in the Dreamworld, which is his alternative universe of stories ("Imperfect Hosts"). This world of different kinds of stories, by the way, is also an interesting element to explore in *Preludes & Nocturnes*. In the main story, the basic plot, Morpheus's kindly act, takes place while he is searching for his sand pouch—a familiar intertextual object of the Sandman in song and other stories—that Burgess took from him. The pouch has been passed from person to person over the decades until a young woman named Rachel gets it and becomes addicted to dreaming, the way one might become addicted to opiate drugs.

By the time Morpheus comes across her, while searching for his pouch, she has stopped eating and exists only to dream. Her condition is described as this by the third-person narrator: "Her skin is flaking, infected and inflamed. Bedsores cover her back and legs. . . . Her stomach shrank, then bloated. Then it shrank again. Hunger subsided to a low nagging in the back of her mind. It's OK. It goes away. Like the pain goes away. Like everything goes away when the dreams come" ("Dream a Little Dream of Me"). When Morpheus and his guide, John Constantine—yes, here's the intertextual insertion of another comic character—find Rachel and the sand pouch, Morpheus is concerned only with the pouch. But Constantine, Rachel's former boyfriend, reminds Morpheus, "You can't leave her like this." Morpheus is unconcerned: "Why not? Her metabolism is obviously destroyed. The sand was the only thing keeping her alive. She will die soon. Painfully, I would imagine" ("Dream a Little Dream of Me"). This is when Constantine explodes in anger at the callous Lord of Dreams. Morpheus is jolted out of self-involvement and compassionately gives Rachel a dream of reconciliation with Constantine as she slips into death.

This act of compassion is in contrast with Morpheus's otherwise self-involved and arrogant behavior. And arrogance is part of the larger problem for the main character of *Preludes & Nocturnes*. It is a key theme of the volume. If Morpheus were more of a godlike character, as godlike characters are imagined to be in the culture of most readers of *Sandman*, he would have followed a clear code of ethics. He never would have dismissed Rachel in the first place. He would have obviously good behavior of a superhero, else he would be a villain.

Instead, Morpheus is more like the main character of a realist novel, but one who just happens to have greater-than-human power. Like the central character of a novel, Morpheus is complex, even if he is something like a god. Two literary critics put it this way: "*The Sandman* features a superhero whose only powers are delusions of grandeur" (Kukkonen and Müller-Wood 154). Traditional near-godlike superheroes, like Superman, don't have delusions of grandeur. They are dedicated to good from the start of a story to its end. Like allegorical figures, they represent what they are on the surface.

Behaving more like a human, Morpheus is interesting for the large number of emotionally or cognitively troubling events that readers might focus on. Morpheus's story, his quest plot, is not of a superhero, but of an aspect of humanity, the aspect of us that dreams of control over our circumstances. Like us, Morpheus dreams of power and human connection and, yes, revenge . . . all "such stuff as dreams are made on." Morpheus describes his dream of power exactly this way shortly after he escapes from his cage: "The Dreamworld, the Dreamtime, the unconscious—call it what you will—is as much part of me as I am part of it. And for the first time since my return, for the first time in 70 years, I reach out my substance . . . and I shape the world" ("Imperfect Hosts").

Because Morpheus is a flawed and emotionally conflicted hero when he begins his quest, he exhibits little compassion for the humans whose dreams or waking life have been negatively affected by his absence. Until the scene with Rachel, his concern is only for the return of his power and the restoration of his grand realm of the Dreaming. To find out who has taken the tools that contain his power, Morpheus calls Clotho, Lachesis, and Atropos, the ancient Fates of Greek mythology ("Imperfect Hosts"). Here, again, is an intertextual moment in the plot. They appear "The one who is three The we who are they. The Hecateae . . . Tisiphone, Alecto, and Magaera . . . Diana, Mary and Florence," they call themselves. As Morpheus calls them, "the three graces" ("Imperfect Hosts"). These names are allusions to similar tripartite demi-gods in different mythologies. They tell Morpheus who has his pouch of sand, protective helmet, and ruby dreamstone amulet. They then laugh derisively at Morpheus as he thanks them for the information. Morpheus thinks he understands their laughter: "I have answers of a sort. This will be an uphill quest" ("Imperfect Hosts").

Morpheus only thinks he is on a quest to retrieve his objects of office, the objects through which he wields power over human dreams. But literary critics might notice another more human quest, a journey through an emotional landscape. Morpheus must deal with the rage he feels at having been trapped by Burgess. He will have to decide what to do with his overwhelming urge to get revenge on those who have wronged him. By the end of the first volume of the ten-volume *Sandman* series, he will have to face his internal hunger for the absolute power of a god. He will be faced, also, with the consequences of his dismissive manner toward a character named Lyta in volume two of *Sandman* (*The Doll's House*, "Playing House"). But that is getting ahead of the story.

It is enough for now to focus on his initial motive for the quest: getting his powerful tools of office back. In the process, Morpheus encounters various forms of evil. One type of evil that he encounters conforms to the allegorical figure of evil common to comics, namely the villain that a superhero must successfully battle. In this case, the villain is a demon from Hell. We might expect the demon to be Lucifer himself, the ruler of Hell, according to Judeo-Christian mythology.

At this point, it is important to note that the following literary interpretation requires use of the word "mythology" over faith-based language. This is not intended to be disrespectful. Instead, it is intended to be neutral, for the sake of academic analytical and critical thought. Lucifer is sometimes presented in literature as a villain, with expressly evil intention. However, in the *Sandman* series, his motives are much more ambiguous, even to the point of abdicating his place as Lord of Hell in volume four (*Season of Mists*, "Episode 2"). Elaine Pagels, a historian of religions, gives insight into the complex mythology of Lucifer figure in *The Origin of Satan*, calling him a "luminous falling star" and identifying him as "light-bearer" (48). Her scholarly study of the mythological Lucifer matches the Lucifer character in *Sandman*. This is no coincidence, since Neil Gaiman is well-versed in mythologies and incorporates mythological figures into several of his works, including his novels.

Victoria Nelson, a literary critic who deals with *Sandman's* depiction of Lucifer, explores one of the themes common in comics like *Watchmen, John Constantine: Hellblazer, Swamp Thing*, and *Sandman*, namely the theme of Gothic powers. In *Gothicka*, she describes the Lucifer of *Sandman* as a "Romantic fallen angel" (84). Nelson's focus on "gothic" and "romantic" elements signals a large area of literary study that helps to explain not only works of literature from the early nineteenth-century Romantic period, but also some literature being published today. Her book examines the current revival of gothic romanticism in today's popular media, and she notes that graphic stories of the English and Scottish writers Moore, Ennis, Ellis, Delano, Gaiman, and Morrison "nourish tarnish on their superheroes' souls" (84).

"Tarnish" is a feature of gothic genres, and Lucifer supplies some of it in *Preludes & Nocturnes*. As a character associated with the Judeo-Christian god, Lucifer's presence prompts the critic Rodney Sharkey to ask the question, "Does god exist in *Sandman*?" (par. 7). Sharkey answers his question as follows: "Apparently he does and he does not" (par. 7), and he goes on to explain that there are references to a "Shaper" who "condemns Lucifer to dream of heaven" in "A Hope in Hell" episode (par. 7). At the same time, as Sharkey explains, "the notion of the Shaper as a ruling, monotheistic God is problematic" (8). He gives examples from volume four of the series, *Season of Mists*, and argues that in *Sandman*, "hell is more properly psychological and therefore symbolic" (par. 8).

Sharkey's analysis, like the works of Pagels and Nelson, points us to the thematic complexity of evil in *Preludes & Nocturnes*. Yes, there *is* an evil villain in the volume. He goes by the name of Choronzon, which is yet another mythological figure and an intertextual character from the pages of other DC comics. And yes, Morpheus engages this villain in battle. However, it is not a physical fight, like one would expect from a traditional comic. It is a mind game of concepts that overpower and trump the opponent's concepts. When Choronzon names "anti-life. . . the dark at the end of everything" to vanquish Morpheus's concept of an all-encompassing "universe—all things encompassing, all life embracing," Morpheus trumps the negative force of anti-life with one little word: "hope." With that little word, Morpheus wins the "battle" with the demon and regains his helmet ("A Hope in Hell"). He essentially vanquishes the evil of despair, something that humans experience emotionally, psychologically.

Psychological kinds of evil, then, are brought to the fore in *Sandman*. So are psycho-social forms of depravity. For example, in the "Imperfect Hosts" episode, a dysfunctional relationship is presented. In that episode, Cain and Abel—two more mythological figures who show up in more than one of the DC comics—are introduced. These inhabitants of the Dreamworld are not just dream characters. They are the children of Adam and Eve in the Hebraic Genesis story. Like in Genesis, Cain and Abel in *Preludes & Nocturnes* are caught in a victim/victimizer dynamic. "Imperfect Hosts" begins with Abel fearful of opening a gift box from Cain. In the past, such boxes have exploded, killing him. Cain slyly asks, "Now, why would I give you an exploding present? What kind of a brother would I be if I did that?" Abel replies, "The, uh, kind who kills me whenever he's, uh . . . mad at me, or bored, or just in a lousy m-mood." And that is exactly what happens. Cain gets frustrated with Abel and kills him ("Imperfect Hosts").

Evil, as an emotion-based destructive dynamic, is punctuated in the final page of the "Imperfect Hosts" episode. Abel, now revived from his death and sitting on the porch of his house, tells the dragon hatchling the lie that he tells himself: "It's a story of two brothers and they, uh . . . they loved each other very much and they were always nice to each other" ("Imperfect Hosts"). Abel is an example of a victim who feels powerless to escape the cycle of violence.

Other examples of psychosocial evil in *Preludes & Nocturnes* might not be so obvious. As interpreters of the volume, we might ask whether there are parallels between the dynamic that traps Abel and a culture that might support an addictive state like Rachel's. There are other characters whose evil acts might be studied from a range of socio-psychological perspective, including a character who gets his thrills as a "creeper" cat burglar ("Dream a Little Dream of Me") and a very scary "Granny," who torments the child character who grows up to be "Scott Free" of the Justice League of America ("Passengers").

Even the magician Burgess who has caged Morpheus might be interpreted from a social or psychological perspective, as might the magician's son ("Sleep of the Just"). Of course, a character who is a magician may also be interpreted through the lens of the literary study of gothic characters and gothic narrative structures. The point here is that *Preludes & Nocturnes* invites multiple interpretations of its characters and multiple perspectives on its themes, including the role of the supernatural and the nature of human evil.

One of the elements of *Preludes & Nocturnes* that begs for multiple approaches is the overall intertextuality of the characters. Up to this point, intertextual characters have been mentioned, but the significance of intertextuality itself has not been explored. Intertextuality provides multiple layers of meaning for any reader, who also reads the source texts involved. For example, I teach Shakespeare plays in a college course, so I get extra meaning from the allusions to Shakespeare in *Preludes & Nocturnes*. "Sound and Fury" contains an allusion to Caesar and the soothsayer of Shakespeare's *Julius Caesar* (1.2.12–24) and a direct quote of the famous "tale told by an idiot, full of sound and fury, signifying nothing" speech of the tragic hero of *Macbeth* (5.5. 26–28). These allusions—or intertextual references—echo the mixed motives of characters of those plays. Although not in *Preludes & Nocturnes*, but in other volumes (*The Doll's House, Dream Country, The Wake*), Shakespeare himself appears as a character, and his interactions with Morpheus bring out the psychological features of the main character.

Another prominent intertextual character of *Preludes &*
Nocturnes based on a real person in history is John Dee. This
character engages Morpheus in combat over the ruby amulet in
the seventh episode, "Sound and Fury." John Dee first appears
in "Imperfect Hosts" as an inmate of the Arkham Asylum for the
Criminally Insane, an institution that shows up in other DC Comics
series. This denizen of Arkham is none other than the DC Comics
character Doctor Destiny. He is also the "echo" of the real John Dee,
who might have been used as the model for literary characters like
Shakespeare's Prospero. György E. Szönyi and Rowland Wymer
explain this connection in their essay "John Dee as a Cultural
Hero" (189). They explore the ways in which the actual man John
Dee, a late sixteenth-century alchemist and occult philosopher,
developed a reputation of being both a fraudulent sorcerer and
"someone who could easily be duped" (190). According to Szönyi
and Wymer, several contemporary literary, filmic, and musical
works that include Dee as a character, use him "as the epitome of a
dream of transformation with close analogies to the way the creative
imagination itself operates" (202).

As a figure of transformation in *Preludes & Nocturnes*, Dee
is the catalyst of transformation for Morpheus in the "Sound and
Fury" episode. Like all true catalysts, Dee himself cannot change.
He is trapped in a mind without dreams. And his internal torment
matters, not just as a foil for Morpheus, but for what it says about
the psychological torments that can lead to violence, to evil. In the
"Imperfect Hosts" episode, Dee's tortured mind is evident. He moans
to his mother, who visits him in his Arkham cell, that "I would have
dreamed of you . . . if I could dream. It's been a long time. . . .
They took my dreams away from me!" As he cries to his mother, his
face matches the extreme distress in his voice: he is wide-eyed with
pinpoint irises, his scalp bald except for two tufts of uncombed hair,
his mouth a mass of broken teeth and overflowing slobber, his hands
fisted around the bars of his cell ("Imperfect Hosts").

Experiencing such extreme powerlessness, Dee's "dream" of
absolute power takes over, resulting in violent behavior that, on the
surface, looks like the pure evil of a villain. This is the kind of evil

that the "Passengers" episode of *Preludes & Nocturnes* presents. Here Dee escapes from Arkham and kills a kind woman who gives him a ride in her car. Then Dee gets possession of Morpheus's powerful ruby amulet and wields the amulet in a murder spree at an all-night café in the "24 Hours" episode. But this murder spree involves psychological mind games. Echoing the mind-game battle between Morpheus and Choronzon, Dee uses the amulet to insert warped visions in the minds of people in the café, causing them to kill each other. This, then, is psychological horror with physical consequences.

After the mass-murder scene, Morpheus engages Dee in battle over the power ruby. Here, the thematic elements of the nature of evil, the dangers of absolute power, and the urge to exact revenge converge in a literally explosive battle ("Sound and Fury"). Dee appears to win the battle, only to find that he has simply freed Morpheus from dependence on the ruby for power. Morpheus has been transformed, and in his transformed state, he forgives Dee for stealing the amulet and using it to manipulate and kill others. Again, the psychological and emotional state of Morpheus is stressed, which allows a reader to interpret the various plot elements and character interactions that contribute to an outcome of transformation and forgiveness. One interpretation might be that Dee's power as a catalyst of transformation comes in part from his echo of the *real* sorcerer, John Dee, Shakespeare's contemporary.

Interpreting the theme of forgiveness might take a reader to a *Preludes & Nocturnes* episode that comes before the battle between Morpheus and Dee. In "A Hope in Hell," as Morpheus is led toward his encounter with Lucifer and Choronzon, he is taken by a set of cages, one of which contains a crying woman named Nada. She calls out to Morpheus—calls out in her African language to Kai'ckul—saying "Free me, Lord! You ordered me confined here! Your forgiveness can free me! I implore you . . . Don't you love me?" Morpheus, or Kai'ckul, replies stonily, "It has been ten thousand years, Nada. . . . yes, I still love you. But I have not forgiven you" ("A Hope in Hell"). An interpreter might argue that this brief scene, taking up only seven story panels, signals a central theme of the whole *Sandman* series, that of forgiving and being forgiven. Maybe having been confronted by Nada, Morpheus's conscience is pricked, making it easier to forgive Dee. Maybe. This theme is one of many surrounding the complex, realist character.

True to many realist novels, where the struggling central character comes to self-awareness about his human flaws in a particular scene, Morpheus finds himself sitting in a public square feeding pigeons and feeling sorry for himself in the final episode of *Preludes & Nocturnes*, "The Sound of Her Wings." Along comes a smiling young woman, wearing black lipstick, black skinny jeans, and a black spaghetti-strap camisole. She lounges near Morpheus, while he explains his dark mood. He admits something has felt wrong ever since he got his power back. He is baffled by how the destruction of the ruby did not kill him but, oddly, freed him. "More than that," he says, "It freed everything of me that was in the stone. I got it all back . . . I was more powerful than I had been in eons. . . . You see, until then I'd been driven. I'd had a true quest, a purpose beyond my function—and then, suddenly, the quest was over. I felt . . . drained. Disappointed. Let down" ("The Sound of Her Wings"). Morpheus's ennui, he recognizes, is related to a false quest for power.

The response of the young woman is to berate Morpheus for his self-involvement. She declares, "You are utterly the stupidest, most self-centered, appallingest excuse for an anthropomorphic personification on this or any other plane! . . . Feeling all sorry for yourself because your little game is over, and you haven't got the — the balls to go and find a new one!" ("The Sound of Her Wings"). She sounds like an older sister bawling out a younger sibling, and that is exactly what she is: Morpheus's big sister, Death. Victoria Nelson, who describes Death as a "cute, caring bisexual Goth girl with a philosophical streak," notes that she is a true allegorical figure, the kind that was believed to be real in the worldview three centuries ago, but not so for our "secular twentieth-century sensibility" (173). As an allegorical figure, Death is all about the *idea* of death that we humans hold in our minds. She is that against which we finally judge what it means to be human in a human community, as philosophers like Alphonso Lingus remind us. In a chapter of *The Community of*

Those Who Have Nothing in Common, where Lingus explores the relationship between death and meaningful communication among humans, Lingus identifies the moment that we attend the death of someone as a "limit-situation" (113). In that moment, what we say may be meaningless, "the end of language" (113), but also "the beginning of communication" according to Lingus (114).

The final episode of *Preludes & Nocturnes* has that quality of beginning communication, as Morpheus attends Death on her "rounds." She gently gathers the dying and ushers them, with soft comfort, into the state beyond ("The Sound of Her Wings"). This way of thinking about Death soothes us. It pushes that *other* version of Death, the Grim Reaper skeleton, out of our minds. We accompany Death intently, just as Morpheus does. We see why he loves his big sister, Death, and relies on her. Maybe we, too, rely on Death to give "voice" to our lives, to give our lives meaning.

The way I have just inserted us into the final scenes of *Preludes & Nocturnes* in this past paragraph is designed to illustrate a creative philosophical approach to literary criticism that has developed in our postmodern world. This is a "lyric essay" approach that David Shields describes in *Reality Hunger* (24–31). It is a process-based approach that lets interpreters focus on how a piece of literature relates to their own lived experience. An interpreter may even imagine experiencing the process that Morpheus goes through while reading. Such process and relationship-to-reader approaches are associated with the type of literary interpretation called "reader response," which has been popularized by literary theorist Stanley Fish.

Whatever our approach to interpretation, we reader-critics of *Preludes & Nocturnes* will find much to analyze: the way in which Morpheus has developed as a realist character with the potential for growth, the theme of the death/human relationship, the nature of evil, the reason an intertextual character like Death would be so different from the traditional figure of the Grim Reaper in hooded robe with harvest scythe, and the purpose of allegory.

We can't forget allegory, for Morpheus *is* our dreams. His quest may be our own. When we contemplate *Preludes & Nocturnes* as allegory, then another, older kind of literary interpretation might open up in a fresh way. The narrative structure of the hero myth that Joseph Campbell described in *The Hero with a Thousand Faces* in 1949 endures for its relevance to stories like *Preludes & Nocturnes*. Stephen Rauch examines the quest of Morpheus in relation to the hero myth, reminding us that "the central plot of *Sandman*, Dream's process of becoming human, is a kind of hero myth, with new implications for the classical model" (138). Campbell even went so far as to argue that the "modern hero" must guide society (391). Whatever the purpose and meaning that interpreters assign to Morpheus, there is, indeed, something both very classical and very contemporary about Gaiman's character. Morpheus can be interpreted as something very old, the grand allegorical idea of what a dream is, what a quest is. Morpheus is also something still fairly new to comics, a non-superhero, who has the capability of human flaws and human heroics. Neil Gaiman's most famous character is all this . . . and so much more. It's just up to us to interpret.

Works Cited

Bevington, David. *The Complete Works of Shakespeare*. 6th ed. New York: Pearson-Longman, 2009.

Campbell, Joseph. *The Hero with a Thousand Faces*. Princeton: Princeton UP, 1949. 17. Bollingen Ser.

Castaldo, Annalisa. "'   .'" *College Literature* 13.4 (Fall 2004): 94–110.

Constandinides, Costas. *From Film Adaptation to Post-Celluloid Adaptation: Rethinking the Transition of Popular Narratives and Characters across Old and New Media*. New York and London: Continuum, 2010.

Gaiman, Neil. *The Sandman: The Doll's House*. Fully recolored ed. Vol. 2. 1989–90, episodes 9–16. Illus. Mike Dringenberg et al. New York: DC Comics, 2010.

_____. *The Sandman: Dream Country*. Fully recolored ed. Vol. 3. 1990, episodes 17–20. Illus. Kelley Jones et al. New York: DC Comics, 2010.

_____. *The Sandman: Preludes & Nocturnes*. Fully recolored ed. Vol. 1. 1988–89, episodes 1-8. Illus. Sam Kieth, Mike Dringenberg, and Malcolm Jones III. New York: DC Comics, 2010.

_____. *The Sandman: Season of Mists*. Neil Gaiman. Fully remastered ed. Vol. 4. 1990–91, episodes 21–28. Illus. Kelley Jones et al. New York: DC Comics, 2010.

_____. *The Sandman: The Wake*. Vol. 10. 1995–96, episodes 70–75. Illus. Michael Zulli, Jon J. Muth, and Charles Vess. New York: Vertigo-DC Comics, 1997.

Gardner, Jared. *Projections: Comics and the History of Twenty-First-Century Storytelling*. Stanford, CA: Stanford UP, 2012.

Kukkonen, Karin and Anja Müller-Wood. "Whatever Happened to All the Heroes? British Perspectives on Superheroes." *Comics as a Nexus of Cultures: Essays on the Interplay of Media, Disciplines and International Perspectives*. Ed. Mark Berninger, Jochen Ecke, and Gideon Haberkorn. NC: McFarland and Company, 2010. 153–63. Critical Explorations in Science Fiction and Fantasy 22.

Lingus, Alphonso. *The Community of Those Who Have Nothing in Common*. Bloomington: Indiana UP, 1994.

Nelson, Victoria. *Gothicka: Vampire Heroes, Human Gods, and the New Supernatural*. Cambridge, MA: Harvard UP, 2012.

Pagels, Elaine. *The Origin of Satan: How Christians Demonized Jews, Pagans, and Heretics*. New York: Random House, 1995.

Rauch, Stephen. *Neil Gaiman's* The Sandman *and Joseph Campbell: In Search of the Modern Myth*. Holicong, PA: Wildside Press, 2003.

Shakespeare, William. *Julius Caesar. The Complete Works of Shakespeare*. 6th ed. Ed. David Bevington. New York: Pearson-Longman, 2009. 1051–90.

_____. *Macbeth. The Complete Works of Shakespeare*. 6th ed. Ed. David Bevington. New York: Pearson-Longman, 2009. 1255–92.

_____. *The Tempest. The Complete Works of Shakespeare*. 6th ed. Ed. David Bevington. New York: Pearson-Longman, 2009. 1570–603.

Sharkey, Rodney. "'Being' Decentered in *Sandman*: History, Dreams, Gender, and the 'Prince of Metaphor and Allusion.'" *ImageTexT: Interdisciplinary Comics Studies* 4.1 (2008): 32 Dept. of English, U of Florida, 2008. Web. 16 Sep. 2013.

Shields, David. *Reality Hunger: A Manifesto*. New York: Alfred A. Knopf, 2010.

Szönyi, György E. and Rowland Wymer. "John Dee as a Cultural Hero." *European Journal of English Studies* 15.3 (2011): 189–209.

Frank Miller's *Sin City*

Terrence Wandtke

Frank Miller's *Sin City* first appeared in 1991, during an era in which comic books moved beyond their widespread characterization as kids' stuff and during a time in which comic books were redeveloped as "graphic novels" for adult readers in the United States. In regard to comic books' characterization as kids' stuff, *Sin City* arrived about forty years after Fredric Wertham's anti-comic book campaign; the related 1954 Senate hearings; and the industry's self-regulation, which removed adult-oriented crime comics from newsstands. It also arrived about fifteen years after Will Eisner announced the creation of the "graphic novel"—only to be roundly ignored by the public at large. In regard to comic books' redevelopment as "graphic novels," *Sin City* arrived about ten years after the direct market boom in comic book sales, which showcased unconventional adult comics like *Maus*, *Love and Rockets*, and *Mister X* and about five years after the sophisticated deconstruction of the superhero in *Watchmen* and Miller's own *The Dark Knight Returns*. All of these titles would reach their largest audiences once they were bound as square, book-length collections and marketed as "graphic novels." With the appearance of creator-owned publishers, like Dark Horse, this would seem like the perfect time for a well-known creator, like Miller, to extend the creative freedom he enjoyed with the DC-published title *Ronin*: to craft a space outside the still-limited world of company-owned properties and elevate graphic novels to the level of art form. Often referring to Will Eisner and the artistry of comics during his early interviews, Miller was thought to have the vision to usher in a new age of the graphic novel by most readers of mainstream comics and many readers of independent comics. Curiously, Miller would set forth a work that would indeed change the industry, but with a presentation hardly expected. After working with Dark Horse to produce the four-issue *Give Me Liberty* (collected as a square-bound book) and the three-issue *Hard Boiled* (collected in a European-style deluxe format book), *Sin City* was published not exactly as a limited series, but rather as several eight- to fifteen-page installments in an increasingly rare anthology format found in *Dark Horse Presents*.

With an explicit presentation of profanity, sex, and violence that would have scandalized critics like Fredric Wertham, *Sin City* brought crime comics to a time and place outside the confines of the Comics Code and in a purer form—not synthesized with other genres (like the superhero or science fiction story), as in Miller's past work. With an unstoppable hulk of a fall guy, named Marv, *Sin City* presents a tale of suffering in the middle of thoroughly corrupted urban landscape, which harkens back to classic film noir in both its themes and chiaroscuro play of light and dark. While celebrating genre conventions long lost to comics in the United States, *Sin City* does something else by pushing its narrative to extremes: to critically represent comics and culture. And therein lies the importance of the original monthly anthology format for *Sin City*. Even though most creators and critics agree that the term "comic book" poorly describes the medium, there is little agreement on the meaning of the term "graphic novel" and its difference, if any, from the comic book. Much of the popular associations with the graphic novel imply adult content that is presented to a longer, more expensively produced—and therefore non-disposable—book format. Conversely, during the pre-collector age of comic books, their cheaply printed, pamphlet-style publication format made comic books readily disposable and, therefore, beyond the consideration of purveyors of high culture.

While Miller advocates forcefully for comic books as art in his early career, he passes over that idea in his later career, preferring to identify comic books as a marginally regarded outlaw medium. The first arc of the *Sin City*, retroactively titled *The Hard Goodbye* in its collected form, represents Miller's attempt to resist the gentrification and high culture commodification of graphic novels through its evocation of a bygone era of pulpy comic book anthologies with questionable content. With the potential to upset the status quo, comic books work in the same way as the protagonist of *Sin City*: a socially unapproved voice that undermines all the superficial things held sacred in order to expose the dirty world beneath those things.

Crime fiction in general and crime comics in particular would serve as a point of inspiration for Miller in two significant ways: as a source of narrative and artistic material and as a reminder of what comics should have been. After the end of World War II, the popularity of the superhero stories began to fade and that of crime stories began to rise. Initiated by titles like *Crime Does Not Pay*, crime comic books developed from the simultaneous attraction and repulsion Americans felt toward real gangsters in the 1930s and 1940s. After the violent life of a major gangster is gratuitously presented at length in *Crime Does Not Pay*, the comic book supposedly sent the message of its title via a much too hasty presentation of the terrified gangster in the electric chair (Benton 25). A more coherent and sophisticated crime story would evolve in the pages of various EC anthology titles, such as *Crime SuspenStories*. Most often depicting the criminal as the ordinary man or woman living next door in suburbia, this type of story insisted satisfaction could not be found in the realization of the American dream (Wright 137); it did this regularly with gruesome details of the criminal act revealed in a surprise twist at the end. However, as is well known in the history of comics, crime comics evoked the ire of socially-minded commentators, like Fredric Wertham. Working with Cold War anxieties about adolescent delinquency, Wertham assumed that EC's crime stories were intended for young readers and condemned them as horribly inappropriate (likely to lead to mental disease and criminal behavior). Due to the pressure of Congressional hearings convened by the Senate Subcommittee on Juvenile Delinquency, the industry would agree to self-regulate via the prohibitions of the Comics Code, which effectively erased crime comics, revived the superhero, and stigmatized comics as kids' stuff for generations to come (Duncan 40–43). When Miller first came to New York City to make a break into the comics industry, he tried to demonstrate his talent with illustrations depicting type characters and situations drawn from crime stories (published in the fan press *APA-5*).

As he settled into his early career as a superhero comic book artist (eventually writing *Daredevil* as a superhero crime story), Miller stated:

> Entranced by Will Eisner's work and really wanting to do crime comics, I did everything I could to pull [Daredevil] over into a crime world. . . . I think heroes by their nature have to be challenging the status quo. I think heroes are much less interesting when they are a force *for* the status quo (Bissette and Wiater 20).

With his description of the hero as an indication of things to eventually come in *Sin City*, he regularly talked in interviews about the greatness of the EC crime comics and the cowardice of an industry that allowed the fear of the masses to influence artistic choices (George 52).

With a femme fatale, a mob boss protected by the powers-that-be, and a protagonist undone by his own belief in the system, *Daredevil*, cleverly disguised like a superhero, brought crime comics back to mainstream popularity. After dissecting superhero tropes in "Roulette," the last story in his initial run on *Daredevil*, Miller moved from Marvel to DC Comics, where he was given more creative freedom. This was seen evident in his first work with DC, *Ronin*: a limited series, published on high quality paper, without advertisements, and promoted primarily to direct-market comic books stories. And this was followed by his work with Batman, most notably including *The Dark Knight Returns*, published in a similar way, but also square bound (with the limited series quickly published as a trade paperback and read widely outside conventional superhero comic book readership).

In reference to the format used for *Ronin* and refined with *The Dark Knight Returns*, Miller acknowledged an important shift in comics readership outside the traditional fan base and toward the graphic novel format: "[T]he format definitely went over well with whoever saw it. Mostly the reaction I got from people outside the industry was they wanted to see the entire thing collected together, because they like reading it at once" (George 38). *The Dark Knight Returns* also uses crime story conventions to fundamentally rework, question, and undermine the traditional superhero with a deeply flawed Batman at odds with the corruption of the civilized world, including the conformist Superman. Frustrated with the mainstream comic book industry and finding many opportunities outside the big two publishers, thanks to the 1980s boom in comic book publishing, Miller participated in steps taken toward sophisticated adult content and presentation, which took comics beyond their literal pulp paper origins. In addition to being an outspoken advocate of comics as art, Miller was also a supporter of creator rights and Denis Kitchen's Comic Book Legal Defense Fund. Poised to become a creator at the forefront of a movement in American comics beyond typical genre and cheap presentation, Miller embraced the crime comics history he had always loved, put together a black-and-white series without the complex color available via new printing technology, and presented it in an anthology, a nearly extinct format that was based on pulp fiction precedents. With *Sin City*, Miller produced a series that evokes the most disturbing pre-Code aspects of EC crime comics and, ironically, becomes one of the most influential graphic novels in American comics history.

Before producing *Sin City* for *Dark Horse Presents*, Miller developed two science fiction limited series, *Give Me Liberty* and *Hard Boiled*, for Dark Horse, one of the comic book publishers born of the market expansion during the direct market boom. Dark Horse gave creators full rights to their work. Also, returning from a short-lived sojourn in Hollywood, Miller described the experience in this way: "For me, the biggest jump came when I sat down at my board to start *Sin City*. I'd just finished two years working as a screenwriter writing *Robocop 2* with all the bosses in the world, left exhausted and existentially confused" (George 91). Connecting his oppressive stint within the Hollywood system with his existential confusion, Miller confronts that confusion with what would become his signature series. And with a certain celebrity status as a comic book creator, Miller brought readers to *Dark Horse Presents* with the debut of *Sin City*. In Basin City, a muscled ex-con named Marv spends the night with Goldie, a beautiful prostitute, and wakes up to find her dead the next morning. After brutally dispatching a SWAT team sent to catch him, Marv cuts a bloody swathe through the underworld of Basin City, in order to find out who set him up to take the fall for Goldie's murder. Ultimately, his brutal investigation leads to corruption at the highest levels, uncovering city and church leader, Cardinal Rourke, in league with a serial killing cannibal. The plot itself treads familiar territory for Miller, with a hero hopelessly set against the system, and yet it also seems new, perhaps due to the exaggeration of the very content specifically prohibited by the Comics Code. Marv is pill-popping, sexual, and hyper-violent in ways that walk a line between a protest of content prohibitions and a parody of crime comics conventions; Marv gleefully smashes his way through a police cruiser, questions a thug by dunking his head in a dirty toilet, and chases after one of his antagonists with a hatchet in his hand and an eye on the nice coat the man is wearing. The only thing that serves as a clear motivation for Marv is honoring the gift of a one-night stand from Goldie, who merely sought shelter out of fear for her life.

As comics critic R.C. Harvey notes, Marv would become a template for all *Sin City* protagonists:

> Beginning with the brute force named Marvin, all the so-called good guys are . . . uncompromising barbarians, ruthless outlaws, whose inarticulate sufferings and single-minded motivations and deeply, deeply frustrated yearnings for human affection in any form are all that make them humanly recognizable for most of us who read about them (Harvey, "Introduction" 2).

While Marv is a loner whose actions may seem justified by the extremes of the institutionalized evil around him, Marv is not a typical hero, seems delusional, and identifies himself as a psychopath: "Then it hits me. What if I'm wrong? I've got a condition. . . . What if I'm imagining things? Like I did when I thought Goldie attacked me after she was already dead? . . . What if I've finally turned into what they always said I was going to turn into—a maniac, a psycho killer?" (Miller, *Sin City* 132). While the narrative eventually reveals Goldie had a twin and Marv was not hallucinating, this introspection, at least temporarily, calls into question the story as a whole through the subjectivity that produces it.

However, his mental instability eventually becomes a moot point in the next *Sin City* story (*A Dame to Kill For*), in which the main character considers Marv as a character born at the wrong time, someone who'd have been well respected on an ancient battlefield (Miller, *Sin City: A Dame* 93). In this light, Marv's mental instability is a faulty social construction that he must overcome to exact an ancient standard of retribution on the guilty. In an interview, Miller states: "My feeling is that the hero has now been defined by phrases like the odious one that we were all raised with—crime does not pay. Of course it pays, you schmuck. That's not why we don't do it. We don't do it because it is wrong" (Mitchell). Criticizing the simplistic moral of one of the first American crime comic books, Miller establishes a different sort of standard for his hero outside a conventional notion of a just world. After Marv realizes Goldie knew too much and was killed to cover up Cardinal Rourke's deranged partnership with the serial killing cannibal, Marv kills both Rourke and the cannibal and is sentenced to death for his crimes. In addition to *Sin City*'s narrative, suggesting Marv's execution is unjust, Marv faces his death in an angry, fearless way that rewrites the facile ending of most stories in *Crime Does Not Pay*.

In reference to his crime-tinged, pre-*Sin City* work, Miller would reminisce, "When I was fourteen years old I thought Mickey Spillane's stuff would make some *great* comics. Even though it took me twenty-one years to get around to it, I still hadn't felt that it had been done in the meantime" (Bisette and Wiater 219). Undisputedly, *Sin City* realizes classic crime fiction and film noir more fully than any of his previous work with the use of first person narration, snappy ironic banter, and bad seed typology. However, rather than wholly recreate pulp fiction elements, it complicates its setting by integrating period elements with the presentation of contemporary fashions, technology, and slang; additionally, the urban landscape is often rendered in block-like shapes, which form abstract, negative space constructions and suggest the setting be any city in any time. Miller commented on the location of *Sin City* by saying, "I'm never gonna name where it is, because it's nowhere" (Brownstein 61). Abandoning the moody colors of Lynn Varley, Miller's long-time artistic partner, Miller's black-and-white aesthetic shaped the design and noir identity of the city and generally required a level of technical mastery not previously seen from him. Due to his effective use of the dramatic contrasts between black-and-white, comic scholars Randy Duncan and Matthew J. Smith would state, "Frank Miller . . . is known for his ability to depict moments of powerful action using stark contrasts of shadow and light" (117).

Yet while the crime story in its American context had always tended toward realism, Miller moves toward abstraction. Leaving behind the Neal Adams-influenced work of his earlier years, he integrates the more abstract manga tradition of *Lone Wolf and Cub* and the finely detailed work of Moebius; aerial perspectives that stress the height of buildings and distance from the subject are highly detailed achievements, which effectively present the isolation of Marv and other characters in *Sin City*. Moreover, as suggested by R.C. Harvey, "The next development in the evolution of this style saw Miller discard the mechanical device of a light source and work purely in contrasting black-and-white." (Harvey, "Introduction" 4). Often, in order to develop greater thematic resonance, Miller deepens, exaggerates, or virtually ignores the realistic presentation of a scene. An example of this appears when Marv walks down an alley; he is a diminutive figure, set against impossibly tall buildings represented only as blocks of black space. Another example is when Marv shares his tirades with his sympathetic parole officer: he becomes a figure made entirely of black space, relieved only by the white crosses of his bandages .

The strange sense of familiarity, displacement, and abstraction adds up to an experience of hyper-reality as Miller expands on experiments begun in other work, like *The Dark Knight Returns*. R.C. Harvey comments on that previous work in a way that unintentionally, but effectively describes *Sin City*: "[Miller] often simplified his rendering of the heroic figure into abstraction; the pictures, frequently almost caricatures—cruel in their exaggeration—give the story a raw edge" (Harvey, *The Art* 148). Harvey goes on to show how Miller's art is a radical departure from the "realistic" house style prescribed by DC and Marvel, a style also influencing much of the output from independent publishers of the 1980s, such as First, Eclipse, and Comico. The depiction of Marv's physiognomy does work in a limited way within the basic confines of realism, as he is rendered with exacting attention to detail that notably includes the lines on his face and the wrinkles on his coats; however, even this level of detail defies the long history of monthly comic book publication in the United States that, in the interest of speed, couldn't accommodate artists interested in complex line and brushwork. Moreover, Marv's hulking frame is only somewhat believable, disproportionate from his surroundings, with his facial characteristics often cartoonishly exaggerated for effect.

Miller emphasizes Marv's outsider status by making him into a strangely abstract grotesque, which is most notable when Miller devotes a splash page to Marv's face during one of his many violent confrontations; Marv's face is divided between black-and-white with more attention to the symbolic split within Marv than the light source. The lines on Marv's face more closely resemble cracks in a hard surface than lines on skin. Other figures are caricatured for the sake of parody, such as the barroom stooge Marv easily dispatches (an exaggeration of Marvel's bad boy Wolverine) and the prostitutes of "Old Town," with whom Marv is eventually allied for the sake of revenge. The prostitutes are too-perfect, curvaceous male fantasies, whose costumes include one of Wonder Woman.

In addition, Miller changes the stereotypical content of the comic book panel at the very beginning, when Goldie meets Marv; both figures are displaced to the upper right of the splash page, with the rest of the panel simply a white space. While it certainly accentuates the unbalanced drama of their meeting, it also goes against a long-standing editorial standard within the industry to fill up every part of every page with color illustration and thereby give readers their money's worth. Likewise, in the superhero story genre, which long dominated the industry, the narrative moves at a breakneck pace from one event to the next to satisfy a modern reader's supposedly short attention span. While creators like Jack Kirby changed some of the dynamics by stretching out action (as Miller does himself in *Sin City*), the industry would frown on sequences, like the ten pages of character development visually devoted to Marv walking in the rain. Miller states, "That was me saying, 'This is where I'm going.

I've been away from comics for two years, and I'm back.' . . . That was my walk in the rain" (Brownstein 22).

Miller's celebrity status brought readers in significant numbers from the well-tread ground of mainstream comics publications to the sometimes unfamiliar territory of independent comics publications. He was certainly part of a trend that started with direct market comic book stores (where comic book readers purchased independents in increasing numbers) and continued with bookstores that carried publications like *The Dark Knight Returns* (where non-comic book readers purchased trade paperback publications of superhero stories). However, *Sin City* might be his most significant contribution to the evolution of late twentieth-century comic book readership because it brought comic book readers and non-comic book readers to a genre other than the superhero story. The genre of the crime story not only was long dormant in comic books, but it was also representative of an adult readership that could have been established for comic books in the 1950s. Perhaps aware of his potentially contradictory roles as both a rebel and an increasingly well-known celebrity author, Miller maintained his status as a renegade by exaggerating the controversial characteristics of the genre by adding even more explicit profanity, nudity, sex, and violence, seemingly flaunting its space outside what had been defined as appropriate by the Comics Code.

Certain types of approval were quick to follow, such as nomination for seven Eisner Awards and the winning of three (the award, of course, was named after one of Miller's heroes and the man who popularized the term 'graphic novel'). However, that approval was far from universal, with criticism from people inside and outside the industry, who felt *Sin City* didn't represent a celebrity's successful move toward art outside the mainstream, but instead portrayed a celebrity's celebration of clichés and sexist preoccupations shaped by mainstream culture's power fantasies. Comics creator Ed Brubaker, the eventual inheritor of Miller's reintroduction of crime comics, suggests that *Sin City* should be understood as superheroes in trenchcoats (Phegley). Alan Moore, author of *Watchmen* (like *The Dark Knight Returns* is credited for remaking the superhero for adults), characterized *Sin City* as "unreconstructed misogyny" ("The

Honest"). Perhaps the most famous criticism came from outside the industry, as Ray Suarez devoted an episode of NPR's *Talk of the Nation* to adult comics and interviewed the popular comics creator and theorist Scott McCloud. Suarez quoted Marv's description of his parole's officer's body, lamenting her life as "a dyke" as "a damn crime"; for Suarez, it was meant to represent the adult content of the "new comics": "adolescent guy power trips, sexual fantasies . . . and in many cases blood, blood, blood!" (McCloud 81).

Undoubtedly, Sin City pushes the boundaries of culturally acceptable content; in addition, through Marv's quest for revenge, it evokes the masculine ideals seen in classic crime fiction and through Goldie's presentation as the hooker with the heart of gold, it employs certain typology to represent both men and women. Moreover, women are represented in various states of undress, with impossibly perfect bodies and as objects of masculine desire (represented by male characters or the constructed gaze of the reader). However, critics have been divided on whether this presentation was intended as a straightforward reconstruction of the genre, or if by its excess, this presentation was intended to question, parody, and/or undermine the genre. When quoting Ray Suarez, McCloud himself would identify the series as "a tongue-in-cheek, over-the-top, hyper-noir send-up. Unfortunately, the more ironic aspects were lost in the translation" (McCloud 81). However, McCloud's near-identification of Sin City as hyper-reality doesn't necessarily mean that the work is subversive (since in the traditional definition by Jean Baudrillard, hyper-reality is a preferred substitute for reality).

Other theorists and academics have disputed McCloud's position, such as Christopher Pizzino in "Art That Goes BOOM," a critique of another Sin City arc: "[Miller] evokes the features of noir, fully participating in it, more than he represents its values in a mediated fashion" (124). Miller himself hasn't done much to settle this dispute. Sometimes, he has emphasized Sin City as absurd, connecting to works like Dr. Strangelove (a clearly satiric film by Stanley Kubrick): "I'm not going to go into a lengthy defense of the complexity of my work, but my stories aren't just people killing each other. . . . part of what I find entrancing about current times is the sense of absurdity" (Brownstein 8). However, he has also clarified that his intent is to reinterpret rather than parody (George 82) and has defended his sexualized representations of prostitutes by simply saying Sin City is not realistic, and he didn't want it to be depressing (84). Moreover, he extols Dirty Harry as a profoundly moral force (35) and resists the attempt to identify multiple levels in his works; when receiving a lifetime achievement award at the Scream Awards on the SPIKE TV network, Miller would say, "Drama is drama, character is character, death is death, sex is sex, and blood is blood" (Spike TV's Scream Awards). In the decades since the initial publication of Sin City, the general tendency has been to not read it as nuanced or parodic because Miller's political beliefs have become more stereotypically conservative (seen in his comments on the Middle East ["Writers"] and the Occupy movement [Miller, "Anarchy"]) as have his aesthetics (seen in the self-described propaganda of Holy Terror).

However, it's difficult to accept Miller's statements that limit *Sin City* as a sophisticated, multi-layered work; even if only developed by Miller at an intuitive or unconscious level, there are portions of *Sin City* that clearly employ, reinterpret, and undermine comic book conventions in fundamental ways. One of the most famous sequences in the text is structured around one of its shocking violations: killing a priest and using religious language to describe the act. After revealing that Cardinal Rourke is connected to Goldie's murder, the priest asks whether "that corpse of a slut is worth dying for." Marv responds with continued narration for his own story: "Worth dying for. Worth killing for. Worth going to hell for. Amen" (Miller, *Sin City* 67–68). In this full-page design, the first three sentence fragments are respectively associated with the silhouette of Marv's gun, of the priest shot in the head, and of the cross atop the church. The three panels are shaped by the sound of his gun fired three times (BLAM, BLAM, BLAM), with the interior of the letters filled with the above-described images. In "BLAM! The Literal Architecture of *Sin City*," Luke Arnott has argued that, while Miller may have shown little interest in the implications of this complex design, it nevertheless interrogates the relationship between image and perceived sound created by the use of words intended to convey sounds other than speech.

Regardless of Miller's own opinions, Arnott identifies it as a bold experiment that challenges the fundamental grammar of comics, which usually makes space for sound effects rather than using sound effects (in this case, a sound emblematically associated with a weapon) as the space itself to be occupied. While this discussion of subverting form as it depicts violence doesn't refute criticisms of *Sin City* as a derivative, sexist power fantasy, it does suggest that Miller, in his attempt to undermine more complex readings of his work, might not be the best source to settle this dispute.

Sin City would by subtitled *The Hard Goodbye* in the 1993 trade paperback, when it was clear that Miller would revisit Basin City in other story arcs (in limited series and self-contained graphic novels). As he did so, his narrative and visual style would evolve over that time, but for reasons similar to ones just mentioned, it might not be fair to judge the initial installment too much by the subsequent ones (anymore than it would be to judge it by the film adaptation, co-directed by Miller, that redefined the use of green screen technology and knowingly explored artificial/hyper-real presentation in film). Regardless, as both a moment in time and a continuing influence, *Sin City: The Hard Goodbye* is significant to the history of comic books, especially the history of American comic books. It marks a new era of extremely popular crime comics in the United States and thereby marks the return of the repressed in American culture. It synthesizes mainstream comics culture with previously prohibited content that had only been seen in the US with the underground Comix movement. It serves as a prominent example of a creator's popularity, enabling not the conglomerate, but the individual with the long-held hope for creator rights (made part of the business model by upstart publishers). It demonstrates approaches to comic art connected to international styles seen in the samurai comics of the manga tradition and the science fiction comics of the Franco-Belgian tradition.

However, the ironies of this work are that it thoroughly inaugurates the graphic novel despite being serialized in a nearly obsolete anthology format; it is hailed as self-conscious art, while being derided as a gratuitously violent and sexist celebration of the male preoccupations that had long dominated the American market; and it realizes the desire of Miller's early career to have comics books legitimately recognized as an art form, just as Miller turns a corner that would make him see embracing the pulp origins of comic books a important political act. In a conversation with Will Eisner, Miller would state, "I think we are in a young and vital form that has a rather dangerous outlaw aspect to it, and that's one of the things I love about it" (Brownstein 162). With *Sin City*, Miller makes a concerted choice to evoke a time and format, wherein the comic was less respectable, not only telling stories of outlaws, but also celebrating the outlaw nature of the medium. Despite—or perhaps due to—its gratuitous, possibly stereotypical presentation of sex and violence, *Sin City: The Hard Goodbye* refuses to be co-opted as a graphic novel by the culture at large and maintains its identity as a critical voice by positioning itself between the mainstream and the margin.

Works Cited

Arnott, Luke. "BLAM! The Literal Architecture of Sin City." *International Journal of Comic Art*. 10.2 (2008): 380–401.

Benton, Mike. *Crime Comics: The Illustrated History*. Dallas: Taylor Publishing, 1993.

Bissette, Stephen R. and Stanley Wiater. *Comic Book Rebels: Conversations with the Creators of the New Comics*. New York: Plume, 1993.

Brownstein, Charles. *Eisner/Miller*. Milwaukie, OR: Dark Horse, 2005.

Duncan, Randy and Matthew J. Smith. *The Power of Comics: History, Form, and Culture*. New York: Bloomsbury Academic, 2009.

George, Milo. Frank Miller: The Comics Journal Library. Vol. 2. Seattle: Fantagraphics, 2003.

Harvey, R.C. *The Art of the Comic Book: An Aesthetic History*. Jackson: UP of Mississippi, 1996.

_____. Introduction. *The Art of Sin City*. By Frank Miller. Milwaukie, OR: Dark Horse, 2002. 1–4.

Honest Publishing. "The Honest Alan Moore Interview—Part 2: The Occupy Movement, Frank Miller, and Politics." Honestpublishing. com. 3 Dec. 2011. Web. 11 Sep. 2013.

McCloud, Scott. *Reinventing Comics*. New York: Harper Collins, 2000.

Miller, Frank. "Anarchy." *Frank Miller Homepage*. 7 Nov. 2011. Web. 10 Dec. 2011.

_____. *The Dark Knight Returns*. New York: DC Comics. 1996.

_____. *Give Me Liberty*. Milwaukie, OR: Dark Horse. 1992.

_____. *Hard Boiled*. Milwaukie, OR: Dark Horse. 1993.

_____. *Holy Terror*. Burbank: Legendary, 2011.

_____. *Ronin*. New York: DC Comics. 1995.

_____. "Roulette." *Daredevil: Visionaries 3*. New York: Marvel Comics, 2001. 199–221.

_____. *Sin City*. Milwaukie, OR: Dark Horse. 1993.

_____. *Sin City: A Dame to Kill For*. Milwaukie, OR: Dark Horse. 1995.

Mitchell, Elvis. "Frank Miller." *The Treatment*. KCRW, Santa Monica. Radio. 30 Mar. 2005. Radio.

Phegley, Kiel. "Ed Brubaker: Crime, Superheroes, and Comic Book History."
Publishers Weekly. 15 Sep. 2009. Web. 15 Aug. 2013.

Pizzino, Christopher. "Art that Goes BOOM: Genre and Aesthetics in Frank Miller's Sin City." English Language Notes. 46.2 (2008): 115–128.

Spike TV's Scream Awards. SPIKE TV. 10 Oct. 2006. Television.

Wright, Bradford W. *Comic Book Nation: The Transformation of Youth Culture in*
America. Baltimore: Johns Hopkins UP, 2001.

"Writers, Artists Describe the State of the Union." *Talk of the Nation*. National Public Radio. 24 Jan. 2007. Radio.

Max Allan Collins' *Road to Perdition*_____

Jared Griffin

In *Reading Comics: How Graphic Novels Work and What They Mean*, Douglas Wolk argues that the "superhero genre . . . [is] an ideal framework for discussing the complexities of morality and ethics" (99). The postmodern comic form, specifically in its correlation to the superhero narrative context, Wolk claims, presents a new challenge to the nearly religious demarcation of "good guy vs. bad guy" in modern literature, where the "good guy" is consistently virtuous and the "bad guy" is inevitably evil. Wolk points to Alan Moore's seminal *Watchmen* as the initiation of this discussion, where such moral complexity in heroes and such challenges to public narrative codes stand in high relief. Max Allan Collins's *Road to Perdition* maintains this comic innovation in vivid visual detail, character gravitas, and thematic weight. As Wolk declares that the comic form has "grown up" (3) to confront typical definitions of morality and heroism, so too does *Road to Perdition*, which tells the story of a young boy "growing up" to tackle a similar dissonance: that the (myth)ological male American (super)hero is a complicated and contradictory figure, underscored by an, at times ironic, reliance on a religious sense of violence.

At first glance, *Road to Perdition* does not seem like a typical superhero story, especially in the sense to which Wolk refers. *Road to Perdition* does not have a protagonist who can fly, shoot lasers out of his eyes, or bear the weight of a supernatural origin story (though his background is foggy, which lends itself to spectacular mythmaking by others). Instead, our "hero," the elder Michael O'Sullivan, is initially granted the mythos of superhumanness by the narrator, his son, who shares his father's name, and by other characters and true crime writers. While an understated agreement exists among these observers about the elder O'Sullivan's capabilities, superhumanness is still in the eye of the beholder: the younger Michael imagines his father as an incarnation of Tom Mix (a popular paperback cowboy, who influenced John Wayne), with the requisite super-abilities to dodge bullets, speedily react to threats, and sense danger around a corner; Michael's enemies take the myth further and grant him a supernatural moniker—the Archangel of Death. Historians, too, take pleasure in embellishing acts of violence and heroism, a practice that the younger Michael-as-adult is not too fond of, for his view of his father changes from myth to human, from superhero to vulnerable man. Younger Michael even warns his audience in the first frame about this mythmaking through unreliable memory (17); despite the story being written in black-and-white, there is plenty of gray in this story.

The younger Michael's journey through his memories (his road) is as much about his own survival as it is about the survival (and death) of the super-human image of his father; his journey to the realization that his father is, indeed, real. That realization seems to encapsulate what many male coming-of-age stories, such as this, are primarily about: a young boy seeing the "real world" through the eyes and experience, through the legacy and weight, of his father. Making their contribution to this genre, Collins and artist Richard Piers Rayner attempt to capture this spiritual, existential, and physical verisimilitude of the father/son relationship through the O'Sullivan boys. Readers journey along with the younger Michael, experiencing this slow-growing epiphany with him; the elder O'Sullivan gradually becomes more real, not only to the younger Michael, but also to readers. One way the artist accomplishes this is through the iconography of characters' faces and details, which makes them more unique, real, and complicated, and thus more contextualized within the novel's coming-of-age genre and thematic conditions. In many ways, the artistic detail of characters' faces begins to reflect the "gray" nature of morality and ethics within the novel's universe, especially as the details reflect the historical uniqueness of the characters (consider Scott McCloud's discussion of details in comic form). This storied universe, with its generic and thematic contexts, is informed quite heavily by the relationship of violence to spirituality and masculinity in American narratives. A coming-of-age story does not occur in a vacuum, after all. This essay will thus attempt to understand the moral complexities of *Road to Perdition* by synthesizing its many circumstances—for instance, the generic framework, the dynamism of the O'Sullivan characters, the spiritual thematic perspective—within a violent American context.

American Violence

The frames of *Road to Perdition* are filled with graphically violent imagery. While some graphic novels do exist to titillate an audience through such imagery, the violence of *Road to Perdition* is no mistake or marketing ploy. Some caveats should be added to Collins's and Rayner's visualization of violence. The first is that violence itself is a theme and provides much of the framework for the younger Michael's coming-of-age epiphany. Second, Collins uses violence to comment on the nature of memory and mythmaking. Much of the dramatization of violence was created (or inferred) by true crime writers, and perhaps never "really" happened. Collins uses that device to show that that kind of narrative (un)reliability is, essentially, irrelevant as fact, but important in understanding how different text-makers contribute to mythmaking. What is important for Collins is to demonstrate the development of the younger Michael as he tries to figure out who his father is. Third, a responsible analysis of *Road to Perdition* must consider its cultural context (that is, the cultural environment in which it is set and in which it is written), a context burdened with violence.

The world that the O'Sullivans (the world of Collins and Rayner, as postmodern text-makers) inhabit is a world subsumed by a religious dedication to violence, a dedication to violence so intricately tied together with religious ideology, that it is difficult to imagine them separate. This is not a unique world, but one that accompanies the American conception of "America as a wide-open land of unlimited opportunity for the strong, ambitious, self-reliant individual to thrust his way to the top" (Slotkin 5). This perseverance for self-actualization in America carries with it a penchant for violence, as individuality is of the highest regard. Richard Slotkin, in *Regeneration Through Violence*, calls this American impulse "regeneration," the idea that whoever you are, you can leave the burden of society behind and re-create yourself in America. Slotkin observes that "the means to that regeneration ultimately became a means of violence, and the myth of regeneration through violence became the structuring metaphor of the American experience" (5). We can see this in the process of the O'Sullivan boys escaping the corrupt world of the Tri-Cities and Chicago, which could only come through violent action.

Forgiveness was out of the question for the father, so whatever redemption, or justice, or regeneration they were looking for, whatever safe place they sought, will always be influenced by violence. And this regenerative process is spiritual in nature, too, as it pit early American Christians against those, whom they saw as pagan natives, in the Christian quest to regenerate their community in the image of John Winthrop's eminent "city on a hill." As Stephen Stein postulates, this "religious apocalypticism . . . involves in some fashion the quest for salvation, righteousness or wisdom" (211). The narrative of *Road to Perdition* is infused with this pretext.

Readers are confronted with that religious sense of violence in the first chapter title: "Archangel of Death." Immediately visible are: first, the complexities that the comic form can discuss, which Wolk observed and, second, the American reliance on the myth of religion and violence, extrapolated by Slotkin. This is a relationship that the O'Sullivans thematically try to negotiate: their ideology proclaims that they should not kill, yet they do out of a sense of honor and justice; the elder Michael's violent quests lead to the killing of innocents, despite church teachings; while confession makes them feel better, the O'Sullivans are still plagued by the consequences of sin. The consequences of their sins are where the road that the title speaks of leads to—perdition; it is a title, in which we can continue to sense that moral tension. As with many texts, the title is indicative of an influential narrative theme, and in the case of *Road to Perdition*, we are presented with two themes that, combined, create the sense that the O'Sullivans are victims of the myth of American regeneration, that their physically violent journey is also a religious journey that creates more questions about the roles of violence and spirituality in a male coming-of-age story than it answers.

The Road

The idea of the "road" in narrative fiction is a popular theme many writers use to frame their characters' development, perhaps to the point of being cliché. Likely, many readers will see the word "road" and draw synonyms of "street," of a thoroughfare that guides someone from one place to another. Looking at the etymology of the word "road," though, gleans nuanced understanding of the theme. "Road" is an Old English word, dating as far back as the mid-fifth century. Derived from the Germanic *rad* (pronounced "rawd"), the word "road" originally meant a journey on horseback (we also get the word "ride" from the same Germanic root), or "hostile incursion." The sense that "road" means "street" did not exist until Middle English, around the 1590s. But taking into account the original denotation of "road," we can understand that the context is already violent; the very word "road" carries with it a violent context: in the novel, the O'Sullivans are sure to encounter "hostile incursions" on this figurative (and literal) road. Granted, what journey would be worth reading if it did not have some sort of violence, that is, hostility or complication? And perhaps that is why we are so fond of the word "road" when we talk about journey (instead of "street," "avenue," or "boulevard")—because the word itself is rife with progressive conflict.

With its violent connotation, "road" implies two other readings: a physical journey that incurs violence, and an existential or spiritual one that also invites violence. Speaking about this dual-nature of violence, Norman Mailer noted that, when one is confronted with violence:

> The first reaction, the heart of the violence, is the protection of the self. The second question [is] the moral question. . . . [M]en who are otherwise serious but ready for personal violence, are almost always religious. They have a deep sense of dread, responsibility, of woe, of reluctance to make an error in violence and a grim, almost tragic sense of how far violence can carry them (29).

As a frame for the O'Sullivans' story, then, the road comprises two paths: a physically violent road and spiritual/existential road, that is, a road that challenges the body and a road that challenges one's identity and ideology.

These two visions of the "road" are mirrored in the elder and younger Michaels. The elder O'Sullivan is a relatively static character, and his road as the more literal road, the road to a place called Perdition, Kansas, where his family will be safe. His hope (his promise of regeneration) lies in the place called Perdition, and the way is paved with violence. Just as a physical road is generally unmovable and rigid, so is the elder O'Sullivan, who is static in his convictions and quest; he does not change along this road, which is dedicated to physical retribution and carnal justice. The younger Michael hints at his father's stationary mental state when describing the scene at the Lexington Hotel: "Why did he . . . go out into inevitable carnage?" (Collins 151). The elder Michael fulfills his tragic, inevitable destiny with no major change in his character, no real reflection on violence, except in his (unheard) confessions to priests.

His fixedness is also reflected dramatically in his nickname: Archangel of Death. This is a title that he assuredly fulfills; he does not question it, at least from the narrator's perspective. Instead, all we see is action, of the father walking and driving down this road (even as we witness him teaching his son to literally drive). The elder Michael is acting in a world, in a society, that needs him to act that way. This core, static element of Michael's identity is reinforced through his actions, but that doesn't seem to affect how he is visually manifested by Rayner. Noticing how Rayner's illustrations of Michael shift, one may suspect that the artist was never sure how he wanted to portray Michael. However, taking into account the context of the unreliable and contradictory nature of personal memory (Collins 17), of photographic evidence (22), of the cultural mythologizing (48), and academic (or popular) historicizing (301), we can begin to understand how different people and readers see and read others differently, especially when focused on their deeds and motivations, and not given much insight into their thought processes, emotional states, and spiritual and identity crises. In many panels that feature his profile, O'Sullivan's face matches Dick Tracy's (184, 232) with the prominent Roman nose and chiseled chin. In others, he resembles Kevin Costner (146), Kirk Douglas (127), and panels near the end illustrate him as Al Pacino (241), Eric Roberts (243), and, ironically, Paul Newman (265).

The younger Michael says that he relies on other accounts to picture his father, and the varying illustrations underscore that ambiguity in a narrative point of view. To what extent is the younger Michael's and other historians' accounts of this figure reliable? It probably doesn't matter. What matters is that readers are given insight into how these perspectives affect one character and, from our own readerly reflection, how they affect us. What readers see is a man of action who follows through in body and (as far as we know) soul on his unquestioned ideals. Unlike his physical representation in the novel, though, the elder O'Sullivan's name and legacy is unquestioned, except by his son. No one denies that he is the Archangel of Death; in fact, they respect it. So he walks his road with assurance and conviction, knowing how it will end. Whatever moral questions he asked about his work and his ideals, he answered long ago, outside the comic panel and scope of this narrative. He is unchanging and decisive, an Old Testament deity, which makes his providential lust for justice via carnage that much more unsettling and confusing for his son.

The son's "road" is designated by its spiritual temperament, reflected in his character's dynamic nature. The younger Michael's dynamism leads us to classify his story as a *Bildungsroman*. R.B. Kershner explains that the *Bildungsroman* is a "novel of formation" (110), a novel about a young person being formed into an adult; a coming-of-age story. "Bildung" is a German word meaning "formation" or "growth," and "roman" is the term for what we now refer to as the "novel," which is "predominately concerned with the situation of a protagonist in society" (110). We may see *Road to Perdition* as a story that explores how the younger Michael becomes disillusioned to some extent with the society that his father has come to represent. Readers can sense the beginning of this change in Michael's character as he releases a balloon after he hears the gunfire that signals the death of his mother and brother, Peter (69). As a symbol of Michael's childhood naivety about his father's world, which is very much his own world, the balloon flies away, thereby initiating Michael's journey as a *Bildungsroman* protagonist. And readers might get the sense that he didn't let go of his balloon willingly; it was shaken, startled, perhaps even forced out his hand. The harmony and joy he once felt in his family (in the small society built by his father) is now in disharmony, which leads to a crisis that is never truly resolved.

In the visual representation of the younger Michael alone, Rayner's artistry points to that crisis. Consider the sketch of the younger Michael as he waits outside of Rance's office. He's shadowed, his face angled down, eyes peering up (reminiscent of Jack Nicholson as Jack Torrence in *The Shining*), holding a gun near his jaw (183). He looks much older in this panel than he does in previous ones: his bangs swoop down over his narrowed eyes, and his face appears longer, punctuated by a square chin. Compare this perspective to the full-frame illustrations of the younger Michael before and after the shooting, which feature the boy with shorter hair and a rounder chin (173 and 186). In fact, the representation of Michael after he shoots a man attacking his father is startling because his whole persona is childlike (186). A play on point of view and characterization occurs here: a picture of how Michael sees himself, beginning to grow up and protect his family (183), complicated by how his father sees him, still a child (186). The younger Michael negotiates his identity in the shadow of a myth. That clash of point of view is the heart of the tension between father and son in a *Bildungsroman* narrative. This tension is not about control (as in many parent-versus-child narratives); the tension is about reality-versus-myth and, according to Franco Moretti, "happiness" (or harmony, in this case) versus "freedom" (557–58).

As the reality of his father's world becomes more apparent, the younger Michael nonetheless retains great respect for and loyalty to his family. He heeds his father's advice about seeking help on the literal road and extends that direction to his spiritual life. The elder

O'Sullivan instructs his son, "If I'm not back in half an hour, go . . . . [t]o the first church you see in the first town that isn't Chicago" (122). Michael does just that much later in the narrative, making a decision to be free of the cycle of violence (by breaking the American regeneration myth) and becoming a priest. So while he does not follow in his father's footsteps as a literal soldier, he does become, what the novel alludes to earlier, a "Christian soldier," by obeying his father's command to seek out a non-corrupted church. This road to perdition is the younger Michael's journey toward ordering his own values, just as his father ordered his (44), and it allows him to remain in the business of judgment, as his father was, but of a different kind of judgment: instead of punishment, he deals in absolution.

Michael's father placed his highest value on his "nuclear" family, and it does, at least initially, seem ironic that the younger Michael chose the priesthood, a vocation that bars priests from creating a family like that. Michael substitutes the nuclear family (filiation) for a larger, corporate family (affiliation), so the idea of family seems to be a more existential decision and point of growth for Michael. In this decision is the fulfillment of the Kazuo Koike epigraph to "choose a road for yourself." Michael imagines his father making a different choice: the elevator operator in the Lexington Hotel asks the elder Michael, "Going . . . down?" as Michael points a gun in his face. He does not merely choose his fate, his descent into perdition, but also demands it. The novel seems to argue that in this world, the road to perdition is relentless; the road out of perdition, however, is the existential one (190).

Perdition

The second half of the title bears as much gravity as the first half. Similar to "road," "perdition" has both a literal meaning in the narrative context—that of Perdition, Kansas, a place invented for the book—and a spiritual one, meaning hell or punishment in Christian theology. After the fourteenth century, notably after the publication of Dante's *Divine Comedy* (which includes an infamous volume on hell called *Inferno*), the word "perdition" began to connote severe, sustained judgment on one's soul. Before perdition's appropriation by Catholic theologians, "perdition" referred to a more general sense of ruin and destruction. The original usage of "perdition" connoted the destructive elements of, say, an apocalyptic event; only later did the term come to refer to the punishment of an individual's soul as a consequence of sin. In both a Christian and pre-Christian soteriological understanding of the word "perdition," the unifying theme is that of apocalyptic entropy: that something is being destroyed, and in its destruction, it is being (or becoming) fallen and lost. The idea or threat of perdition-as-apocalypse is conflated with violent imagery in *Road to Perdition*, and contextualizes Michael's spiritual journey as a *Bildungsroman* figure.

The O'Sullivans' Christian spirituality and its rudimentary apocalypticism reflects their relative dynamism. Collins first introduces the O'Sullivan family in a photograph, placed in front of a church (one of those historical documents Michael employs to sketch an impression of his father). The O'Sullivan family members pose for a photographer, with only the younger Michael smiling, an indication of his assumptions about the world. The "photograph" is coupled with the younger Michael's voice describing his father as "honorable" and a "family man" (22). Placing the family by this church, the younger Michael creates a frame through which to understand his father and the entire narrative. His father, like the church in the background and its connotation to the younger Michael-turned-priest, values honor and family.

At this point in the story's chronology, this church is probably one corrupted by the Looney family, which further reinforces the younger Michael's naivety and the elder Michael's loyalty to the Looney family—two virtues that will be challenged. The cross in the upper right corner of that panel accents the picture, automatically carrying religious (and literary) ideas of sacrifice and judgment. In a way, this is the younger Michael's rebuttal against the true crime writers who seem to have used historical data to mythologize the elder O'Sullivan as a violent renegade, when Michael has a piece of history himself—this photograph—to justify the humanity behind his father's decisions. Additionally, this frame is made whole at the end of the story (the church itself is redeemed) when readers discover that the younger Michael has chosen a life of service as a priest, as a *father*, no less (302). It's no mistake that the first and final visuals we see of Michael are at church: first on the outside (representing his superficial understanding of the world), then within the innermost sanctum, the confessional booth (representing his knowledge and acceptance of a particularly ordered society).

The religious life proves to be a point of contention between father and son, a point of ambiguity for the younger Michael, as he learns the ways of his father's world. He struggles to ease the cognitive dissonance he feels as his loyalties are divided by his father's actions. Are the commandments "thou shalt not kill" and "honor thy father and mother" mutually exclusive, Michael frets. What's more important: loyalty to one's family or loyalty to one's god? And what happens to someone's identity when loyalties such as these collide? Divided loyalties and disorder seem to be one of the consternating definitions of perdition, that something is broken and disordered when virtue does not even make sense anymore. As the elder Michael explains, "We're all sinners, son. That's the way we enter this world, but we can leave it forgiven" (190). In what is probably the most important statement in the book about this theme, the elder O'Sullivan's theologizing here encapsulates the traumatic spirit of this perdition road—that the world is messed up—and becomes a moment of enlightenment for the younger Michael. In the previous panels, Michael describes this hellish road with vivid sensory details: "It was hell. And I'll never forget the smell of it— gunpowder, blood, urine, excrement . . ." (188). He is knee-deep in sin, and he realizes the weight of that knowledge, just as Adam and Even did in the Garden of Eden.

But perhaps redemption can be found. After experiencing "hell," the younger Michael receives a gentle kiss on the cheek from his father and notes that he'll "never forget the tenderness of how Papa carried [him]," adding: "When I was much smaller, he'd carried me up the stairs and to bed like this" (188). They find a Catholic church in a little town, and here's the first moment the younger Michael is seen in the confessional booth, after which he claims he "felt better"

(192). The dynamism of Michael's character stands out more from his father's static character here: the commissions and confession of sin actually serve to change the younger Michael, to encourage his choice to go down a markedly different (in some ways, but as I mentioned earlier, perhaps not all that entirely different) road, as one who understands the road to perdition to help others traveling that same road, to help other archangels. Instead of committing statically to one particular road (as Koiko suggests) Michael decides to choose a road that combines both of those loyalties (to life and to family); his solution is order-in-synthesis.

While this character association with perdition seems somewhat simplistic, the book presents another complex picture of spirituality and perdition-as-apocalypse. The montages of violence, for instance, implicate the religious context in a more ambiguous way. In chapter one, as the elder O'Sullivan is delivering a message (of forgiveness through violence—an indication of Looney's disordered value system), the scene erupts into carnage. Contrasting the action inside Lococo's office with the outside, Collins creates a scene that conflates Mailer's sense of religious violence with actual religious content using a rendition of "Oh When the Saints Go Marching In." The song is typically performed with an upbeat, jazz cadence, reminiscent of a victory march for the souls of Christians proceeding through the heavenly gates after judgment, of the saintly spirits who escaped (or avoided) perdition. The irony is that the people Michael kills are not really saints. They are judged and punished for their wickedness (at least in the elder O'Sullivan's point of view). Michael, as a heavenly/earthly archangel, the instrument of God's justice, commits brutal acts of violence against the backdrop of this light-hearted, joyous musical number. No one is a saint in this scene.

In the same sense that a road is simultaneously a place and a state of being, so is Perdition/perdition. In the consideration of theme and characterization, the road to perdition carries additional meaning in the context of the novel's setting. Perdition as a physical place (at least in the world of the novel) and perdition as the spiritual state of being punished for one's sins, carries over to the idea of perdition signifying American tensions between urban and rural settings.

As much of Michael's exposition explains, Collins establishes the primary setting of the novel in 1930 Tri-Cities metropolitan area, about 200 miles west of Chicago. Michael characterizes these places to further establish the themes of violence and perdition: he notes the unemployment and industrialization of the agricultural lifestyle; the mob's money-grabbing through bootlegging, prostitution, gambling, and blackmail; and, of course, the military industrial complex, manufacturing guns and tanks for the arsenal. Even the church is defiled (83) and the concept of forgiveness is tainted (147). The setting is infused with a dirty violence. Michael even notes that he cannot remember summertime, that is was "always winter . . . snow and sludge and sleet mixed with dirt and cinders" (17).

The opening panels are packed with urban imagery—people, buildings, cars—and the skies are essentially blank. No clouds or sun accent the sky or horizon. The panels showing the skies over Davenport across the Mississippi River (18) and over the *Quinlan* (20) are overwhelmingly white, with only the smog of the factories smudging the glaring white-scape. The first natural or pastoral setting readers are introduced to is the exterior of the O'Sullivan house in Rock Island, which includes sky, trees, grass, and bushes; it is a place set apart from city life, a place where Michael and Peter can play outside in peace. The corruption that defines the city (likely because of its alliance with the über-sinful Chicago) does not exist here. When the elder O'Sullivan exacts justice (i.e. commits his sin), he is always in the city or in city-related places, such as hotels or banks. When the gangsters, who represent a disordered society, commit violence, they attack homes and farms.

The inciting event, the first major "turn" in the narrative, occurs when these two settings collide as Michael sneaks away with his father to the city. Because of that act, these two worlds—the cityscape and the domestic household—are now intertwined; what happens in one must now affect the other. Now that the younger Michael has surreptitiously invaded the city-world, Conner Looney, the devil that he is, is allowed to invade the domestic site. The elder Michael attempts to preserve that domestic value: he places his dead wife and son in bed and bids them good night even though he tells his son that this is not their "home anymore—just an empty structure" (78–79). That sanctuary he tries to create for his family is too fragile. His instinct, then, is to flee the city (and/or civilization and society) in times of trouble and tragedy to a pastoral site because that order has broken down (115), a common American trope: consider Nick Carraway in *The Great Gatsby* and Henry and Catherine in *A Farewell to Arms*. In characteristically American fashion, the O'Sullivans try to escape to a farm in Kansas, far from the Tri-Cities and Chicago, to a natural, pastoral setting that has avoided the disorder and corruption of the modern-day Zenith.

Wolk's assessment of the comic form to discuss the moral ambiguity of American heroism is most adept. On one hand "perdition" in *Road to Perdition* represents the American ideal of redemption in nature, of a hero's quest to escape the sinful city; and on the other, it represents the inescapable violence that accompanies such regeneration. This ambiguity is extended to the character of the elder Michael O'Sullivan, as he attempts to redeem his son by rescuing him from perdition (the 'to Perdition' in the title), yet simultaneously, he represents the violence and judgment (as the Archangel of Death) that makes such redemption necessary in the first place. He is both his son's redeemer and persecutor, the bane of most male *Bildungsroman* characters. Such violent soteriology is a staple of the American *Bildungsroman* experience.

Works Cited

Collins, Max Allan. *Road to Perdition*. New York: Pocket, 2002.

Kershner, R.B. *The Twentieth-Century Novel: An Introduction*. Boston: Bedford, 1997.

Mailer, Norman. "W.J. Weatherby: Talking of Violence." *Pontifications*. Boston: Little, Brown, 1982. 28–31.

McCloud, Scott. *Understanding Comics: The Invisible Art*. Northampton, MA: Tundra, 1993.

Moretti, Franco. "The Way of the World: The *Bildungsroman* in European Culture." 1987. *Theory of the Novel*. Ed. Michael McKeon. Baltimore: Johns Hopkins UP, 2000. 524–65.

Slotkin, Richard. *Regeneration Through Violence: The Mythology of the American Frontier, 1600–1860.* Middletown, CT: Wesleyan UP, 1973.

Stein, Stephen J. "American Millennial Visions: Towards Construction of a New Architectonic of American Apocalypticism." *Imagining the End: Visions of Apocalypse from the Ancient Middle East to Modern America.* Eds. Abbas Amanat and Magnus Berhnhardsson. New York: I.B. Tauris, 2002. 187–211.

Wolk, Douglas. *Reading Comics: How Graphic Novels Work and What They Mean.* New York: DeCapo, 2008.

Marjane Satrapi's *Persepolis*_____

Adam Capitanio

Marjane Satrapi's *Persepolis: The Story of a Childhood* was originally published in a two-volume French edition in 2000 and 2001, with an English-language translation appearing in 2003. The English-language follow-up, *Persepolis: The Story of a Return,* was published in 2004. In its entirety, *Persepolis* is an autobiographical graphic novel, telling the story of Satrapi's childhood and maturation from age ten to twenty-four.

A native Iranian, Satrapi grew up during her country's revolution and subsequent war with Iraq, both of which form the backdrop of *Persepolis*. Coming from a liberal, Westernized family, Satrapi grows from a precocious child into a combative and thoughtful teenager, outspoken against the daily indignities she suffers as a young woman in a fundamentalist Islamic society. Fearing for their opinionated daughter's safety, Satrapi's parents send her to Europe, where *Persepolis* ends. No longer a child, Satrapi's experiences in Europe are recounted in the sequel.

Persepolis was highly regarded when it was published and is one of the few graphic novels with massive acclaim to reach a mainstream audience. Appearing at the same cultural moment as the 9/11 terrorist attacks, *Persepolis* provided a new perspective on Iranian society at a moment when Middle Eastern, Islamic cultures were the subject of increased international concern, and a moment when Iran positioned itself as the major geopolitical power in the region. Ultimately, *Persepolis* remains significant for its ability to powerfully render the experience of growing up and discovering oneself amidst historically significant events and within a rapidly changing cultural environment.

Historical Background
The major historical context that readers need to understand *Persepolis* fully is the Iranian Revolution and the subsequent war

between Iran and Iraq. Although Satrapi explains some of this background in *Persepolis* itself, it is worth reiterating some of the major events.

The seeds of the Iranian Revolution were sown during the course of the twentieth century, which saw Iran—formerly Persia— vacillate between its religious and cultural traditions as a wave of modernization swept through Middle Eastern societies. That wave brought with it meddling and manipulation by Western powers, such as the United States and United Kingdom.

During the early part of the twentieth century, Great Britain took an interest in Iranian politics and economics after the discovery of massive oil reserves in the country. They supported, somewhat begrudgingly at times, the military coup of army officer Reza Khan in 1921. Over the course of the 1920s and 30s, Khan put into place a number of secularizing and modernizing reforms, which continued when his son, Reza Pahlavi, was crowned in 1941. Pahlavi was not particularly popular with either religious conservatives or leftists, and an uprising in 1953 installed Mohammed Mossadeq as prime minister (Murphy 702).

Mossadeq was not in power for long, however. A CIA-backed coup removed Mossadeq from power and reinstalled Pahlavi, poisoning the relationship between the Iranian people and the United States for decades to come (702). After the Shah returned to power, he began the so-called "White Revolution," which sought to rapidly modernize and transform Iranian society, using oil revenues as funding. The White Revolution angered religious leaders, as its secular programs threatened their power base. At the same time, the Shah's intolerance for dissent and political organizing turned intellectuals and leftists against him as well (Felton 380).

Protests against the Shah began in 1976, but did not swell into a mass movement until 1978. They eventually grew so large and widespread the Shah and his wife were forced to flee the country. Into the power vacuum stepped Ayatollah Ruhollah Khomeini, a popular religious leader and symbol, for religious conservatives, of the resistance against the Shah. Khomeini established an Islamic theocracy that reversed many of the civil rights the people had gained, betraying the secular and leftist parts of Iranian society that had worked with the Islamists to overthrow the Shah (381).

Just as the Islamist government began to consolidate power, Iraq, Iran's neighbor to the West, attacked. The Iraqi dictator Saddam Hussein was hoping to seize valuable oil fields during the disorganization that followed the Revolution, and to gain a measure of revenge against the Iranian government, which encouraged Iraq's Shia Muslims to revolt against him (Lorentz 134-135). The war lasted from 1980 until 1988, with neither side willing to capitulate to the other, despite both suffering heavy casualties. The new Iranian government, however, was able to use the war to consolidate its power by rallying the people against a clear enemy. *Persepolis* ends with the war still raging, and Marjane sent away because her outspokenness is particularly dangerous during a jingoistic period.

Storyline and Narration

Persepolis opens "in media res," with a portrait of Marjane ("Marji" to her parents and friends) wearing her headscarf after the Islamic Revolution in Iran. The next panel shows Marji's classmates, all seated in a row and similarly bedecked. Satrapi opens the graphic novel this way to give a clear message about its thematic content: the focus is on the impact of the Islamic Revolution on regular individuals, in particular women and children. Satrapi's experiences are especially relevant in this context, as she was developing into a young woman at the time of the revolution and the subsequent Iran-Iraq War. The comparison between the two panels introduces another theme important to *Persepolis*, that of the tension between individuality and imposed collectivism. While the first panel shows Marji by herself, the second shows her four classmates, and the artwork and framing reveals how veiling made the girls barely distinguishable from one another.

After introducing the effect of the Revolution through women's protests against headscarves, Satrapi returns to her young childhood, and the entirety of *Persepolis* proceeds chronologically from there. The narrative extends from Marjane's birth to the age of fourteen, when her parents send her to live in Europe. It does, however, concentrate heavily on the years 1979-1984, as Marji transitions from childhood to young adulthood, and the Iranian Revolution solidifies into the Islamic theocracy that still rules the country today.

Although the basic narrative trajectory of the graphic novel is straightforward, it unfolds in an episodic format, with each episode bearing a distinct title, theme, and brief narrative event or connected series of events. In other words, each episode of the graphic novel could stand on its own. When reading *Persepolis,* the episodes can be interpreted as distinct texts, or, compared to the larger themes of the entire work, as a particular iteration.

The narration comes from Satrapi's own voice and serves a number of simultaneous functions. First, it serves simply to explain events depicted in an individual panel and to create narrative momentum from one incident to the next. The narration is first person in the typical literary past tense. Second, it also serves to motivate and smooth over transitions and leaps that Satrapi makes between past and present, reality and imagination, and personal experience and historical events.

The first chapter, "The Veil," demonstrates how the narration shifts between these different registers. The first events of the graphic novel, the protests against the veil, shift to a discussion of Marji's very early childhood, and her youthful desire to become a prophet. In one transitional panel, showing a frontal view of Marji divided between the signs of science and modernity (gears, tools) and those of religion and tradition (curved Islamic design, the chādor), she says "I really didn't know what to think about the veil. Deep down I was very religious but as a family we were very modern and avant-garde" (6). Both the art and the narration work in concert to move the reader from the present experience of protest against the veil to Marji's memories of her childhood and significant religious feelings and fantasies. It explains her feelings about the events in her life, while simultaneously smoothing over the temporal transition between the protests and her youth. As the subjective, imaginary panel dividing her between modernity and tradition shows, however, the artwork also plays an important role in understanding the ideas Satrapi pursues.

Artwork

The art in *Persepolis* occupies a midpoint between naturalism and abstraction. Characters are rendered in a way that differentiates them and makes them recognizable, but there is a clear "cartoonish" style. Satrapi's art uses clean lines and shapes, with simple, contrasting lines to create a sense of depth or shadow. *Persepolis* is entirely in black-and-white; there is absolutely no color, nor are there any shades of gray, contributing to the heavy contrast in the art. Many panels do not have extensive backgrounds, depicting the characters against a flat black or white block.

When asked why she decided to write *Persepolis* as a graphic novel, Satrapi defended her artwork and the notion of a graphic novel itself: "Image is an international language…You cannot draw someone crying, and in one culture they think that he is happy" (Satrapi). Aside from its universal quality, Satrapi argues that her iconic, cartoonish images make *Persepolis* "more accessible. People don't take it so seriously." This "lack of seriousness" enables her to incorporate humor in narrating the tragic circumstances of her childhood. As the graphic novel shifts between those poles, it makes both emotions resonate by contrast.

One critic, Kimberly Wedeven Segall, argues that Satrapi's art "offer[s] a measure of detachment…the cartoon visual detaches [the reader] from traumatic events" (40). In other words, Segall claims the visuals shield the reader from the full force of the terrible and traumatic events occurring around Marji. And indeed, as Segall points out, the visual images often fail to capture the nature of Marji's feelings. In one episode, Marji's friend Neda is killed by an Iraqi bombing; when Marji realizes that Neda is dead by spying her bracelet amidst the rubble, the final panel of the episode is fully black. Her narration reads "no scream in the world could have relieved my suffering and my anger" (142, Segall 41). Segall suggests that the artwork and narration are in conflict, with the latter narrating and reacting to horrible events, while the former struggles to adequately present them to the reader.

If this is the case, however, the artwork actually reinforces the perspective of the graphic novel; in providing a "detachment" from events, Satrapi's drawings mirror her experience as a child growing up in a traumatic environment. Many of the terrible events occurring in Iran are kept from her because she's a child, or are told to her second hand, meaning that Marji is detached from many events and must imagine them. The tortures that Siamak and Mohsen describe in "The Heroes" are a case in point, as is Marji's feeling of being small, rendered in the image itself, when Siamak's daughter proclaims her father's heroism (51–52). The cartoonish images allow Satrapi to freely blend actual events with her imagination and ideas. They function as a subjective version of events; much of what Satrapi tells the reader is true, but filtered through her own memory, imagination, and childhood understanding of those events.

This can be seen clearly at the end of "The Sheep," when Marji rejects God after the execution of her favorite uncle, Anoosh. A full-page image of Marji, splayed against the dark background, provides a sensation of her floating in space, which is emphasized by a few small planets and stars. The emptiness of space reflects her own feelings of sadness and spiritual emptiness, which is rudely interrupted by the more immediate physical danger of the war: a large splash balloon cries out "Marji! Run to the basement! We're being bombed!" at the bottom right corner of the panel (71).

Satrapi will also utilize graphic abstraction and symbolism to make a larger point or provide the reader with a subjective sensation. In these moments, the subjectivity of the narration and the artwork come to reinforce each other, giving readers access to one unique individual's experience and reaction to events. A good example of this occurs in the chapter "The Trip," when Marji and her parents visit Italy and Spain, fearful that the regime will soon forbid them from doing so. In another full-page image, Marji and her parents float on a magic carpet above images signifying the countries they visit: the leaning tower of Pisa, laundry hung outside the windows of Mediterranean architecture, and an abstracted Spanish dancer in the middle. Surrounded by swirls of wind that keep the family aloft, the images combine to connote the happy experience of the trip, expressing a feeling deriving from an entire set of experiences rather than each individual moment. In this way, the nature of Satrapi's artwork can be seen as not just fostering an accessibility and universality, but also enabling access to her subjective experience.

Themes and Critical Perspectives

A text as rich as *Persepolis* cannot be reduced to a single idea; but it can be argued that the key theme in the graphic novel is the establishment of an identity and self-image forged from personal experience and from the cultural subject positions made available to a particular individual. Many of the larger concerns of the text— the critiques of class and gender inequality, the parallels between family and national history, the conflict between individuality and collectivity, and the overwhelming power of a consumerist global youth culture—all play a part in Marjane's growing up and finding an identity for herself. In this respect, *Persepolis* is, as many critics have noted, a *Bildungsroman*: a novel or story about an individual's coming of age.

The early parts of *Persepolis* involve Marji's attempts to forge her own identity from the political, religious, and historical subject positions available to her. When she is very young, Marji decides to become a "prophet," aware that such an occupation, if we might call it that, has been historically closed to women. Her fealty to God and comfort in religion, however, fluctuates and falters with the course of the Revolution. Marji abandons her plan to become a prophet when becoming a revolutionary seems more attractive. She does, however, note a clear similarity between God and Karl Marx, "though Marx's hair was a bit curlier," a similarity emphasized in a panel depicting them facing one another (13). In any case, there's a subtle critique here in Marji's search for a guiding (grand)father figure: both God and Marx serve a similar function in people's lives, providing them with a guiding ideology to live by. This connection becomes clearer when Marji is introduced to her uncle Anoosh, who had been imprisoned by the Shah for being a communist. Although Marji looks up to Anoosh for his views and his heroic political imprisonment, the first image of him frames his face in a halo, like a religious icon (54). Anoosh's political commitment sanctifies him, and it is his eventual execution that causes Marji to lose her faith in God entirely.

Marji "tries out" subject positions other than religious devotee and communist revolutionary. For example, after learning about the torture of political prisoners, Marji takes to the streets with her friends to play a game where "the one who loses will be tortured" (53). She takes on the persona, in other words, of one of the Shah's secret police, something that gives her a "diabolical feeling of power" (53). This feeling is reflected by Marji's vision of herself in a mirror, sprouting devil horns. She quickly rejects this play-identity, however, as it is both counter to her existing religious and political feelings.

The cruel irony of Marji's development from child to teenager is that her "coming of age" aligns with the consolidation of the Islamic regime's power. At one point, Marji notes that the survival of the regime was dependent on the continued waging of war with Iraq, and part of maintaining that survival was the execution of those who opposed it: "Naturally, the regime became more repressive. In the name of that war, they exterminated the enemy within" (116–117). As she narrates this revelation, Marji lights a cigarette and smokes it, her "act of rebellion against my mother's dictatorship" by which she "kissed childhood goodbye" (117). In other words, Marji's maturation into a young adult, and her departure from childhood, is presented simultaneously with the regime's maturation into a fully repressive, wartime state.

This is only one instance of the conflation drawn among Marji, her family's experiences, and the larger historical context in which they live and which has structured their lives as well as Marji's own growth as an individual. A clear example of this comes in the chapter "The Water Cell," where Marji learns of her own personal connection to the protests taking place against the Shah. Her father tells her that her grandfather had been a prince, who lost his nobility after Reza Khan seized power. Marji learns that her own family history is intertwined with the series of historical events that lead to the current protests against Khan's son, the Shah Reza Phalavi. This personal, familial connection to events is reinforced when

Marji learns from her Uncle Anoosh about his part in an attempt to establish an independent Iranian Azerbaijan.

Although Marji is in an unusual position regarding the connection between her family and her nation's historical events—most Iranians would not have such clear links to significant historical figures—she still desires a more experiential "feel" for that history. Thus, as Kimberly Wedeven Segall points out, after learning how her grandfather was tortured by being suspended in a cell filled with water for hours, Marji takes a long bath in an effort at "an uncanny re-creation" of her grandfather's experience (25, Segall 40). The closest she comes is examining her hands afterwards, which "were wrinkled when I came out, like Grandpa's" (25). She therefore manages to have some, however tangential, physical connection to her grandfather and the torture he suffered at the hands of the Shah. In these illustrative moments, Satrapi suggests that our family and personal histories are always intertwined somehow with historical events, even if the physical evidence and signs of those connections remain indistinct or only suggested.

Another way that Marji attempts to assert an identity for herself is through the consumption of the products of a global youth culture. Although the Iranian government becomes more repressive over the course of the graphic novel, Satrapi reminds us that Iran is by no means a closed society. Part of its heritage of modernization over the course of the twentieth century, and the development of a bourgeois middle class of which Marji's family is part, was Iran's involvement in a popular culture that grew steadily more global over the course of the postwar era. Thus, even with the establishment of a strict Islamic theocracy, Marji is not cut off from the important cultural icons and consumer goods that youth around the world use to signify their identities.

The episode entitled "Kim Wilde" is the best example of Marji's consumption of global youth culture. On a trip to Turkey, Marji's parents buy her a number of artifacts of Western popular culture—posters of Kim Wilde and Iron Maiden, Nikes, a denim jacket, and a pin of Michael Jackson. Babak Elahi discusses how Marji uses these signs of Western culture to "try out" a counter-cultural identity. In one panel, Marji mimics Kim Wilde's pose in a poster, as if it were a reflective mirror. Moreover, Wilde's song "Kids in America" takes on an added dimension in the Iranian context: not only does it celebrate the energy and enthusiasm of youth, but it also becomes a paean to the freedom and culture of the United States.

Significantly, the song appears twice in the chapter. First, after Marji has left the house decked out in her Western garb (denim jacket and Nikes), and second, she listens to it loudly on the stereo after being harassed over her outfit by the Guardians of the Revolution (131–134, Elahi 317–318). In the first circumstance, the song reiterates Marji's adoption of a Western counter-cultural identity; and in the next, it reflects how that identity helps her to protest, albeit only in a small and private manner, her treatment at the hands of the repressive state authority. The fact that Marji is a girl makes her particularly vulnerable and targeted by the authorities; but at the same time, her class status protects her from some of the most terrible consequences of her actions.

Reading a Single Episode

Satrapi is particularly skilled at drawing together multiple thematic strands in single episodes. Let's take one chapter from about halfway through the volume, "The Key," as an illustrative example. In this chapter, the Iran-Iraq conflict has become a war of attrition, and it opens with Marji looking at a "list of martyrs" in the newspaper, each with his own picture and name listed. The sheer number of dead men shocks Marji, who asks her mother "Have you seen all these causalities?" to which her mother responds, "how can I not see?...the streets are packed with nuptial chambers." Marji then plays an expository role in her narration, explaining to the graphic novel's largely Western readership that Shiite Islamic tradition builds nuptial chambers for unmarried men who die, so they "can symbolically attain carnal knowledge" (94).

While Marji narrates her individual horror at the sheer volume of dead soldiers, the mass collectives mobilized by the state's fundamentalist ideology is on display throughout the chapter. The martyrs depicted in the newspaper images and the nuptial chambers lined up in the street are mirrored by a full-page panel on the next page, depicting Marji and the girls in her school beating their breasts to mourn the dead. Later Marji's cousin Shahab, a member of the army, tells her about the many young boys used as cannon-fodder for the war, and two panels show the boys being propagandized and sent into the fight. Each boy wears a headband; like the girls in their veils, they are barely distinguishable from each other—a group without individuality.

The juxtaposition of Marji's conversation with her mother and the experience of "mourning the martyrs" at school establishes a conflict between Marji's private, home experience, where she and her parents remain skeptical and pragmatic about the revolution and war, and the public sphere of institutions like the school, where the official state ideology of the fundamentalist government is enforced. Satrapi links this in-school indoctrination to the history of Iranian religious expression. Throughout the graphic novel, Satrapi connects the history of her country to present events, offering both an explanation for how and why things happen, and demonstrating continuity between the past and present, even in the face of massive, discontinuous upheaval. In this circumstance, the beating of breasts has a particular context—the girls are forced into a ritual mourning for the soldiers—connected to a common historical and cultural practice. The discontinuity is demonstrated in Satrapi's juxtaposition of illustrations. While the breast beating is undertaken entirely by girls, religious flagellation is depicted as done by men, even sometimes as an individual feat of devotion, as Satrapi's narration attests: "It could go very far. Sometimes it was considered a macho thing" (96). Thus, while there is a historical connection at work, the re-application of the historical practice to women represents the discontinuous dimension introduced by the revolution.

The ritual mourning inflicted upon the girls represents a larger enforcement of strictly defined gender roles on society in the wake of the Islamic Revolution. The most visible dimension of this division was the enforcement of dress (74–75); thus the image of the girls beating their breasts both demonstrates the symbolic behavioral expectations placed upon them—to be the embodiment of the nation's mourning of its lost soldiers—but also their symbolic interchangeability and lack of distinction (95).

The gendered expectation of behavior also has a class dimension. Later in the chapter, the Satrapis' maid, Mrs. Nasrine, comes with gold-painted plastic key that was given to her son, who was told the key would get him into heaven should he be "martyred" in battle. Marji worries about her cousin Peyman, who is the same age, but when she asks if he received a gold key in school, he answers quizzically "keys to what?" (100). Thus, it is not merely boys who are asked to run into combat and die, but specifically lower-class boys. At the end of the chapter, Satrapi makes the class distinction all too clear and tragic. She depicts a group of boys in silhouette, all with keys around their necks, dying in a minefield. The jagged, scratched lines of the drawing suggest the violence done to the boys as they die. In the panel directly below, Marji and her upper-class friends jump and dance at a party. Their bodily contortions echo those of the dying boys in the panel above, both drawing and denying a connection between the two. While both groups consist of young people whose thoughts are focused on joy and pleasure (the murdered boys are prepared for war by being told that "the afterlife is even better than Disneyland" and "in paradise there will be plenty of food, women and houses made of gold of diamonds" [101, 100]), only the privileged group enjoys it. While her peers die needlessly, Marji goes to the party in "a sweater full of holes...and a necklace with chains and nails" because "punk rock was in" (102). Because of her class, Marji is able to continue to explore her identity and consume the iconography of global popular culture without serious consequence, unlike those boys unlucky enough to be born to poor parents.

Reception, Impact, and Legacy

When the first part of *Persepolis* was published in France in 2000, it was greeted with outstanding reviews, which continued with the English translation a few years later. However, the impact of the graphic novel was not limited to excellent critical reviews. *Persepolis* affected the reception of graphic novels and influenced the course of the memoir form in the subsequent decade. Moreover, it also contributed significantly to discussions of the contemporary Middle East at a time when the world's attention was centered on the region.

The attention *Persepolis* received on its publication contributed to the improving reputation of the graphic novel as a form of literature and art, a process that began in the 1980s with superhero stories like *Watchmen* and with the family Holocaust memoir *Maus*, which served as an inspiration for Satrapi. *Persepolis*'s reputation is such that it regularly appears on lists of the greatest graphic novels of all time, with *The Herald Scotland* placing it first in 2013 (Jamieson). It also appeared on the cusp of a flood of memoirs, a genre that exploded during the 2000s (Yagoda 3). Moreover, *Persepolis* inspired a new wave of memoirs specifically by Iranian women, many of whom live in the West (Nahai, Paköz), and it was at the forefront of a new movement of memoirs in graphic novel form. It was followed by acclaimed works, like *Fun Home* by Alison Bechdel, *Blankets* by Craig Thompson, and *Stitches* by David Small.

However, the release of *Persepolis* in the wake of the 9/11 attacks and the subsequent War on Terror might be where its impact was most felt. Ahu Paköz writes that recent memoirs by Iranians have been especially significant in raising "the consciousness of foreigners towards the issues of women in Iran." Satrapi herself has been particularly outspoken about writing *Persepolis* to counter the image of Iran and its people that had spread in the West in the years since the Revolution. "There's a misconception in the West that every Iranian is scum, that all men force women into marriages, then beat them, and that everybody is a fanatic," she has said. "I want to show that I'm a human being, like my fellow Iranians" (Burns). Satrapi's goal of changing American and European perceptions of Iranians grew particularly important after George W. Bush identified Iran as one of the "Axis of Evil" countries, along with Iraq and North Korea, which each threatened the rest of the world with terrorism.

After the success of *Persepolis: The Story of a Childhood* and its sequel *Persepolis: The Story of a Return*, a film adaptation was produced and released in 2007. The film was critically acclaimed, just as the graphic novels had been, and brought Satrapi's message of tolerance to an even greater audience.

Despite its positive message, critical acclaim, and influence, *Persepolis* has also sparked controversy in a number of circumstances. The film version prompted a protest by the Iranian government of the Cannes Film Festival, where it first screened ("Iran Protests..."). A few years later, a screening of the film on Tunisian television resulted in outraged Islamists setting fire to the TV station, and the station's owner was put on trial for "inciting public disorder" (Hayoun).

Although one might expect *Persepolis* to have a hostile reception in countries where Islamic fundamentalists are influential, the graphic novel was recently also the subject of a brief controversy in the United States. The Chicago public school system, arguing that *Persepolis* contained material unsuitable for children and that students were not developmentally ready to understand it, issued a district-wide ban of the graphic novel in March 2013. A number of educational and civil rights organizations protested the ban, and the Chicago Teacher's Union (CTU) connected the book's "questioning of authority" with the reason why the school system banned it (Gupta). In the face of such objections, the school system eased the ban, enforcing it only for certain age groups. However, the CTU's analysis of the situation demonstrates the universal quality of *Persepolis* as a work supporting equality and freedom of speech.

Works Cited

Burns, Charles. "Marjane Satrapi: Princess of Darkness." *The Independent*. 1 October 2006. Web. 20 October 2013.

Elahi, Babak. "Frames and Mirrors in Marjane Satrapi's *Persepolis*." *symploke* 15.1-2 (2007): 312–325.

Gupta, Prachi. "Chicago Teacher's Union Calls 'Persepolis' Ban 'Orwellian'." *Salon*. 20 March 2013. Web. 20 October 2013.

Hayoun, Massoud. "How a 5-Year-Old Foreign Film Sparked a Free-Speech Fight in Tunisia." *The Atlantic*. 30 April 2012. Web. 20 October 2013.

"Iran-Iraq War." *Historical Dictionary of Iran.* Ed. John H. Lorentz. 2nd ed. Lanham, MD: Scarecrow Press, 2007. 133–135. *Gale Virtual Reference Library.* Web. 12 Oct. 2013.

"Iran Protests 'Persepolis' Screening." *USAToday.* 20 May 2007. Web. 21 October 2013.

"The Iranian Revolution: Document in Context." *The Contemporary Middle East: A Documentary History.* Ed. John Felton. Washington, DC: CQ Press, 2008. 379–383.

Jamieson, Teddy. "The 50 Greatest Graphic Novels of All Time." *HeraldScotland.com.* 18 August 2013. Web. 14 October 2013.

Murphy, John F., Jr. "Iran." *Encyclopedia of Politics: The Left and The Right.* Ed. Rodney P. Carlisle. Vol. 2. Thousand Oaks, CA: SAGE Reference, 2005. 700–703.

Nahai, Gina. "So What's with All the Iranian Memoirs? An Original Tries to Explain." *Publisher's Weekly.* 26 November 2007. Web. 13 October 2013.

Paköz, Ahu. "A Reawakening of Memories in Comic Form: *Persepolis* by Marjane Satrapi." *Scan: A Journal of Media Arts Culture.* 5.2 (September 2008). Web. 14 October 2013.

Satrapi, Marjane. *Persepolis: The Story of a Childhood.* Trans. Mattias Ripa and Blake Ferris. New York: Pantheon, 2003.

Segall, Kimberly Wedeven. "Melancholy Ties: Intergenerational Loss and Exile in *Persepolis.*" *Comparative Studies of South Asia, Africa and the Middle East* 28.1 (2008): 38–49.

Yagoda, Ben. *Memoir: A History.* New York: Riverhead Books, 2009.

Robert Kirkman and Tony Moore's *The Walking Dead*

Michael J. Blouin

Robert Kirkman and Tony Moore's *The Walking Dead: Days Gone Bye*, first released in 2003, has served as a major catalyst for the recent surge in popularity of the undead, spawning the hugely popular television series *The Walking Dead* on AMC (2010–present). The flesh-hungry fiends have experienced resurgence of late in other corners as well, rivaled only perhaps by their vampiric cousins. They crop up in video games, hawk board games, steal the spotlight in a commercial for Sprint Unlimited, and appear on the silver screen in seemingly endless variations.[1] By analyzing a key theme in *The Walking Dead*, this essay grapples with an epidemic that spans the previous decade. Specifically, this graphic novel re-animates for readers the zombie apocalypse, as well as the infamous rhetoric of Charlton Heston, in order to contribute to a dialogue concerning gun control in the United States.

Kirkman and Moore tell the story of policeman Rick Grimes and his struggle to survive the aftermath of a zombie apocalypse. Upon waking from a coma, he gradually finds his way back into the arms of his wife, Lori, his best friend Shane, and his son Carl. They are members of a caravan of individuals struggling to come to terms with a rapidly decaying society. Once re-united, the extended family must learn how to survive under increasingly harsh conditions. The graphic novel concludes with a dramatic fracturing of the family unit, opening the door for a lengthy continuation of the series (nineteen volumes and counting).

The Walking Dead recognizably changes the tenor established by previous zombie narratives. For one, by placing less stress upon the gore of attacks by the living dead, it subtly shifts focus away from the metaphor of "the zombie" and onto a direct appeal to the struggles of human beings. The plot spends far more time considering the inner-turmoil of personal relationships than it does crafting gruesome sequences (though it is not without a couple of unnerving encounters). The greatest tension of this volume, it can be argued, remains Lori's betrayal of Rick with his best friend Shane during his absence. Thus, rather than rehearsing the symbolic ties between contemporary society and the mindless march of mobile corpses, Kirkman and Moore allow readers to bypass familiar analogies and confront pressing issues of the day, including the quagmire of gun policy.

In order to transform the trajectory of the zombie tale, the graphic novel must first complicate the all-too-familiar correlation between consumerism and the living dead. William Seabrook's 1929 novel, *The Voodoo Island*, was one of the first texts to popularize the zombie in American popular culture and presents the creature to his readers against the backdrop of Hasco, an American conglomerate that produces synthetic sugar.[2] He describes the scene as "like a chunk of Hoboken" while recognizing that his nativist commentary (*zombi* as a Haitian phenomenon) faces an "incongruous background," resonant of "modern big business, and it sounds like it, looks it, smells it" (Seabrook 22).

George Romero further develops the link between zombies and an over-industrialized modern world. In *Dawn of the Dead* of 1978, he ingeniously positions the zombies inside of the epicenter of modern-day commercialism: a shopping mall. Theorists Gilles Deleuze and Félix Guattari, pleased by this correlation, subsequently declare the zombie to be our only modern myth. Since the initial connections drawn by Seabrook and Romero, critics of the living dead almost always critique the *ennui* of late capitalism. We ARE the zombies, they announce with a common refrain; we blindly consume, and we possess fewer and fewer signs of our humanity.

Yet Kirkman and Moore complicate this association. The earlier anti-capitalist vision of the undead establishes the victim of the attacks (and, vicariously, the audience) within a pre-determined space aligned with the political Left. If you survive the violence of consumption, you align yourself with idealized "outsiders"; for Romero, these "outsiders" are the 1960s counter-culture. In *The Walking Dead*, human beings are "outsiders," too. But this time, the goal is not to upset the established order. Instead, the goal is to regain a sense of tradition from within the rubble. The restoration of Rick and Lori's marriage following the apocalyptic surge suggests, for the reader, a resurrection of conservative "family values." Throughout the story, women spend their time cleaning clothes, while the men go off to hunt. Lori admits, "I don't know about you but I can't even shoot a gun... I've never even tried. To be honest... I wouldn't trust any of those guys to wash my clothes" (Kirkman and Moore). Most importantly, any claims for pacifism or signs of antipathy to violence—usually expressed by Lori—become the object of ridicule by other characters. In short, during the year that saw the launch of the Iraq war—specifically, 2003—Kirkman and Moore appear to cast zombies as a threat *against which* society can restore its "lost traditions."

Both versions of the zombie narrative privilege the "outsider"; however, the slippery politicized terms of Left and Right become inverted in this contemporary rendering. For Rick and his group, to enter back into a more "conservative" mode is the sole way to survive in a time of excess. To justify such a transformation, characters must also engage in awkward debates regarding the acceptability of firearm use. These debates are awkward not due to their timely content, but due to the supernatural forces stacked up against them. It can be jarring when, in this novel and in the zombie fad to follow, characters pause amidst an overwhelming onslaught of the walking dead to iron out the finer points of responsible gun ownership.

The issues surrounding firearms—who should be allowed to possess one; how can we safely regulate them; is it a right, a privilege, and/or a necessity; and so forth—were heated in 2003. The Columbine shooting of 1999 still haunted the public imagination. The following year, Michael McDermott shot and killed seven co-workers in Massachusetts. In 2003, Doug Williams massacred fourteen African Americans. Indeed, the question of gun control has never been very far from the public eye in the United States. The Wild West imagery of the Bush administration in the years following 2001 further served to illuminate issues of justifiable retaliation, quick-draw thinking, and self-preservation at any cost. *The Walking*

Dead, therefore, emerges from a cultural moment in which debates surrounding firearms were widespread and the slogan "shoot first, ask questions later" echoed in the language of American domestic and foreign affairs.

Yet Kirkman and Moore do not simply champion gun possession; rather, their graphic novel delves into the complexity of a debate that has enthralled Americans since the perceived opening of the frontier. Although to harness the power of a firearm can be a vital necessity when facing the living dead, it can also do irreparable harm to friends and family, hence creating a cycle of despair fueled by the utter pervasiveness of the weapon. Guns are the problem as well as the solution. As a result, readers may feel, at times, as though the zombies fade into the background of the story or function as mere target practice within a contest where their existence remains secondary. Julia Round writes, "Zombies are slowly being excised from their own stories and replaced with a critique of humanity" (Round 155). Whether or not this shift diminishes the larger role of the undead, the emphasis on firearms has certainly resonated with practitioners of the zombie tale over the past decade.

Gunslingers and Zombies

The Walking Dead successfully blends tropes from the Western genre into the milieu of a zombie apocalypse. One specific example is the memorable panel, which depicts Rick riding his horse off into the sunset of a cityscape that is being feasted upon by the living dead. Richard Slotkin, one of the preeminent scholars of the Western genre in American culture, outlines its scope in his 1998 book, *Gunfighter Nation: Myth of the Frontier in Twentieth-Century America*. The persistence of "the gunslinger" as a motif helps to explain the persistence of the popularity of guns in the United States. Discussing filmmaker John Ford, Slotkin writes: "We are to continue to believe our myths despite our knowledge that they are untrue... we will behave as if we did not know the history whose truth would demystify our beliefs" (Slotkin 342). Proponents and opponents of gun control alike prefer the fantastic stuff of myth to the hard facts of the cases at hand. By merging the sentiments of the

Western with the zombie thriller, Kirkman and Moore expose to the reader how issues surrounding firearms have been buried beneath layer after layer of cultural mythology.

Early on in *The Walking Dead*, Rick transforms into a stereotypical cowboy by donning an over-sized cowboy hat. The transformation is triggered by Rick's entrance into a deserted police station closet, which is filled with guns and ammunition. "If whacking those things over the head with the shovel does them in… I'm sure those things will work," he comments. "Should save you some effort" (Kirkman and Moore). As soon as he takes custody of the weapons, he adopts a heroic swagger, tipping his new hat and claiming to "protect and serve." He even secures a horse for himself when his patrol car runs out of gas on the highway. In one memorable sequence, Rick rides his horse across a Georgia field and over a tall fence, calling out: "Let's go!" Thus, as the reader follows him into the bleak desert, the mythos of the gunslinger moves steadily to the fore.

However, circumstances almost immediately check the overzealous use of these firearms. Rick has to be reminded by a neighbor that he must preserve his bullets and not waste them on harmless targets. A young boy named Glenn saves him from an onslaught by scolding him for recklessly firing into a crowd: "Stop using that gun! You'll have the whole city on us!" These weapons serve the essential purpose of *hunting* in the early stages of the plot. Rick and Shane spend a fair amount of time in the wilderness, tracking down food for their cohort. Kirkman and Moore's text establishes clear parameters for the proper, and improper, employment of arms.

Despite an established limit regarding the utility of the guns, Rick relentlessly strives to accrue more. He ignores an abandoned army tank on his way into the city, in order to secure firearms for the group. By so doing, he overlooks a clear sign of awesome firepower laid to barren waste. He brings an abandoned shopping cart along to the gun store to exit with the largest number of weapons he can possibly transport. With no apparent regard for the task at hand (hunting), he commands Glenn to grab "a little bit of everything." Rick is so eager to load up on firearms that his accomplice has to remind him: "We need to make sure we don't grab anything that won't work in the guns we get." The sense of comfort and empowerment that he receives from these weapons pushes Rick to cling desperately to an armful of them, risking his life to retain as many as he can possibly hold. Slotkin explains the transformation of the Western genre during the Cold War as follows: "In the world of the gunfighter… moral suasion without violent force to back it is incompetent to achieve its civilizing ends" (Slotkin 402). To regain a sense of moral order within his own world, Rick sees no alternative to uninhibited violence; for him, "civilization" remains synonymous with heavy armament. Cold War "moral suasion" and the reckless accumulation of weapons are rooted deep in Rick's psyche.

To counter-balance this longing, a number of characters in the story insist upon preaching the benefits of gun safety. The same neighbor who advises Rick to conserve bullets admonishes his son for touching one of the firearms. "I'm gonna teach you how to use one of them tomorrow… but until then they're off limits" (Kirkman and Moore). Later, Rick and Shane begin to lead a training course for the group. They instruct other members (in particular, women) on how to safely and effectively use their munitions. The narrative maintains a significant tension between an obsessive lust for guns and an equally obsessive lust for benign usage.

In particular, this cultural tension comes to the fore when Rick decides to teach his son Carl about a supposedly essential skill. Donning his father's over-sized cowboy hat and his very own gun holster, Carl joyfully runs at his father's call: "Nobody better be using my gun!" Rick beams with pride at his son's enthusiasm for the task. After a successful shooting session, he agrees that his son has earned the right to carry a gun like everyone else. He announces to the rest of the crew, "I know he's young, but just for safety's sake, he's going to be carrying his own gun from now on." Lori, conversely, does not agree with this decision and bitterly reminds her husband that their son is seven years old. Rick's zeal and Lori's antipathy illuminate the central crisis of this narrative: not the encroachment of a massive zombie hoard, but the debate surrounding America's ever-swelling gun culture.

A resolution for this tension does not readily appear. At first, the graphic novel seems firmly pro-gun. A stray zombie pack invades camp. Lori, caught off guard, fumbles away her gun and endangers her family. At the last possible moment, Carl rushes to the rescue, blasting the creature with a direct shot. His mother is visibly shaken. Rushing into her husband's arms, she apologizes and acknowledges: "I was so stupid." Nevertheless, although Carl's access to a firearm rescues her in this instance, this very same weapon will later greatly complicate conclusions drawn from the episode.

The final scene of the narrative restores an overarching sense of ambivalence. Shane, unnerved by Lori's unwillingness to leave her husband, loses all control. With unbridled fury, he turns his gun on Rick. Ironically, when one recalls the absurdity of Rick's armload of firearms limiting his mobility back in the city, Rick now pleads with his old friend: "Can you please just *put the gun down*?" And then, with Rick's weapon of choice at last turned against him, Carl once more races to the rescue. He kills Shane with a clean shot. He has now saved both of his parents. But sadness permeates the concluding panels of *The Walking Dead*. Carl weeps, "It's not the same as killing the dead ones, daddy." To which Rick responds, "It never should be, son." The presence of guns endangers Rick in unexpected ways. They threaten his life, they allow his friend to lunge from the precipice, and they rob his son of his innocence. Gone is the immature exuberance of the gunslinger. The story ends with swirling questions. Without firearms, would Shane have been capable of confronting Rick in such a fatal fashion? Would Carl have preserved his youthful outlook – or would he be an orphan? This graphic novel, moving from police armory to gun store to target range, cannot escape the entanglements of the gun debate. After all, it has long been this debate that undergirds both Western and apocalyptic narratives. Carl's concluding discharge stuns the reader into deeper inquiries and encourages them to resist easy answers to a broader impasse.

A Haze of Smoke and Shells

This branch of the debate was only just beginning with the appearance of Kirkman and Moore's work. In fact, the correlation between gun control discourse and the zombie phenomenon grew ever stronger over the past decade. For example, in the second volume of the series, *The Walking Dead: Miles Behind Us*, the issue of whether or not we should arm our children—in a general sense, the question of how to pass on the legacy of our gun culture to the next generation—remains as powerfully present as in the original narrative. Tyreese, one of Rick's companions, is approached by his daughter and her new boyfriend. The two teenagers admit that they still have the firearms given to them by Rick for target practice. Tyreese begrudgingly allows them to hold onto the weapons for their safety, but reminds them that it would be wiser to keep them holstered unless an emergency situation arises. The sagacity of this advice immediately falls under the reader's scrutiny. Once out of earshot, the young man says, "I thought that bastard would never let us have guns. It's going to be much easier now" (Kirkman and Adlard 22). These ominous words cloak a mysterious intent and, once more, draw the reader's attention to the conundrum of how to arm future generations in a suitable manner. Will Tyreese's child use sound judgment? Or does some darker deed lie in store? These two teenagers position themselves in a doorway in a later panel, handguns on display at their hips. They watch as Tyreese's partner admits: "You never know what's going to happen next." Nor would these uncertainties remain within the confines of the *Walking Dead* series. A brief survey of several zombie narratives since the appearance of *The Walking Dead: Days Gone Bye* will demonstrate to the reader the increased prevalence of this theme.

In one variation, firearms are part and parcel of the "zombification" of modern life. Max Brooks' 2006 horror novel, *World War Z: An Oral History of the Zombie Wars*, considers this over-reliance in one scene featuring a Japanese *otaku* (a tech-savvy shut-in). The young man, recalling his initial encounters with the zombies, laughs: "This was not America, where there used to be more firearms than people" (Brooks 263). Instead of lamenting the absence of guns, he returns to his cultural "roots" and picks up his ancestor's scabbard to fight off the invasion. By seizing the ancient weapon, this anti-social character regains a sort of vibrancy, channeling a life force that had previously drained away. A similar rejuvenation later occurs in the American military. One soldier tells of his unit's return to guns styled after weapons used in World War II as having a "retro feel" (337). The text, therefore, refashions our relationship to our weapons. Guns that are "too advanced" cause decay in our connection to the act of self-defense; when experiencing the tactile feel of an antique gun, nostalgia washes over the soldier and pushes him to seize his firearm with a renewed sense of empowerment.

Ruben Fleischer's 2009 movie *Zombieland* similarly plays like a love letter to a fading gunslinger culture. Tallahassee (Woody Nelson) re-instills a passion for weapons among his young crew. In one particular bonding scene, he teaches a young girl named Little Rock (Abigail Breslin) how to fire a gun with Zen-like mastery (a skill that will later save them all). Tallahassee's final shoot-out with the zombies celebrates the glorious discharge of a favorite American pastime at fever pitch. As in *The Walking Dead*, zombies seem, at times, to be little more than moving targets, affording the crew a chance to get reacquainted with their weapons and, subsequently, their humanity.[3] Yet, also like the graphic novel, *Zombieland* pauses to consider this overzealous reliance. In one memorable scene, Columbus (Jesse Eisenberg) accidently shoots and kills Bill Murray (playing himself) in a prank gone horribly wrong. Cloaked in comedy, the audience nonetheless does not pause to meditate on the irony for long. During a zombie invasion, survivors must take the bad with the good when it comes to heavy armament.

Likewise, Stephen King contemplates the nation's gun laws in his 2006 zombie novel, *Cell*. Protagonists Tom and Clay wander across state lines and end up in Massachusetts, a state with the most stringent gun laws in the country. They acknowledge that if more people had guns, there would likely be isolationist thinking and a widespread willingness to kill one another in order to reach shelter. While they mock their neighbor, with his NRA sticker and Bush-Cheney bumper sticker, they are reassured that his house will be well stocked with weapons. The two men recognize that the neighbor might shoot them as they approach (a definite vote in favor of the Massachusetts laws), but they cannot avoid the prospect: "Do you want to go with just knives for protection? I'm asking you as one serious man to another, because some of the people we run into *are* going to have guns" (King 83). Despite his resignation, Clay still hopes that his son is alive "in a place where people aren't putting guns into the hands of children who were good at video games" (171). The ongoing debate—reiterating a theme we locate within the pages of *The Walking Dead*—is of interest less because it offers definitive answers to these big questions (it remains unclear exactly which side the novel advocates), but because of the astounding degree to which contemporary zombie narratives have absorbed the gun control debate.[4]

A cyclical trajectory of *The Walking Dead* positions this debate appropriately as one driven by a kind of *self-cannibalism*. In the opening panels, it is the proliferation of guns that triggers the zombie onslaught. An escaped convict shoots Rick with his handgun. He awakens, sometime later, in the midst of a dangerous new world. Essentially, the unlawful possession and use of a firearm transforms Rick into a sort of zombie. After all, what is Rick's subsequent coma, if not an example of the "living dead?" The pages that follow trace Rick's attempt to "become human" once more. The process includes, as we have seen, a voracious appetite for stockpiling. In the end, this compulsive armament leads to another lost soldier in a depleted army against the total apocalypse (this time, his best friend, Shane). If guns create a growing number of dead bodies, but a lack of guns only allows for an increase in dead bodies, what remains to be done? The human race appears doomed to exist in an endless cycle of violence and decay.

By channeling conventions from the Western as well as the zombie tale, Kirkman and Moore present readers with a grim illustration of how the gun debate offers no readymade outlet for twenty-first century citizens. As the graphic novel propels itself forward, with a resounding shot fired at its protagonist, it closes with an equally resounding blast. A lack of firearms surely guarantees death from zombie hordes, while a plethora of firearms guarantees destruction from a different, though equally ominous, source. When we stop to lament the tragic events of the Navy Yard shooting in Washington, D.C., or to question the outcome of a recall election in Colorado, where politicians in favor of stricter gun laws were ousted by the concentrated maneuvers of gun lobbyists, or any number of gun-related events in America (and they seem destined to repeat *ad nauseum* for many years to come), recent zombie narratives offer a productive avenue for thinking through these issues. Moving targets with a hunger for brains force us to take a hard look at our gun policy.

There may still be hope. Slotkin argues, "Myth is not something *given* but something *made*" (Slotkin 659). Kirkman and Moore's revision of the Western genre, now populated by the undead, allows readers to confront the mythic structures they have been given and then to construct something new. Moreover, for individuals who routinely proclaim their respective views as "common-sense," *The Walking Dead: Days Gone Bye* reminds readers on both sides of the issue to appreciate the complexity of the crisis. By visualizing a vicious cycle, this narrative helps the reader to seek a productive compromise as the species continues to cannibalize itself in a haze of smoke and shells.

Notes

1. A far from exhaustive list of these variations includes the film *Warm Bodies* (2013), the board game *Last Night on Earth: The Zombie Game* (2007), and the self-proclaimed "Zombie Sonics" (fans of the recently dismantled NBA franchise, the Seattle Supersonics).

2. Many erroneously give credit to Seabrook as the very first writer to introduce the zombie into popular culture in the United States. In truth, travel writer Lafcadio Hearn popularized the zombie years earlier, during the 1880s in his writings on New Orleans.

3. As Kim Paffenroth notes, "We will always be our worst enemies, and the ones we can never fully eliminate" (Paffenroth, 20).

4. For more on Stephen King's contribution to the gun control debate, see his essay *Guns* (Philtrum Press, 2013).

Works Cited

Brooks, Max. *World War Z: An Oral History of The Zombie War*. New York: Broadway Paperbacks, 2006.

King, Stephen. *Cell: A Novel*. New York: Scribner Book Co., 2006.

Kirkman, Robert and Tony Moore. *Walking Dead, Vol. 1: Days Gone Bye*. Berkeley, CA: Image Comics, 2006.

Kirkman, Robert and Charlie Adlard. *Walking Dead, Vol. 2: Miles Behind Us*. Berkeley, CA: Image Comics, 2009.

Paffenroth, Kim. "Zombies as Internal Fear or Threat" *Generation Zombie: Essays on the Living Dead in Modern Culture*. Eds. Stephanie Boluk and Wylie Lenz. Jefferson, NC: MacFarland & Co., 2011. 18–27.

Round, Julia. "The Horror of Humanity" *The Walking Dead and Philosophy: Zombie Apocalypse Now*. Chicago: Open Court, 2012. 155–167.

Seabrook, William. *The Voodoo Island*. New York: Lancer Books, 2009.

Slotkin, Richard. *Gunfighter Nation: The Myth of the Frontier in Twentieth-Century America*. New York: Altheneum, 1992.

Zombieland. Dir. Ruben Fleischer. Perf. Jesse Eisenberg and Woody Harrelson. Columbia, 2009. Film.

RESOURCES

Additional Works in the Graphic Novel Genre

The Superhero Narrative Graphic Novel

Animal Man by Grant Morrison, Chas Truog, and Tom Grummett, 1991

Batman: Black and White by Jim Lee, et al., 2007

Batman Vol. 1: The Court of the Owls (The New 52) by Scott Snyder and Greg Capullo, 2012

Batman: Hush by Jeph Loeb, Jim Lee, and Scott Williams, 2003

Batman: The Killing Joke by Alan Moore and Brian Bolland, 1988

Batman: The Long Halloween by Jeph Loeb and Tim Sale, 1998

Captain America, Volume 1: Winter Soldier Ultimate Collection by Ed Brubaker et al., 2010

Civil War by Mark Millar and Steve McNiven, 2006–2007

Crisis on Infinite Earths by Marv Wolfman and George Pérez, 2001

Crisis on Multiple Earths Vol.1 by Gardner Fox and Mike Sekowsky, et al., 2002

Crisis on Multiple Earths Vol.2 by Gardner Fox, Dennis O'Neil, Mike Sekowsky, et al., 2003

Daredevil by Frank Miller and Klaus Janson, 2013

Daredevil, Vol. 1: Yellow by Jeph Loeb and Tim Sale, 2011

The Death of Captain America, Volume 1: The Death of the Dream by Ed Brubaker and Steve Epting, 2008

Fantastic Four: Crusaders & Titans by Roy Thomas et al., 2013

Final Crisis by Grant Morrison, J.G. Jones, and Doug Mahnke, 2010

The Flash Vol. 6: The Secret of Barry Allen by Geoff Johns and Howard Porter, 2005

Green Lantern: Legacy by Joe Kelly and Brent Anderson, 2002

Green Lantern: Secret Origin by Geoff Johns and Ivan Reis, 2010

Hulk: Gray by Jeph Loeb and Tim Sale, 2011

Identity Crisis by Brad Meltzer and Rags Morales, 2006

Iron Man: Armored Vengeance by David Michelinie, 2013

Justice Vol.1 by Jim Krueger, Alex Ross, and Doug Braithwaite, 2008

Kick-Ass by Mark Millar and John Romita, Jr., 2011

Kingdom Come by Mark Waid and Alex Ross, 1997

Marvel Super Heroes Secret Wars by Jim Shooter, Mike Zeck, and Bob Layton, 2011

Mystery Men by David Liss and Patrick Zircher, 2012

The Rocketeer: The Complete Adventures by Dave Stevens, 2009

Spider-Man: Blue by Jeph Loeb and Tim Sale, 2011

Spider-Man: Death of the Stacys by Stan Lee, et al., 2012

Superman/Batman: Public Enemies by Jeph Loeb and Ed McGuinness, 2004

Superman: Birthright by Mark Waid and Leinil Francis Yu, 2004

Superman: Red Son by Mark Millar, Dave Johnson, and Kilian Plunkett, 2004

Tales of the Batman by Tim Sale et al., 2007

Thor Vol. 1 by J. Michael Straczynski and Oliver Coipel, 2008

Ultimate Fantastic Four, Vol. 1: The Fantastic by Brian Michael Bendis, Mark Millar, and Adam Kubert, 2004

Wonder Woman: Gods and Mortals by George Pérez et al., 2004

X-Men: Days of Future Past by Chris Claremont, et al., 2014

X-Men: God Loves, Man Kills by Chris Claremont and Brent Anderson, 2011

The Horror Narrative Graphic Novel

American Vampire by Scott Snyder, Rafael Albuquerque, and Stephen King, 2010

Anne Rice's The Vampire Lestat by Faye Perozich and Daerick Gross, 1991

Courtney Crumrin and the Night Things by Ted Naifeh and James Lucas Jones, 2003

Hellboy, Volume 1: Seed of Destruction by Mike Mignola and John Byrne, 2003

Locke & Key, Vol. 1: Welcome to Lovecraft by Joe Hill and Gabriel Rodriguez, 2010

Lucifer: Book One by Mike Carey, et al., 2013

Marvel Zombies by Robert Kirkman and Sean Phillips, 2006

Spawn Origins, Volume 1 by Todd McFarlane, 2009

30 Days of Night by Steve Niles and Ben Templrsmith, 2007

Y: The Last Man by Brian K. Vaughan and Pia Guerra, 2008

The Crime Narrative Graphic Novel

The Big Fat Kill: A Tale from Sin City by Frank Miller, 1995

The Goon: Nothin' But Misery by Eric Powell, 2003

The Kille Omnibus, Volume 1 by Matz and Luc Jacamon, 2013

Nemesis by Mark Millar and Steve McNiven, 2011

Pride of Baghdad by Brian K. Vaughan and Niko Henrichon, 2006

Ruse, Vol. 1: Enter the Detective by Mark Waid and Butch Guice, 2002

The Reality/Fantasy Narrative Graphic Novel

Age of Bronze, Vol. 1: A Thousand Ships by Eric Shanower, 2001

Asterios Polyp by David Mazzucchelli, 2009

Cursed Pirate Girl: The Collected Edition, Volume 1 by Jeremy A. Bastian, 2010

Enemy Ace: War Idyll by George Pratt, 1990

The League of Extraordinary Gentlemen, Vol. 1 by Alan Moore and Kevin O'Neill, 2002

The Marquis: Danse Macabre by Guy Davis, 2001

Marvel: 1602 by Neil Gaiman, Andy Kubert, and Richard Isanove, 2004

Mysterius the Unfathomable by Jeff Parker and Tom Fowler, 2010

Neil Gaiman's Neverwhere by Mike Carey and Glen Fabry, 2007

Planetary, Vol. 1: All Over the World and Other Stories by Warren Ellis and John Cassady, 2000

Swallow Me Whole by Nate Powell, 2008

The War that Time Forgot, Vol. 1 by Bruce Jones and Al Barrionuevo, 2008

The War that Time Forgot, Vol. 2 by Bruce Jones and Al Barrionuevo, 2009

Bibliography

Barker, Martin. *A Haunt of Fears: The Strange History of the British Horror Comics Campaign*. London: Pluto Press, 1984.

Beaty, Bart. *Fredric Wertham and the Critique of Mass Culture*. Jackson, MS: UP of Mississippi, 2005.

Chapman, James. *British Comics: A Cultural History*. London, UK: Reaktion Books, 2011.

Comer, Todd A. and Joseph Michael Sommers, eds. *Sexual Ideology in the Works of Alan Moore: Critical Essays on the Graphic Novels*. Jefferson, NC: McFarland, 2012.

Di Liddo, Annalisa. *Alan Moore: Comics as Performance, Fiction as Scalpel*. Jackson: UP of Mississippi, 2009.

Duncan, Randy and Matthew J. Smith. *The Power of Comics: History, Form and Culture*. New York: Continuum, 2009.

Eisner, Will. *Graphic Storytelling and Visual Narrative: Principles and Practices from the Legendary Cartoonist*. New York: W.W. Norton & Company, 2008.

Fingeroth, Danny. *Disguised as Clark Kent: Jews, Comics, and the Creation of the Superhero*. New York: Continuum, 2008.

Fish, Stanley. *Is There a Text in This Class? The Authority of Interpretive Communities*. Cambridge, MA: Harvard UP, 1980.

Gravett, Paul. *Graphic Novels: Everything You Need To Know*. New York: Collins Design-HarperCollins, 2005.

Hajdu, David. *The Ten-Cent Plague: The Great Comic-Book Scare and How It Changed America*. New York: Farrar, Straus and Giroux, 2008.

Haslem, Wendy, Angela Ndalianis, and Chris Mackie, eds. *Super/Heroes: From Hercules to Superman*. Washington, DC: New Academia Publishing, LLC, 2007.

Hatfield, Charles, Jeet Heer, and Kent Worchester, eds. *The Superhero Reader*. Jackson, MS: UP of Mississippi, 2013.

Howe, Sean, ed. *Give Our Regards to the Atomsmashers: Writers on Comics*. New York: Pantheon, 2004.

Jones, Gerard. *Men of Tomorrow: Geeks, Gangsters, and the Birth of the Comic Book*. New York: Basic Books, 2004.

Kannenberg, Gene, Jr. *500 Essential Graphic Novels: The Ultimate Guide*. New York: Harper Design, 2008.

Kovacs, George and C. W. Marshall, eds. *Classics and Comics*. Oxford, UK: Oxford UP, 2011.

Kwitney, Alisa. *The Sandman: King of Dreams*. San Francisco: Chronicle Books, 2003.

Lee, Stan and George Mair. *Excelsior!: The Amazing Life of Stan Lee*. New York: Touchstone, 2002.

Madrid, Mike. *Supergirls: Fashion, Feminism, Fantasy, and the History of Comic Book Heroines*. Minneapolis: Exterminating Angel Press, 2009.

Marshall, C. W. "The Furies, Wonder Woman, and Dream: Mythmaking in DC Comics." *Classics and Comics*. Eds. George Kovacs and C.W. Marshall. Oxford, UK: Oxford UP, 2011. 89–101.

Maslon, Laurence and Michael Kantor. *Superheroes!: Capes, Cowls, and the Creation of Comic Book Culture*. New York: Crown Archetype, 2013.

McCloud, Scott. *Understanding Comics: The Invisible Art*. New York: William Morrow, 1994.

Millidge, Gary Spencer, Smoky Man, Leah Moore, et al. eds. *Alan Moore: Portrait of an Extraordinary Gentleman*. Leigh-On-Sea, UK: Abiogenesis, 2003.

Morrison, Grant. *Supergods: What Masked Vigilantes, Miraculous Mutants, and a Sun God from Smallville Can Teach Us About Being Human*. New York: Spiegel & Grau, 2012.

Nevins, Jess. *Heroes & Monsters: The Unofficial Companion to The League of Extraordinary Gentlemen*. Los Angeles: Monkeybrain, 2003.

Normanton, Peter. *The Mammoth Book of Best Horror Comics*. Philadelphia: Running Press, 2008.

Nyberg, Amy Kiste. *Seal of Approval: The History of the Comics Code*. Jackson, MS: UP of Mississippi, 1998.

Reynolds, Richard. *Super Heroes: A Modern Mythology*. Jackson, MS: UP of Mississippi, 1994.

Rhoades, Shirrel. *Comic Books: How the Industry Works*. New York: Peter Lang Publishing, 2007.

_____. *A Complete History of American Comic Books*. New York: Peter Lang Publishing, 2008.

Rogers, Brett M. "Heroes Limited: The Theory of the Hero's Journey and the Limitation of the Superhero Myth." *Classics and Comics*. Eds. George Kovacs and C.W. Marshall. Oxford, UK: Oxford UP, 2011. 73–86.

Sadowski, Greg. *Four Color Fear: Forgotten Horror Comics of the 1950s*. Seattle: Fantagraphics Books, 2010.

Salkowitz, Rob. *Comic-Con and the Business of Pop Culture: What the World's Wildest Trade Show Can Tell Us About the Future of Entertainment*. New York: McGraw-Hill, 2012.

Sanford, Jonathan J., ed. *Spider-Man and Philosophy: The Web of Inquiry*. Hoboken, NJ: Wiley, 2012.

Sandifer, Philip. "Amazing Fantasies: Trauma, Affect, and Superheroes." *Graphia: Literary Criticism and the Graphic Novel*. Ed. William Kuskin. *English Language Notes* 46.2 (2008): 175–92.

Selby, Chip. *Tales from the Crypt: From Comic Books to Television*. Reistertown, MD: CS Films, 2004.

Spooner, Catherine and Emma McEvoy. *The Routledge Companion to Gothic*. London and New York: Routledge, 2007.

Uslan, Michael E. *The Boy Who Loved Batman: A Memoir*. San Francisco: Chronicle Books, 2011.

Voger, Mark. *The Dark Age*. Raleigh, N.C: TwoMorrows, 2006.

Weiner, Stephen. *Faster Than a Speeding Bullet: The Rise of the Graphic Novel*. New York: NBM Publishing, 2004.

White, Mark D. and Robert Arp, eds. *Batman and Philosophy: The Dark Knight of the Soul*. Hoboken, NJ: Wiley, 2008.

_____, ed. *Superman and Philosophy: What Would the Man of Steel Do?*. Malden, MA: Wiley-Blackwell Publishing, 2013.

Wright, Bradford W. *Comic Book Nation: The Transformation of Youth Culture in America*. Baltimore, MD: Johns Hopkins UP, 2003.

Zunshine, Lisa. "What To Expect When You Pick Up a Graphic Novel." *SubStance #124* 40.1 (2011): 114-34. *Project MUSE*. Web. 16 Sept. 2013.

About the Editor

Gary Hoppenstand is a professor in the Department of English at Michigan State University. As a graduate student, he studied with Professor Ray Browne, one of the most important scholars involved in the creation of popular culture studies at the university level. Hoppenstand's major research areas are genre and formula studies in fiction and film. He has published numerous books and articles and has won many awards for his teaching and research. Currently, he is serving as associate dean of undergraduate academic affairs in the College of Arts and Letters at Michigan State University.

Contributors

Michael J. Blouin is an assistant professor of English and the humanities at Milligan College. His research interests include cultural studies, the Gothic, and critical theory. He is the author of the recent monograph *Japan and the Cosmopolitan Gothic: Specters of Modernity* (Palgrave Macmillan, 2013).

Adam Capitanio is a writer, editor, and independent scholar based in New York City. He has a PhD in American studies from Michigan State University and an MA in cinema studies from New York University.

Daniel D. Clark is an associate professor of English at Cedarville University and teaches courses in writing, film, the graphic novel, and contemporary East Asian literature. Before teaching at Cedarville, he taught various English courses in Okinawa, Japan for the Okinawa Prefectural Government Language Center and the University of Maryland's Asian Division. Clark has presented papers on the traditional Japanese aesthetics of Jiro Taniguchi and representations of Jesus in comics. He has also published four entries in Salem Press's *Critical Survey of Graphic Novels*. His interests include Christianity, Japanese culture and literature, and their intersection with comics.

Brian Cogan is an associate professor in and chair of the Department of Communications at Molloy College. He is the author, co-author, and co-editor of numerous books, articles, and anthologies on popular culture, music, and the media. He is the author of *The Punk Rock Encyclopedia* (Sterling, 2008); co-author, with Tony Kelso, of *The Encyclopedia of Popular Culture, Media and Politics* (Greenwood Press, 2009); as well as co-editor, with Tony Kelso, of *Mosh the Polls: Youth Voters, Popular Culture, and Democratic Engagement* (Lexington, 2008). Cogan is also the co-author, along with William Phillips, of the *Encyclopedia of Heavy Metal Music* (Greenwood Press, 2009) and editor of a collection of essays on the popular television show *South Park* (Lexington, 2012). He is currently co-writing the autobiography of legendary punk drummer Marky Ramone.

Joseph J. Darowski is a member of the English faculty at Brigham Young University – Idaho and a member of the editorial review board of *The Journal of Popular Culture*. He received his PhD from the American Studies program at Michigan State University. He has published work on several aspects of the comic book industry and is the editor of *The Ages of Superheroes* essays series. He has also published research on television shows, such as *The Office, Chuck, Downton Abbey*, and *Batman: The Animated Series*.

Lance Eaton is coordinator of instructional design and part-time faculty member at North Shore Community College in Danvers, Massachusetts. There, he teaches courses in popular culture, comics, and literature. He has written articles and entries for scholarly reference works on horror and comics. He has also presented at numerous regional, national, and international conferences. He holds a master's in American studies from the University of Massachusetts, Boston; a master's in public administration from Suffolk University; and a master's of education from University of Massachusetts, Boston. He also regularly contributes to the *By Any Other Nerd* blog (http://byanyothernerd.blogspot.com).

Jared Griffin is assistant professor of English at the University of Alaska Anchorage, Kodiak College. He earned his PhD in English from Texas Christian University. His research interests include, among others, apocalypticism in American literature, graphic novel and film adaptations, and interwar American culture.

Mary Catherine Harper is professor of English and McCann Chair in the Humanities at Defiance College in Ohio, where she teaches literature and creative writing. She received her PhD in literary criticism and theory and also creative writing at Bowling Green State University. Her undergraduate degree was earned at Montana State University. Her creative projects include both poetry and website visuals, and she explores the intertextuality of various literatures, the visual arts, cultural representations, and the philosophical Sublime. She has publications in *Studies in American Indian Literatures*, *Science Fiction Studies*, *Extrapolation*, *FemSpec*, and *The New York Review of Science Fiction*. Harper also has publications in poetry magazines and has won the 2013 Gwendolyn Brooks Poetry Prize, awarded by the Society for the Study of Midwestern Literature.

Jeffrey Johnson was born and raised in St. Louis, Missouri, where he developed a lifelong love of the St. Louis Cardinals and fried foods (both of which have proven bad for his heart). He received his PhD in American studies from Michigan State University and has written numerous journal articles and book chapter about popular culture. His latest book is entitled *Super-History: Comic Book Superheroes and American Society, 1938 to the Present*. He currently lives and works in Honolulu, Hawaii and enjoys the island's lack of snow and abundant greenery.

Cathy Leogrande is an associate professor of education at Le Moyne College, a Jesuit institution in Syracuse, New York. Prior to her career in teacher education, she was a special education teacher, administrator, and staff developer in K-12 school districts. Cathy's research and teaching topics focus on digital literacies, including media literacy, visual literacy, participatory culture, transmedia texts, and new boundaries of copyright fair use. She seeks to assist pre-service and in-service teachers using new literacies to adapt and extend student skills as consumers and producers of content.

Rikk Mulligan is a visiting instructor at Longwood University. His research focuses on intersections between popular culture and political criticism in science fiction, fantasy, horror, graphic novels, and comic books. His dissertation, "Shattered States," a study of post-apocalyptic SF literature and media and its depiction of American decline, is being revised as a book manuscript. He has presented on these topics at the International Conference for the Fantastic in the Arts, The Southwest Texas and National Popular Culture/American Culture Conferences, and the Science Fiction Research Association. He has also published essays on *Battlestar Galactica* and the zombie apocalypse in contemporary TV and film.

Michael G. Robinson is a professor of communication studies at Lynchburg College in Lynchburg, Virginia. He received his BA in radio-television-film, his BS in psychology from the University of Maryland College Park, his MA in telecommunications from Indiana University

Bloomington, and his PhD in American culture studies from Bowling Green State University. He is the co-creator and co-director of the popular culture minor at Lynchburg College. He has appeared in Biography channel programs on *Britney Spears* and the *Harry Potter Kids*, as well as many local broadcasts. He has published popular culture research and articles in *Critical Survey of Graphic Novels: Heroes and Superheroes*, *Movies in American History*, *Super/Heroes: From Hercules to Superman*, *Popular Music & Society*, *and Studies in Popular Culture*.

Michael Rogers is an award–winning freelance editor and writer living in the New York City area. Previously, he was the senior editor for the trade publication *Library Journal* for more than twenty years and has been a prolific news writer, blogger, and reviewer, as well as an avid photographer. He is a lifelong devotee of film and literature.

Rich Shivener is assistant director of the Office of First-Year Programs at Northern Kentucky University. In 2010, he completed NKU's Master of Arts in English program, focusing on comics and writing technologies. The following year, he helped develop teaching strategies, assignments, and event surrounding David Mack's graphic novel *Kabuki: The Alchemy*, assigned as a common reading program for first-year students. His studies and work have since led him to comics publications and academic conferences at New York Comic-Con and Comic-Con International. In addition to serving NKU, Shivener freelances for such publications as *Publishers Weekly* and *Writer's Digest*.

Terrence Wandtke is the chair of the Department of Film and Digital Media at Judson University in Elgin, Illinois. His scholarship analyzes the connections between twentieth-century literature, film, and new media, and his recent research focuses on the heroic tropes associated with comic books, film, and pulp fiction. He is author of *The Meaning of Superhero Comic Books* and the editor of the collection *The Amazing Transforming Superhero: Essays on the Revision of Characters in Comic Books, Film, and Television* (both published by McFarland). He is also the author of *The Dark Night Returns: The Contemporary Resurgence of Crime Comics* (forthcoming from the RIT Press) and the editor of *Ed Brubaker: Conversations* (forthcoming from the University Press of Mississippi).

He serves as the area chair of comics and comic art for the National Popular Culture Association/American Culture Association Conference. The founder and director of the Imago Film Festival, he has served on the selection committee for the St. Louis International Film Festival's Interfaith Award and on the jury for the Elgin Short Film Festival.

Index
